MAILING ADDRESS

Maritime Studies Research Unit
Memorial University of Newfoundland
St. John's, Newfoundland A1C 5S7, Canada

RESEARCH IN MARITIME HISTORY
NO. 3

PEOPLE OF THE NORTHERN SEAS

Edited by
Lewis R. Fischer and Walter Minchinton

INTERNATIONAL MARITIME ECONOMIC HISTORY ASSOCIATION

In conjunction with the Association for the History of the Northern Seas.

St. John's, Newfoundland
1992

ISSN - 1188-3928
ISBN - 0-9695885-2-6

Research in Maritime History is available free of charge to members of the International Maritime Economic History Association. The price to others is US$15 per copy.

Back issues of *Research in Maritime History* are available:

No. 1 (1991)	David M. Williams and Andrew P. White (comps.), *A Select Bibliography of British and Irish University Theses about Maritime History, 1792-1990*
No. 2 (1992)	Lewis R. Fischer (ed.), *From Wheel House to Counting House: Essays in Maritime Business History in Honour of Professor Peter Neville Davies*

Research in Maritime History would also like to thank Memorial University of Newfoundland for financial assistance.

CONTENTS

CONTRIBUTORS

About the Editors

LEWIS R. FISCHER is Professor of History at Memorial University of Newfoundland. As well as being the Series Editor of *Research in Maritime History*, he is Editor-in-Chief of the *International Journal of Maritime History*. His research interests are primarily in nineteenth-century international maritime economic history.

WALTER MINCHINTON is Professor Emeritus at the University of Exeter. He was President of the Association for the History of the Northern Seas from 1982 to 1988.

Contributors

JUDITH BALL BRUCE is a graduate student at the University of California, Berkeley. Her research is concentrated on Russian history and the relationships between European business and religious organizations and indigenes in northern North America.

MERJA-LIISA HINKKANEN is a Docent at the University of Helsinki and a Visiting Fellow at the University of London. Her current reserach interests concern the mentality of Finnish sailors in the nineteenth century as well as marginal groups in British history.

POUL HOLM is Senior Curator at the Fiskeri- og Søfartsmuseet in Esbjerg, Denmark. He has a doctorate in history from the University of Aarhus and has published widely on Scandinavian maritime history. He is currently investigating the history of Danish fishing from the sixteenth to the nineteenth centuries.

JONATHAN M. HUTCHINGS is a history graduate of the University of Leicester and the winner of an award from the European Social Fund for graduate work in information technology. This essay comes from a project on which he has been working.

OLAF UWE JANZEN is Associate Professor of History at Sir Wilfred Grenfell College of Memorial University of Newfoundland. His research and teaching interests are in eighteenth century Newfoundland social, naval, and commercial history.

YRJÖ KAUKIAINEN is Professor of Econcomic History at the University of Helsinki. A past President of the Association for the History of the Northern Seas, he is the author most recently of *Sailing into Twilight: Finnish Shipping in an Age of Transport Revolution, 1860-1914* (Helsinki, 1991).

IAN G. LAYTON is Associate Professor of Geography at the University of Umeå. His teaching and research interests include historical and economic geography, particularly in relation to ports, maritime transport, international trade and regional development in northern and western Europe.

GEORGE MUNRO is Professor and Chairman of the Department of History and Geography at Virginia Commonwealth University and a specialist in eighteenth-century Russian history. His translation (with D. M. Griffiths) of *Catherine II's Charters to the Nobility and the Towns of 1785* was published in 1991 and his study of St. Petersburg in the reign of Catherine will be available soon.

HELGE W. NORDVIK is Professor of Maritime Strategy at the Norwegian School of Management and Editor of the *International Journal of Maritime History*. He is a specialist on nineteenth and twentieth-century Norwegian and international maritime economic history.

RICHARD H. WARNER is Professor of History at Mary Washington College in Fredericksburg, Virginia. A specialist in Russian history, he has recently published a study of Admiral George Paddon in *Mariner's Mirror* and is preparing a new edition of Captain John Deane's *History of the Russian Fleet under Peter the Great* for the Navy Records Society.

DAVID M. WILLIAMS lectures in economic history at the University of Leicester and has written widely on north Atlantic commerce, maritime labour, government intervention, and the free trade movement. He is currently Secretary of the British Commission for Maritime History and Chair of the Editorial Board of the *International Journal of Maritime History*.

People of the Northern Seas: Introduction

Lewis R. Fischer and Walter Minchinton

For too long the most common definition of maritime history encompassed little beyond the study of ships. Obscured in the mists were not only those who manned the vessels, such as mariners and fishermen, but also a host of others who both facilitated and benefitted from seagoing activities. This myopia often relegated maritime issues to the scholarly periphery, since much of what was accepted as maritime history was both antiquarian and untouched by the types of intellectual debates that animated the larger discipline. This collection of eleven articles reflects an emerging trend toward situating maritime questions within the context of broader historical concerns. Nonetheless, we make no claims for the uniqueness of this approach. Indeed, over the past two decades a plethora of monographs and essays have tried to broaden the focus of maritime history,[1] and since 1989 the *International Journal of Maritime History* has also been devoted to this task.

This volume focuses upon some of the "people of the northern seas." Collectively, the contributions convey some of the flavour and diversity of maritime life along the littoral of the world's northern seas in the seventeenth, eighteenth and nineteenth centuries. While the majority deal with Europe, we have also included essays on the north Pacific and eastern North America. The papers were originally presented at a conference sponsored by the Association for the History of the Northern Seas in conjunction with the city of Kotka, Finland, in August 1992. This was the ninth Baltic seminar of the Kotka Provincial Museum and the sixth conference of the Association for the History of the Northern Seas. A variety of factors, including space, precluded the

[1]Some of the best of the more recent studies that have focused upon "people of the sea" include Eric W. Sager, *Seafaring Labour: The Merchant Marine of Atlantic Canada, 1829-1914* (Kingston, 1989); Marcus Rediker, *Between the Devil and the Deep Blue Sea: Merchant Seamen, Pirates and the Anglo-American World, 1700-1750* (Cambridge, 1987); and N.A.M. Rodger, *The Wooden World: An Anatomy of the Georgian Navy* (London, 1986). See also the essays in Colin Howell and Richard Twomey (eds.), *Jack Tar in History* (Fredericton, 1991); and Lewis R. Fischer, *et al.* (eds.), *The North Sea: Twelve Essays on Social History of Maritime Labour* (Stavanger, 1992).

publication of all the papers, but the eleven selected for inclusion in this issue of *Research in Maritime History* are broad in scope. This diversity also characterizes the contributors, who come from Canada, the United States, Denmark, Finland, Norway, Sweden, and Great Britain. Here then is a collection concerned with the lives and activities of people of the northern seas whose lives were governed to some extent by the diurnal round of the moon and the tides, factors which affected the ebb and flow of human activity on the margins of the oceans.

The people of the northern seas encountered in the following pages may roughly be divided into three groups. The first four articles examine those who wrested their livelihoods from the ocean--fishermen, maritime indigenes, and seamen. The next four contributions explore various components of the maritime mercantile community--merchants, shipowners and shipbrokers. The final three essays look at aspects of the important issue of protection (the navy and the coastguard) and the broad problem of the role played by maritime affairs in shaping national and regional cultures. There are, of course, a variety of additional groups and topics that could have been included, but the pool from which these essays were drawn thwarted the possibility of embracing other relevant topics.

For years anthropologists and historians have been concerned with life in small coastal communities throughout the world. Within Europe, communities in places such as Iceland, Wales, Portugal, Norway, Denmark and the Mediterranean have received attention; outside Europe, scholars have examined maritime settlements along the Indian and Pacific Oceans, as well as in New England and Newfoundland in North America.[2] For example, we have the famous account of the fishing village of Nippers Harbour, an isolated pre-industrial fishing community, and Cat Harbour, a rural fishing settlement on the northeast

[2]See, for example, the essays on Ireland, Wales, Portugal, Norway, the Mediterranean and the Pacific Ocean in Paul Adam (ed.), *Seamen in Society* (Paris, 1980) ; Robin Fox, "An Irish Island," in Fox, *Encounter with Anthropology* (Harmondsworth, Eng., 1975), 113-122; Lawrence Carroll Allin, "The Lime Coast: A Maritime Nexus of Community," in Timothy J. Runyan (ed.), *Ships, Seafaring and Society: Essays in Maritime History* (Detroit, 1987), 184-216.

coast of Newfoundland.[3] As people of the northern seas, men in Cat Harbour were fishermen rather than seamen or sailors. "Fishing," James Faris observed, requires "nerve for the water" and few men simply "love to be at it."[4] The lives of fishermen, as well as sailors, deserve consideration in any discussion of people of the northern seas.[5] These individuals have often gone to sea to escape the lot of lowly-paid unskilled workers ashore but frequently have discovered that they have made a harsh bargain. While the pay might be better, it is earned at the price of working long hours under appallingly severe conditions.

As part of an on-going research project, Olaf Janzen examines the origin and persistence of French fishing settlements in seventeenth and eighteenth-century Newfoundland. Forced to abandon the island in 1713, the inhabitants returned to the southwestern corner of the island during the 1730s and 1740s and continued with one interruption as permanent residents until 1755. Supported by supplies from metropolitan France, the settlers maintained their existence in dispersed communities by fishing in the summer and hunting and trapping during the winter. Using mainly French records, Janzen shows how French--and Irish--settlers were expelled again when England and France resumed their periodic conflicts in 1744. With the return of peace in 1748, some French settlers returned, although how many is uncertain. While the isolation of these settlements enabled the inhabitants to remain unobtrusive in peacetime, the French were again driven out when war recommenced in 1755. At this point French sovereignty ended, to be replaced permanently by British jurisdiction. Concentrating on political changes, the author argues that national differences were insignificant for these inhabitants, who flourished by exchanging fish and furs for supplies from passing ships.

---

[3]Tom Philbrook, *Fisherman, Logger, Merchant, Miner: Social Change and Industrialism in Three Newfoundland Communities* (St. John's, 1966); James C. Faris, *Cat Harbour: A Newfoundland Fishing Settlement* (St. John's, 1972).

[4]Faris, *Cat Harbour*, 23.

[5]For a study of the fishermen of Hull, see Jeremy Tunstall, *The Fishermen: The Sociology of an Extreme Occupation* (London, 1962).

About 250 years ago the eastward migration in search of furs brought Russians into contact with Aleuts. The resulting relationship, as Judith Ball Bruce argues, was not as one-sided as previous scholars have suggested. Although this contact had a substantial impact on the lifestyle of the native inhabitants and drastically reduced their numbers, Bruce demonstrates that both groups were able to adapt. The Aleuts taught the Russians vital maritime and hunting skills, while the Europeans showed more respect for this indigenous society than for others they encountered along the western coast of North America. In the end, with a limited amount of violence, the two groups came to form a single society, a unique example, the author claims, of symbiotic European-indigene contact.

But what was life like for those people of the sea who provided the crews for merchant vessels? In a well-known quotation, Samuel Johnson wrote:

> No man will be a sailor who has contrivance enough to get himself into a jail; for being in a ship is being in a jail, with the chance of being drowned...A man in a jail has more room, better food, and commonly better company.[6]

Although this statement may exaggerate slightly with regard both to the quality of food and drink available and to the nature of the company, it nonetheless has the ring of truth. How difficult was life below the decks?[7] Drawing on Finnish source material and adapting his title from Richard Dana's 1840 reminiscence, *Two Years before the Mast*, Yrjö Kaukiainen argues that compared with earlier centuries when shipboard decisions were based on discussion and consensus, in the nineteenth century legal changes shifted power to the master. This was especially true in the deep-sea sector, where the captain acquired absolute control. In most countries, including Finland, seafaring was a residual occupation; given this, it is not surprising that the Finnish situation was

---

[6]James Boswell, *The Life of Dr. Johnson* (London, 1759), I, 348.

[7]For a study of conditions in the early eighteenth century, see Rediker, *Between the Devil and the Deep Blue Sea*.

distinguished by low pay and lengthy contracts which resulted in high desertion rates. Conditions were ameliorated late in the nineteenth century when vessels which made longer voyages grew in size and wage contracts were shortened. The revolver rather than the whip became the method of social control.

After completing their voyages, seamen often found themselves thrown together ashore in mean neighbourhoods of the type vividly described by John Masefield in "Hell's Pavement." If life at sea were perilous to life and limb, a sailor ashore was not much safer.[8] To attempt to ease some of the more insalubrious conditions in English sailortowns, Finnish missions were established in London and Hull in the 1880s. It is the records of these organizations which provide the evidence upon which Merja-Liisa Hinkkanen draws in her study. The missions offered bases in foreign port and links with home for some of the 6000 Finnish seamen who sailed the world's oceans in the late nineteenth century. The missions were places where sailors could meet fellow Finns, receive mail, forward money to their relations and maintain contact with home. They also provided convenient foci for efforts to reclaim itinerant seamen for the homeland.

The people of the northern seas were of course not comprised solely of seamen and fishermen. Also significant were those who sponsored the voyages, owned the vessels and provided the cargoes--the mercantile community. Using an inventory, a source which has recently been exploited more frequently by historians,[9] Ian Layton describes how Abraham Stenholm, a merchant from Luleå in northern Sweden, rose from a post in an office to ownership of his own prosperous business. In the process he acquired property, including a share in a vessel and farmland, and also engaged in shipping. Apart from trade with Stockholm, his main business was by water along the river valleys in Luleå's hinterland. When the rivers froze in the winter, Saami products were

---

[8]For a study of the world's sailortowns, see Stan Hugill, *Sailortown* (London, 1967). Perhaps the best micro-level study of sailortowns is Judith Fingard, *Jack in Port: Sailortowns of Eastern Canada* (Toronto, 1982).

[9]See, for example, Ad van der Woude and Anton Schuurman (eds.), *Probate Inventories: A New Source for the Historical Study of Wealth, Material Culture and Agricultural Development* (Wageningen, 1980).

delivered by reindeer-drawn sledges from up to 200 kilometres inland. With active interests in fishing as well as trade, Stenholm clearly qualifies as a person of the sea. While the analysis of the inventory of this Swedish merchant, who was only forty-seven years old at his death, shows how the business was conducted--with developing interests in farming and fishing as well as trade--Layton suggests that there are further questions which require answers in order to assess the typicality of Abraham Stenholm's career.

Merchants engaged in international maritime commerce also faced the difficulty of finding suitable mediums of exchange. This problem bedeviled merchants engaged in international commerce until the introduction of the gold standard, and those in eighteenth-century Russia were no exception. In his essay on the development of bills of exchange issued at St. Petersburg, Russia's principal port, George Munro lifts the shroud off this oft-concealed issue. Central to his analysis is a list of 4035 promissory notes protested in 1773 in St. Petersburg which shows that while they were little used by artisans, bills of exchange were employed by Russian merchants from the interior, by Russian merchants in St. Petersburg, and by foreign merchants, mainly wholesalers in the import-export business, based in St. Petersburg. This latter group appears to have been less involved in the use of promissory notes to provide loans to transfer cash than native Russians.

Unless they owned their own vessels, merchants with goods to trade by sea required the services of shipowners. Drawing on *Lloyd's Register* and important ancillary materials, David Williams and Jonathan Hutchings examine the shipowners of an important vessel type neglected by historians--the iron sailing vessel--in the first twenty years of its existence. The authors show that vessel size increased between 1838 and 1857 and that craft with auxiliary steam engines were larger than "pure" sailing vessels. While the rigs employed for iron sailing vessels varied with size as might be expected, on auxiliaries the schooner rig predominated regardless of size. The main ports of registration for iron sailing vessels were Liverpool, Glasgow, and the Clyde ports of Dumbarton and Greenock, while London owned the largest group of auxiliary vessels. These auxiliaries were chiefly employed in European trades while iron sail was used in the long-distance trades. In conclusion, William and Hutchings suggest that more investigation of the uses of iron vessels and the individuals who owned them is required.

Until about the middle of the nineteenth century, the shipowning and mercantile communities were frequently, but not always, identical. But thereafter it became increasingly rare for merchants to own the tonnage necessary to carry their goods to market. This disjunction increased the prominence of shipbrokers. These people of the northern seas served the principal purpose of bringing together the buyers and sellers of shipping services. Using the Norwegian firm of Fearnley and Eger as a case study, Lewis R. Fischer and Helge W. Nordvik examine the development of late nineteenth-century shipbroking. They argue that Norwegians were able to gain a toehold in shipbroking as the result of two factors: the completion of the North Sea cable in 1869, which enabled the rapid transfer of information, and the repeal between 1871 and 1885 of domestic laws which limited entry into the profession. For the first few decades after its founding in 1869, Fearnley and Eger's principal business was to negotiate voyage charters for Norwegian-owned sailing vessels in the short-sea trades. But by 1914 the firm was beginning to develop liaisons with firms outside Europe and also to handle significant numbers of time charters. In making this transition, Fearnley and Eger was able to become truly competitive in the international arena.

While merchant shipping and fishing were doubtless the primary forms of maritime employment everywhere around the northern seas, both required protection from hostile foes. One form of shield was provide by the various navies. Based on Russian as well as British records, Richard Warner has prepared a study of Captain John Deane, an Englishman whose service in the Russian navy was dwarfed by his role as diplomat and spy on the track of the Jacobite movement abroad. Although the number of British naval officers who entered Russian service in the early years of the eighteenth century is unknown, this does not diminish Deane's importance. Despite his clandestine activities, Deane lived to the ripe old age of eighty-three. Deane was thus more fortunate than many British seamen.

Most countries with maritime frontiers have over time taken steps to deal with problems that arise when sea meets land. Navies are normally expected to provide defence from invasion by sea, although some coastguards, notably in the US, have had active wartime roles.[10] But other problems have demanded separate solutions. Some coastguards have been used to counter smuggling; indeed the Finnish coastguard was founded in 1920 to check the smuggling of alcohol from Estonia. Some coastguards have also been used to check illegal immigration. Coastguards of some European countries, notably Iceland,[11] provide protection for fishing vessels. Both the US and Canadian Coast Guards have large fleets of icebreakers to keep shipping lanes open through the winter.[12] But search and rescue, sometimes in association with other organisations such as lifeboat services, is now the major role of coastguards, with developments in technology bringing about changes in operational methods, as Walter Minchinton shows in his essay. Radio communication, satellite surveillance, helicopters and inflatable inshore vessels now form part of the equipment of coastguards. Of particular note is the rapid integration of women into this branch of the people of the sea.

Even if it has become cliched to assert that in many parts of the world seagoing activities have played a decisive role in shaping regional and national cultures, the process by which this might occur has been little explored. In a frankly speculative essay, Poul Holm closes this volume by examining how this issue might be approached and some of the pitfalls to be avoided. Using a recent two-volume collection edited by Kirsten Hastrup as an example of the problems inherent in attempting to answer this type of question,[13] Holm raises serious concerns about the way in which scholars have attempted to handle it in the Nordic region. At the same time, he concludes on a more positive note, reasserting the

---

[10]See Stephen H. Evans, *The United States Coast Guard, 1790-1915: A Definitive History (with a postscript: 1915-1949)* (Annapolis, MD, 1949).

[11]See Jón Th. Thór, *British Trawlers in Icelandic Waters: History of British Steam Trawling off Iceland 1889-1916 and the Anglo-Icelandic Fisheries Dispute 1896-1897* (Reykjavik, 1992).

[12]For Canada, see T.E. Appleton, *Usque Ad Mare: A History of the Canadian Coast Guard and Marine Services* (Ottawa, 1968).

[13]Kirsten Hastrup (ed.), *Den nordiske verden* (2 vols., Copenhagen, 1992).

importance of the topic and the need for international collaboration. Moreover, he argues that while any such exploration must be interdisciplinary and trans-national, it has to be informed by a thorough grounding in historical reality. This essay provides a stimulating climax to the volume.

This book of course presents only selective studies of some of the maritime people of the northern seas. It is our hope that they will stimulate further research into the topic, and that international maritime history organizations will see fit in future to provide additional forums for further exploration of the topic. The people of the world's seas--wherever they may live--deserve the fuller scrutiny of scholarly inquiry.

"Une Petite Republique" in Southwestern Newfoundland: The Limits of Imperial Authority in a Remote Maritime Environment[1]

Olaf Uwe Janzen

Introduction

This paper continues earlier research into the origins and persistence of settlement by French and Irish fishermen at Codroy in southwestern Newfoundland from about 1725 until 1755.[2] A previous paper identified the settlers as French fishermen whose lineage could be traced two generations back to fishing families living on the French coast of Newfoundland during the 1680s who were forced to abandon the island following the Treaty of Utrecht (1713) by which France acknowledged British sovereignty over the entire island. A subsequent paper identified one of the metropolitan French merchant families whose capital had maintained the earlier fishing stations in Newfoundland and who reappeared as traders and investors at the Codroy settlement during the 1730s and 1740s. This paper integrates the results of those earlier studies and extends the analysis beyond 1744, when the outbreak of war caused the abandonment of the Codroy settlement. The community was re-established in 1748, only to be destroyed a second time when hostilities between France and England resumed in 1755. When Codroy reappeared

[1]This paper is based in part on research undertaken with support from the Social Sciences and Humanities Research Council of Canada.

[2]"'Une Grande Liaison': French Fishermen from Île Royale on the Coast of Southwestern Newfoundland, 1714-1766—A Preliminary Survey", *Newfoundland Studies*, III, No. 2 (Fall 1987), 183-200; "'Bretons...sans scrupule': The Family Chenu of Saint-Malo and the Illicit Trade in English Cod During the Middle of the 18th Century," *Proceedings of the Fifteenth Meeting of the French Colonial Historical Society Martinique and Guadeloupe, May 1989* (Lanham, MD, 1992), 189-200.

Research in Maritime History, No. 3 (December 1992), 1-33.

in 1762, it was as part of the British mercantile world, for the principal merchant was English. Though the social and economic character of the community after 1762 resembled the earlier pattern, the "French connection" had been broken. This history of a small fishing settlement, in which two French phases were followed by an English one, suggests certain conclusions about the principal factors governing the social and economic character of an isolated community of "people of the sea." I argue that national differences were relatively insignificant, for the similarities between the earlier and later communities at Codroy were stronger than the disparities. The paper is based largely on manuscript and cartographic evidence gathered in the national and regional archives of littoral England and France.

The Persistence of French Settlement in Newfoundland (c. 1684-1744)

On 25 September 1714, the departure of the *Héros* from the little town of Plaisance in southern Newfoundland marked the end of an era. On board was Philippe Pastour de Costebelle, who had been governor of the French colony since 1695. In the negotiations that ended the War of the Spanish Succession in 1713, France had agreed to cede its fishing colony at Plaisance together with all claims to Newfoundland, even though she had been undefeated on the island.[3] To avoid disrupting the French fishery, which had resumed as soon as hostilities had ended and before the final terms of the Treaty of Utrecht had been defined, England allowed the French to delay their withdrawal from Newfoundland until 1714. Nevertheless, most inhabitants of Plaisance, the neighbouring settlements, and the islands of St. Pierre were already evacuated to Cape Breton by the time *Héros* sailed; Costebelle was one of the last to leave. Henceforth, all Newfoundland, Plaisance included, would belong to the English.[4] After fifty years of effort to develop a viable cornerstone of empire based on the fishery, France had given up on Newfoundland.

---

[3]Jean-François Brière, "Pêche et politique à Terre-Neuve au XVIIIe siècle: la France véritable gagnante du traité d'Utrecht?" *Canadian Historical Review*, LXIV, No. 2 (June 1983), 168-187; J.K. Hiller, "Utrecht Revisited: The Origins of French Fishing Rights in Newfoundland Waters," *Newfoundland Studies*, VII, No. 1 (Spring 1991), 23-39.

[4]Georges Cerbelaud Salagnac, "Philippe Pastour de Costebelle," in *Dictionary of Canadian Biography, II: 1701-1740* (Toronto, 1969), 509-513 (hereafter cited as *DCB*).

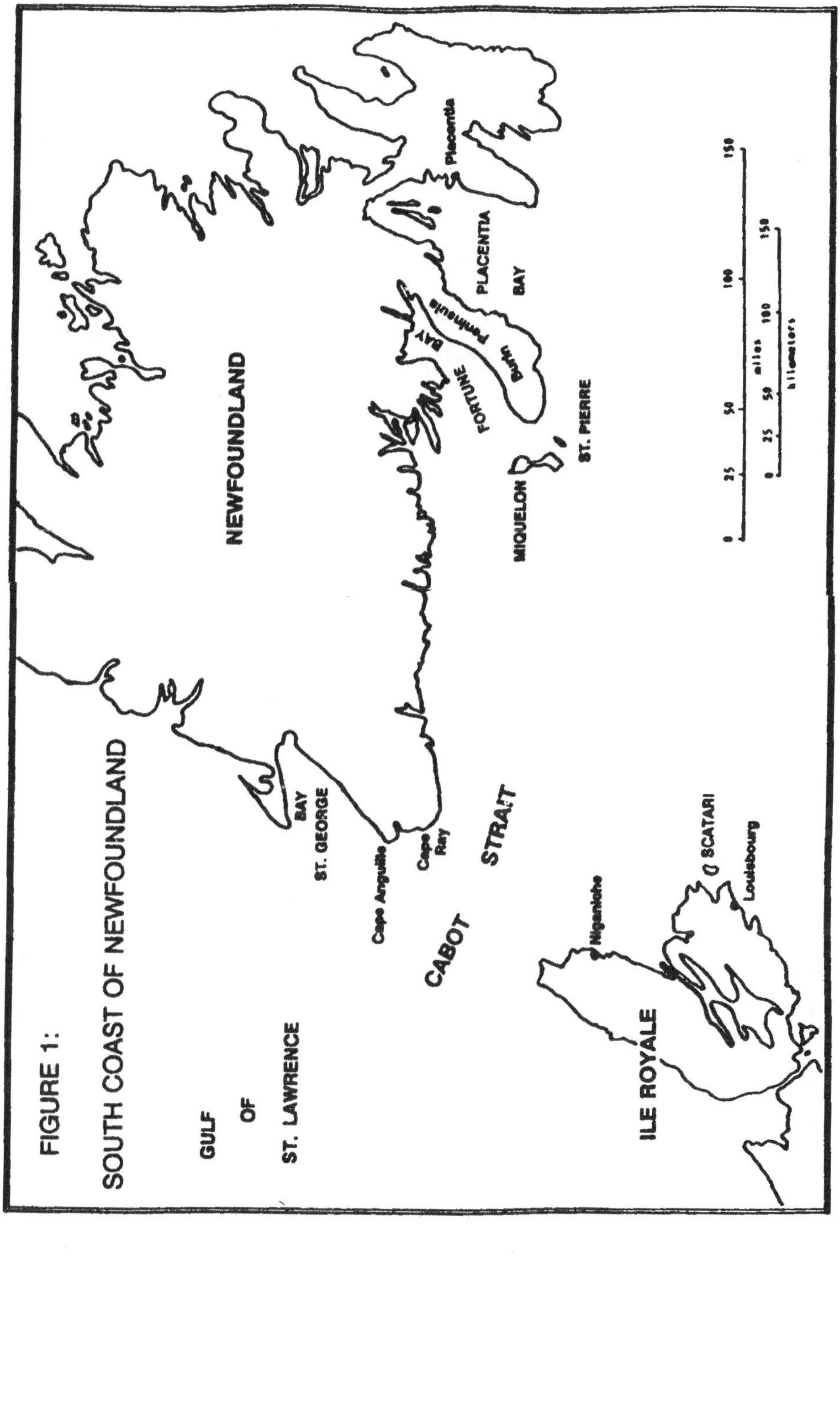

FIGURE 1:
SOUTH COAST OF NEWFOUNDLAND

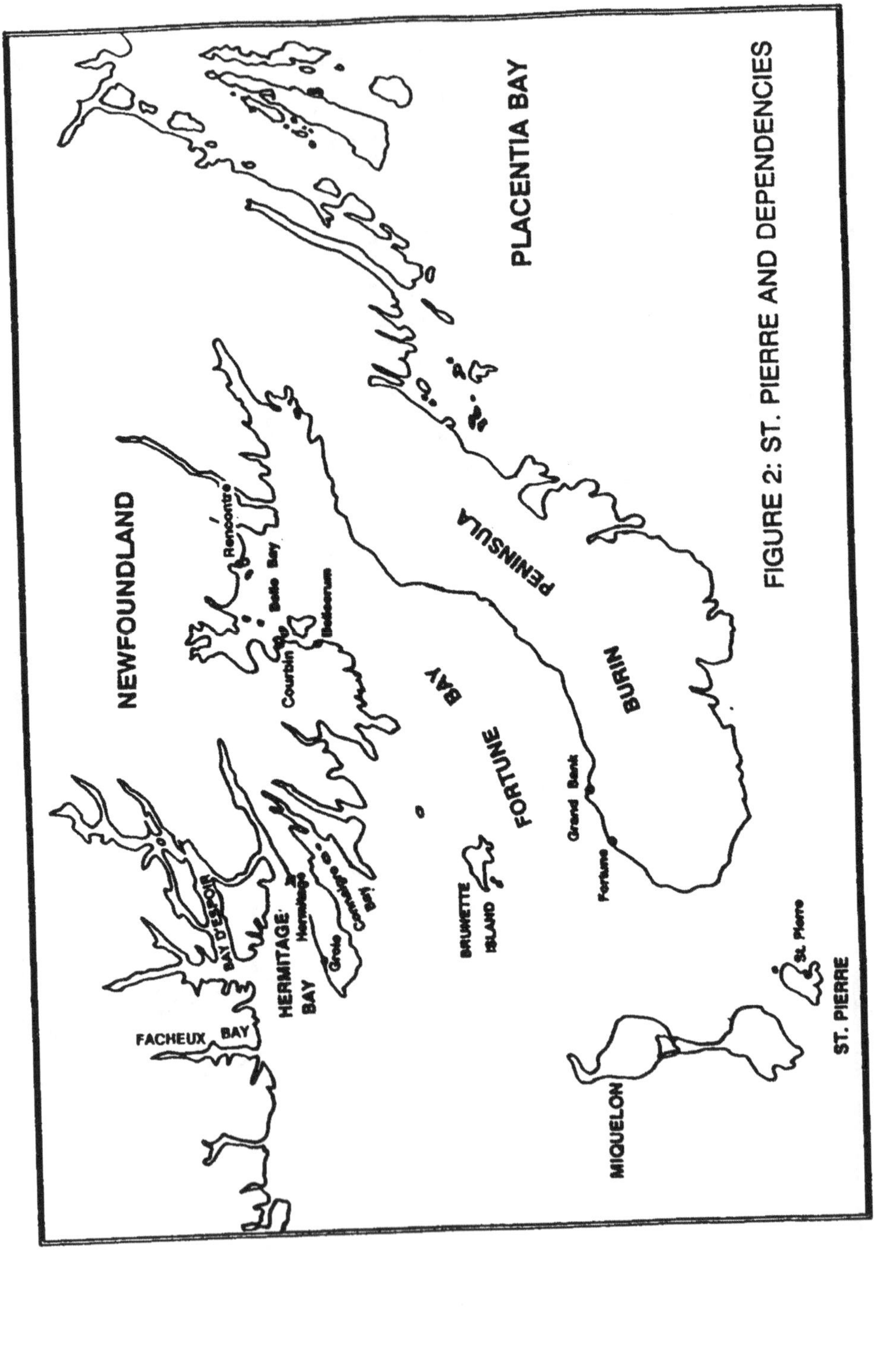

FIGURE 2: ST. PIERRE AND DEPENDENCIES

It seemed a logical decision. The island's limited resources had forced the Plaisance colonists into what one historian described as "a dangerously single-minded concentration on the fishery." This, in turn, had led them into a nearly total dependency on the merchants of the metropolitan fishery for provisions, supplies, and labour. The demands of the fishery, together with a chronic friction between resident and migratory fishermen for beach space, had encouraged a dispersed settlement pattern. While this served the inshore fishery well, it undermined both the centralizing efforts and the authority of government. In the end, Plaisance may have been more a liability than an asset of the French mercantile empire.[5] Turning to Cape Breton Island as a *tabula rasa*, France would try once more to establish her linchpin of empire. French hopes were based on the expectation that Ile Royale (as the new colony was known) offered more fertile soil and would attract a significant number of Acadians away from the Bay of Fundy who would give the new colony the economic diversity that had been missing in Newfoundland; the transplanted Placentians were expected to form the nucleus of a new, more successful fishing community.[6]

Yet if France had abandoned Newfoundland, the same cannot be said for all the French inhabitant fishermen. Of a total population of roughly two hundred, perhaps fifty or sixty chose to remain when the English arrived to take control of Plaisance (or Placentia, as it now became known). A small handful lived in Plaisance itself. Most, however, resided in small outposts and fishing stations scattered around Placentia Bay or even further to the west, beyond the Burin Peninsula at St. Pierre and in neighbouring Fortune and Hermitage Bays, at Fortune, Grand Bank, Havre Bertrand, Connaigre, Courbin and Hermitage (see

---

[5]John Humphreys, *Plaisance: Problems of Settlement at this Newfoundland Outpost of New France 1660-1690* (Ottawa, 1970); B.A. Balcom, *The Cod Fishery of Isle Royale, 1713-1758* (Ottawa, 1984), 14. For a discussion of the rationale behind the efforts of the French crown to develop Plaisance, see Laurier Turgeon, "Colbert et la pêche française à Terre-Neuve," in Roland Mousnier (dir.), *Un Nouveau Colbert: Actes du Colloque pour le tricentenaire de la mort de Colbert* (Paris, 1985), 255-268.

[6]The relatively small population of Plaisance severely limited the role its transplanted inhabitants could play as the "nucleus" of a new fishing society. Most of the fishermen who eventually settled in Ile Royale would come from Europe; John Robert McNeill, *Atlantic Empires of France and Spain: Louisbourg and Havana, 1700-1763* (Chapel Hill, NC, 1985), 18.

Figure 2).[7] These tiny settlements had not only been physically remote from the administrative centre at Plaisance but also had developed a social and economic dependency on St. Pierre that minimized their need for contact with the main colony. The settlements rarely consisted of more than one or two nuclear families. The *engagés* who worked for them were temporary migrants whose presence swelled the total number to nearly nine times that figure.[8] A memorial submitted by merchants of St. Malo some time before 1713 claimed that "il y a à la Baye de

---

[7]Excluding the garrison and the indentured fishermen who were but temporary residents, John Humphreys estimates a permanent population that averaged twenty to thirty male inhabitants in the years between 1671 and 1706, together with more than one hundred dependent women and children; Humphreys, *Plaisance*, 7. However, he excludes the inhabitants of outlying fishing stations such as Petite Plaisance, Pointe-Verte and Fortune in his calculations, residents who are very much central to this paper. Humphreys used data taken from census lists in France, Archives nationales, archives d'outre-mer, série G^1, CDLVII (hereafter cited as ANO G^1/467); these were published under the title "Recensements de Terreneuve et Plaisance" by Fernand-D. Thibodeau in *Mémoires de la société généalogique canadienne française*, X, Nos. 3-4 (juillet-octobre 1959), 179-188; XI, Nos. 1-2 (janvier-avril, 1960), 69-85; XIII, No. 10 (octobre 1962), 204-208; and XIII, No. 12 (décembre 1982), 245-255. In using these census data, Humphreys warned that the "vague terminology and differing methods of enumeration preclude any precise calculation;" *Plaisance*, 22n. This contributes to a large discrepancy in estimates of the numbers of people who remained behind at Placentia after the evacuation. In *Atlantic Empires*, 18, John McNeill claims there were "fewer than ten" while Jean-Pierre Proulx suggests a larger figure of fifty to sixty in "The Military History of Placentia: A Study of the French Fortifications" in his *Placentia, Newfoundland* (Ottawa, 1979), 118-119. This is consistent with subsequent English records that included the more remote settlements of Fortune and Hermitage Bays.

[8]Researchers of the early settlement history of Newfoundland are careful to distinguish between seasonal, temporary, and permanent migrations to the island. The permanent population was much smaller than the total figures in seventeenth and eighteenth-century censuses might suggest. See John J. Mannion (ed.), *The Peopling of Newfoundland: Essays in Historical Geography* (St. John's, 1977), 5; Keith Matthews, "17th Century Settlement in Newfoundland" (unpublished paper, 1974), 5; W. Gordon Handcock, *Soe longe as there comes noe women: Origins of English Settlement in Newfoundland* (St. John's, 1989), 40. Handcock suggests that an accurate measurement of the permanent population of Newfoundland would be to double the number of women and add the children (2F + C), on the grounds that "the number of women and children may be regarded as an index of the more stable and permanent population, since it is axiomatic that these categories have implications for the germination, perpetuation, and continuity of a population and its social capacity to absorb subsequent immigrants (intermarriage)." Handcock, *Origins*, 95.

Fortune et lieux circonvoisins, trois ou quatre habitations qui peuvent avoir 50 à 60 hommes. Ces habitans font la pesche tout l'année lorsque le tems est beau et le permet."[9] The earliest recorded census for the region, taken in 1687, recorded an overall population of perhaps forty adults and children (see Table 1).[10]

Despite their small numbers, the inhabitants of Fortune and Hermitage Bays were permanent residents of Newfoundland. Although the contract labourers were for the most part temporary, some of the families had been living in these tiny communities for a generation by the time Plaisance was evacuated in 1714. Gilles Vincent and his wife, Marguerite Durand, were identified as residents of St. Pierre in 1691, 1693, and 1694; in 1714 he had moved, but only as far as Connaigre. Laurens Millou, his wife Marie LeManquet, and their children were at Fortune in 1693, 1694, and 1711; in 1714, they were at St. Pierre. Julien and Noel Petit were both at Hermitage in 1694; in 1711 Julien was still at Hermitage but Noel was at Fortune, while in 1714 he was reported to be living at Connaigre. One of the most permanently rooted settlers was Jean Bourny, who lived with his wife and children at Grand Bank in 1691, 1693, 1694, 1711, and 1714.[11] Most families were also related by marriage. Bourny's wife, Marie Commaire, was probably related to three other women named Commaire (Anne Marie, Simonne, and Jeanne) who were living with their husbands at St. Pierre in 1693 and 1694. The names Legrand, Durand, Vincent, Commaire and Bourny would all become intertwined through marriage in the decades to come.

---

[9]Cited in Jean-François Brière, *La pêche française en Amérique du nord au XVIIIe siècle* (Saint-Laurent, PQ, 1990), 63n.

[10]ANO G^1/467, No. 4 and No. 5.

[11]ANO G^1/467, Nos. 6, 9, 11; William Taverner, "Survey of the Inhabitants," 1714, London, Public Record Office (hereafter cited as PRO), Colonial Office (hereafter cited as CO) 194/6/243; Second Report for 1714/15 (received 20 May 1718), PRO CO 194/6/226-241. To simplify the citation of the French census material and the Taverner survey, they will be cited in subsequent references simply as ANO Plaisance Census, with the year, and PRO Taverner Survey. Unless specifically indicated to the contrary, the dates on English documents are given in the Julian or Old Style, except that the year is taken to begin on 1 January, not 25 March as was then customary. This puts the dates of English documents eleven days behind those of French documents, which are given in the Gregorian style.

Table 1
Population of St. Pierre and Dependent Settlements, 1687

Place	Men	Boys +15	Boys -15	Women	Girls +15	Girls -15	Engagés	Total
St. Pierre	3	3		3	1		66	76
Fortune	1	1	3	1	2	1	63	72
Grand Banc	3			2		1	39	45
Havre Bertrand	1						35	36
Cap Negre	5	1	2	3	1	1	58	71
L'ermitage	2			1			28	31
Total	15	5	5	10	4	3	289	331

Source: See text.

This pattern, in which dispersed settlements consisted of one or two resident families with temporary contract labourers and seasonal fishermen swelling their numbers, was typical of seventeenth-century Newfoundland, both French and English.[12] If there was geographic mobility, residents did not not move far; some lived at Fortune or Connaigre one year and at St. Pierre another.[13] They supported themselves by fishing in the summer and hunting and trapping in the winter. They marketed their catch not through Plaisance, but through St. Pierre, which served as both a social and economic centre. Most of the fifteen dwellings reported at St. Pierre in 1690 would have been seasonal abodes for French merchants and traders, especially from St. Malo. Their metropolitan connections provided the region's inhabitants with essential

[12]Of the thirty or so English settlements in Newfoundland towards the end of the 1690s, eight contained only one nuclear family and twenty-four had less than five families. The English population fluctuated around 2,000; Handcock, *Origins*, 39-46.

[13]In 1714 at Bandalore, deep in Fortune Bay, there were several structures that belonged to one "Monsr Belorm, a Malouin Gentleman, who hath winter^{d} in that place 20 Years, Successively one after the other...;" William Taverner, "Second Report of his survey work, 1714/15" (received 20 May 1718), PRO CO 194/6/232. This was most probably Simon Belorm or Bolorm, identified in 1714 as a resident of St. Pierre.

services such as outfitting, provisioning, and marketing.[14] Both before and after the French era, St. Pierre was "a considerable Place of Trade;" as the summer ended, and "especially about Mich^mas^ [29 September]...all the Planters & Servants from the Bay de Espère, Capnigro, Grand Bank, Fortune, Courbin &c. bring in their Furrs and Summers Fish to sell for purchasing their Winters Provisions and necessarys."[15] The merchants also brought *engagés* into the area. Some were contracted to the inhabitants; others remained in the merchant's employ, in which case the resident fisherman may have acted more as an agent than as his own master. A few merchants maintained their own fishing stations. Thus, the proprietor named Boismoiris who maintained a station at Fortune in 1714 was almost certainly Claude Chenu, Sieur de Boismoiry, a merchant of St. Malo who with his three brothers played a substantial role in sustaining the resident French fishing communities in southwestern Newfoundland during the 1730s and 1740s.[16] People would also have been encouraged to settle in these remote places by the presence at St. Pierre of a religious cleric, and another at "Cap Negre" (Connaigre).[17]

The disruption and hardship of the war years from 1702 to 1713 must have been difficult. Thus, when some of the buildings at Hermitage were "Burnt by the English" in 1710, at least one resident moved into the Bay d'Espoir.[18] Nevertheless, by the time William Taverner carried out the first English census of the region in 1714, the adult population stood at forty-three, with forty-nine children, for a total of ninety-two; the number of *engagés* was 208 (see table 2). The number of structures had also increased (including at least seven chapels).[19] The people were

---

[14] C. Grant Head, *Eighteenth Century Newfoundland: A Geographer's Perspective* (Ottawa, 1976), 13.

[15] William Taverner to Secretary of State, 22 October 1714, PRO CO 194/5/260v.

[16] A full treatment of the Chenu family and its activities is provided in Janzen, "'Bretons...sans scrupule'."

[17] ANO G[1]/467, No. 4 and No. 5.

[18] Taverner to Secretary of State, 22 October 1714, PRO CO 194/5/260.

[19] Taverner Survey, 1714; Second Report for 1714/15 (received 20 May 1718), PRO CO 194/6/226-241. The improved ratio of inhabitants to *engagés* was a logical reflection of the way in which war had interrupted the annual movement of seasonal labour.

Table 2
Population of St. Pierre and Dependent Settlements, 1714

Place	Name of Planter	Men	Women	Children	Total	Boats	Stages	Houses
Hermitage	Jonathan Micholl	28	-	-	29	6	2	3
Isle Grole	Peter Caroy	6	2	-	9	2	2	5
Canoger	Giles Vincent	17	3	-	21	4	2	4
	Noell Petit	8	-	-	9	2	1	3
	Jonathan Durant	-	-	-	1	-	-	2
St. Peters	Garrª Tulon	19	-	-	20	4	2	6
	Giles Lossout	24	1	-	26	4	1	4
	Simon Bolorm	25	1	6	33	4	1	5
	Larrano Miloro	-	-	-	1	-	1	1
Grand Bank	Jn° Vilden	17	2	1	21	4	1	4
	Stepª Deroch	5	1	6	13	1	1	5
	M. Desallones	21	1	11	34	5	1	4
	Jn° Bourny	4	1	7	13	1	1	2
	Jn° Durand	-	-	-	1	-	-	4
	Julin Durrand	-	-	-	1	-	-	2
	Mr. Mountain	-	-	-	1	-	-	4
	Peter Dupon	-	-	-	1	-	-	2
Fortune	Reno Troquy	9	-	-	10	2	2	2
	Tho. Commes	8	1	6	16	2	1	3
	Jn° Muslow	5	1	-	7	-	-	1
	Nic Boaux	7	1	3	12	3	1	2
	Boismoiris	8	-	-	9	-	1	3
	Larr. Million	17	1	9	28	9	2	6
	Jn° Manhoy	-	1	-	2	-	1	4
Goads	Bossumo				1			
	Jn° Durant	-	-	-	1	-	1	4
TOTAL	26	228	17	49	320	26	11	23

Source: See text.

clearly thriving. And, as the people made quite plain, they were prepared to remain despite the fact that England exercised sovereignty. Taverner reported that most of the male inhabitants and slightly fewer of the *engagés* had sworn the oath of allegiance to the English crown. In effect, the people had been transformed into Newfoundlanders, and the tiny settlements in St. Pierre and Fortune and Hermitage Bays had become homes they preferred not to abandon.[20]

This, however, was much more easily said than done. The authorities at Ile Royale were determined to make a success of the new colony, and sent a priest among the French Newfoundlanders to exhort them to leave.[21] Others were driven away by the British authorities at Placentia, who were quick to abuse their authority, extorting illegal fees and payments from the inhabitants and confiscating their properties for resale to friends and associates. Between 1714 and the late 1720s, this abuse was so persistent that it drove away not only the French but also a significant number of new English settlers.[22] A more subtle yet ultimately more pressing concern was the difficulty of the French inhabitants in adapting to the new mercantile framework after 1714. Long accustomed to exchanging their fish with French merchants for essential supplies and gear, often with the help of credit established over many years of trade, it was not easy to develop similar commercial relations with British merchants. For a while, French trading ships continued to stop at St. Pierre. This, however, was something the British would not tolerate, and soon there were no more reports of French

[20]One factor which contributed to the resiliency of the permanent population was the effort made by the residents to grow more of their own food. At the "Bay of Cap nigro" (Connaigre), Taverner found three plantations which, in addition to its fishery, maintained "2 Corn ffeilds in which growes very good Barley, as ever I saw." Taverner, "Second Report of his survey work 1714/15" (received 20 May 1718), PRO CO 194/6/232v.

[21]Taverner, "Some Remarks," Items F and M, February 1715, PRO CO 194/6/48-48v, 50.

[22]Head, *Eighteenth Century Newfoundland*, 59-60; Capt. St. Lo to Board of Trade, 5 March 1728, PRO CO 194/8/148v, 150.

shipping at St. Pierre or Fortune Bay.[23] Claude Chenu of St. Malo made every effort to maintain his fishing station at Fortune, including the extremely expedient, if not very circumspect, measure of swearing the oath of allegiance to the English crown. Yet as commercial contact with France came to an end, both he and the French inhabitants of Fortune and Hermitage Bays were under growing pressure to leave. By 1724, Lieutenant Gledhill was complaining that the several French families still residing in these bays had fired on "Some of His Maj^ties^ Subjects, and wounded One Man Dangerously...," and he warned that if left alone, they "may in time turn Pyrats."[24] Though it was subsequently established that French Newfoundlanders were legitimate subjects of the English crown, they continued to be viewed with suspicion. By the late 1720s, no French fishermen were left at Placentia; of those who had lived beyond the Burin Peninsula, most had reluctantly drifted to Cape Breton Island.

At Ile Royale, the former Newfoundlanders tried to rebuild their lives, supporting themselves as fishermen, as they had in Fortune and Hermitage Bays. As was characteristic of people who had preferred while living in Newfoundland to maintain some distance from the authorities at Plaisance, they now settled in places like Scatari Island and even Niganiche, away from the emerging administrative and commercial centre of the new colony at Louisbourg. Thus, Pierre LeGrand, once of St. Pierre, settled at Scatari with his family, as did the widow Bourny.[25] Bernard Vincent, possibly an offspring of Gilles Vincent of St. Pierre, settled at Niganiche, while Basil Bourny, an offspring of the Bourny family of Grand Bank, was variously described as a resident of Scatari

---

[23]Elisha Dobree to Taverner, 5 March 1714, PRO CO 194/5/97; Moses Jacqueau to William Lownde (Treasury), 7 May 1714, PRO CO 194/5/117-117v; Taverner, "Report," 22 October 1714, PRO CO 194/5/260v; Taverner, "Some Remarks," Item I, February 1715, PRO CO 194/6/49v.

[24]Gledhill to St. Lo, 16 July 1724, PRO Admiralty Papers (hereafter ADM), series 1, volume 1473.

[25]ANO G^1/466, Nos. 68 and 69, general census of inhabitants at Ile Royale, 1726 and 1734. The widow Bourney, described as a native of Plaisance, could only have been Marie Commaire, wife of Jean Bourny; there were no Bournys in French Newfoundland except the family at Grand Bank.

and Niganiche, and would marry Jeanne Pichot of the latter place.[26] But Ile Royale was not Newfoundland, and the authorities viewed with suspicion those people who deliberately removed themselves from official scrutiny and supervision. France was determined to avoid the mistakes made at Plaisance, with the result that an administrative framework was established in the new colony to regulate all aspects of the fishery in which friction might develop between residents and the seasonal fishermen from France.[27] This strategy quickly became restrictive and burdensome, to the point that a substantial number of fishermen began to drift to a place even more remote, free of control and supervision. They began to re-locate to the southwestern corner of Newfoundland where they settled in several small harbours. The names "Port aux Basques," "Cape Ray," and "Codroy" were used at various times. These names may have been used interchangeably; the name "Codroy" is itself a corruption of Cape Ray (Ca' de Ray). More likely, they referred to individual communities scattered about southwestern Newfoundland (see Figure 3). In any case, this choice of locations placed the inhabitants far enough away from Placentia that they could reasonably expect to avoid interference from the English, who lacked both the will and the means to exercise their authority that far west, and it was effectively beyond the reach of the officials at Louisbourg, whose jurisdiction, according to the terms of the Treaty of Utrecht, did not extend to the coast of Newfoundland. Thus the French Newfoundlanders of Fortune and Hermitage Bays found themselves returning home.

At first, their return was strictly seasonal. In 1724 the Louisbourg authorities accused Basil Bourny, Julien Durand and a fellow

---

[26]ANO G[1]/466, Nos 68 and 69, general census of inhabitants at Ile Royale, 1726 and 1734 (hereafter cited as ANO Ile Royale census, with date); "Journal and Census of Île Royale, prepared by le Sieur de la Roque under the direction of M. le comte de Raymond, in the year 1752," Government of Canada Sessional Paper No. 18, *Report Concerning Canadian Archives for the Year 1905* (Ottawa, 1906), II, 44 (hereafter cited as de la Roque Census); ANO G[2], Greffes des tribunaux de Louisbourg et du Canada (hereafter cited as ANO G[2]), CXCVII, doss. 153 and 196, doss. 124, f.41. Bourny is described in de la Roque's census as a native of Plaisance, born in 1702. Again, this almost certainly made him a son of Jean Bourny and Marie Commaire, for there was no other family by that name living in French Newfoundland at the time.

[27]Balcom, *Cod Fishery*, 14-15.

named Sabot of maintaining a fishing station at Cape Ray.[28] Their choice of Cape Ray and Port aux Basques was dictated in part by the metropolitan French merchants who employed them. Some of these merchants were Basques who were encountering difficulties and discrimination in securing beach space in Ile Royale for their fishing operations and who, like the French Newfoundlanders, gravitated to Niganiche and even Newfoundland in search of a less regulated environment.[29] Certainly that region of Newfoundland had long been associated with the fishing vessels of St. Jean de Luz and Bayonne. The Basques began maintaining semi-permanent shore stations at Codroy in the mid-1720s, leaving crews to overwinter, then picking them up the following year.[30] Other ships showing up at Cape Ray were from Granville.[31] However, it was the merchants of St. Malo who were most strongly linked with the French Newfoundlanders, and one merchant in particular: Claude Chenu. He was identified by Father Marcellin, the missionary at

---

[28]Jacques-Ange Le Normant de Mézy, *commissaire ordonnateur* at Louisbourg, to Jean-Frédéric Phélypeaux, Comte de Maurepas, Minister of Marine, 27 November 1724, AN, Archives des colonies (hereafter AC), série $C^{11}B/7$: 71-71v. Julian Durand, another "native of Plaisance," would marry Madeleine Durand, a native of Niganiche and possibly a granddaughter of Gilles Vincent of St. Pierre; de la Roque Census, 43. Sabot was probably Jean Sabot, husband of Jeanne Bourny and therefore Bourny's brother-in-law.

[29]Laurier Turgeon, "Pêches basques en Atlantique nord (XVIIe-XVIIIe siècle): étude d'économie maritime" (doctorat de 3e cycle, Université de Bordeaux III, 1982), 45-46.

[30]William Taverner, "Second Report" (received 20 May 1718), PRO CO 194/6/237v. Rather than extend his survey to the west coast himself, Taverner relied on information provided by the master of a ship belonging to St. Jean de Luz. The 150-ton *St. Michel*, built and owned by the Sieur Michel de Pedesclaux of Saint Jean de Luz, made fishing voyages to Newfoundland in 1723 and 1724, on each occasion leaving two shallops with their crews to overwinter at Cape Ray; see Pau, Archives départementales des Pyrenées-Atlantiques (hereafter AP-A), série B (supplement), 8724, Registres de l'Amirauté de Bayonne, 1722-1725, entry for 12 January 1724 and 9 August 1725. In 1755, a Basque captain stated that he and his fellow Basques had maintained a shore station at Codroy for thirty years; statement of Jean Lafreche, 9 October 1755, Bayonne, Archives de la chambre de commerce de Bayonne (hereafter cited as ACCB), série I2 (pêche de la moroue), No. 40.

[31]Brest, Archives maritimes au port de Brest (hereafter AM Brest), série $1P^1/1$, 1726, 7/14 and 1727, 5/85, ref. to the *Thomas d'Aquin*, departed Granville in February 1725 and headed to Cape Ray, Newfoundland.

Scatari, as the man who recruited local residents to fish for him in Newfoundland and who, despite the proscriptions of the Louisbourg officials, had encouraged Sabot, Bourny, and Durand to work seasonally at his fishing station at Cape Ray.[32]

Claude Chenu, Sieur Boismory (c. 1678-17?), was one of four brothers: Pierre, Sieur Dubourg (c. 1683-1769); Jacques, Sieur Duchenôt (c. 1687-1758); and Louis, Sieur Duclos (c. 1694-1774). A fifth Chenu, Jerôme, Sieur Dupré (c. 1698-17?) may have been a cousin.[33] They did not belong to the top rank of St. Malo's *négociants*; they lacked the wealth, diversity of commercial activity, and international associations which were definitive characteristics of the great merchants.[34] Instead, their business dealings appear to have been confined to the fishing industry and related activities--outfitting, shipowning, and trade. All appear to have spent their younger adult years as captains of fishing or trading vessels which they either owned individually or in partnership with each other. This in itself was fairly typical of all levels of merchants engaged in overseas commerce, though Louis Chenu seemed content to

---

[32]Joseph Monbeton de Brouillan, *dit* Saint-Ovide, Governor of Louisbourg to Maurepas, 24 November 1723, Archives of Fortress of Louisbourg National Historic Site (hereafter AFL), AC C[11]B/6/193-198v; Maurepas to Saint-Ovide, 26 June 1724, AN AC B/47(ii)/1260-1275; de Normant de Mézy to Maurepas, 27 November 1724, AN AC C[11]B/7/71-71v; affidavit of Rousseau de Souvigny, 23 September, 1724 AFL AC C[11]B/7/72; Maurepas to Saint-Ovide, 25 July 1725, AFL AC B/47(ii)/1260-1275. Since the pagination of the AFL copies of French archival materials does not always accord with the originals, AFL and AN records are distinguished here.

[33]Information on the family was compiled from various registers, reports, declarations, and other manuscripts housed in the Archives départementales de l'Ille-et-Vilaine, Rennes (hereafter cited as AD I-et-V), the Archives de l'arrondissement maritime de Rochefort, Rochefort (hereafter cited as AM Rochefort), the Archives départementales de la Charente-Maritime, La Rochelle (hereafter cited as AD C-M), as well as archival sources already cited. Also of great use was L'Abbé Paul Paris-Jallobert, *Anciens Registres Paroissiaux de Bretagne (Baptêmes-- Mariages--Sépultures): Saint-Malo-de-Phily; Evêché de Saint-Malo--Baronnie de Lohéac-- Sénéchaussée de Rennes* (Rennes, 1902); Paris-Jallobert, *Anciens Registres Paroissiaux de Bretagne (Baptêmes--Mariages--Sépultures): Saint-Malo (Evêché--Seigneurie commune--Sénéchaussée de Dinan)*, (Rennes, 1898), I. The parents of the Chenu brothers were Jean Chenu and Margueritte Porée.

[34]André Lespagnol, *Histoire de Saint-Malo et du pays malouin* (Toulouse, 1984), 152-153.

remain a captain-owner throughout much of the 1730s and 1740s, even as his brothers were establishing themselves as merchants of St. Malo or its suburb, St. Servan. Claude Chenu appears to have been the most mobile. At various times he was identified as belonging to Granville, St. Malo, and La Rochelle, although he always maintained both the business and personal sides of his relationship with his brothers. Together the Chenus maintained fishing stations, owned vessels, and participated in the truck trade at Ile Royale. Their sons provided a large labour pool from which were drawn the captains and junior officers of the Chenu vessels--and the next generation of merchants. This intricate network of shared investment and vessel ownership was fairly characteristic of "une société familiale," by which family connections were used to secure French businesses against the many risks of eighteenth-century commerce.[35] In short, they were a fairly typical, if not yet very powerful, merchant family "on the make," hoping perhaps to duplicate the success of others, like Noël Danycan, who had risen from modest means to the highest ranks of Malouin commercial society.[36]

It was precisely for this reason that the Chenus became intimately involved with the fishing stations in southwestern Newfoundland. Indeed, they played a formative role in their transformation from fishing stations to permanent settlements. The men Claude Chenu recruited to work at Cape Ray were ones he had known, perhaps even employed, at his fishing station in Fortune ten years earlier. During the 1720s, Claude and his brother Pierre frequently visited Scatari Island as owner-captains of vessels engaged in the fish trade, while maintaining a station at Codroy Island near Cape Ray. Brothers Louis and Jacques played junior roles, often serving as second captains. In the early 1730s, Jacques assumed a more prominent part in family trade and even came to dominate it. He

---

[35]The importance of family in eighteenth-century French business is discussed in André Lespagnol, "Une dynastie marchande malouine: les Picot de Clos-Rivière," Société d'Histoire et d'Archéologie de l'Arrondissement de Saint-Malo, *Annales* (1985), 233; Laurier Turgeon, "Les échanges franco-canadiens: Bayonne, les ports basques, et Louisbourg, Ile Royale (1713-1758)" (mémoire de maitrise, Université de Pau, 1977), 86.

[36]Lespagnol, *Saint-Malo*, 131-132. Noël Danycan, Sieur de l'Epine (1656-1734), was the son of a small outfitter who began his career as a captain-outfitter of a Newfoundland fishing vessel. Worth only 15,000 livres at the time of his marriage in 1685, he was worth millions twenty years later, thanks to investments in the South Sea trade.

owned and outfitted many of the vessels; went frequently to Ile Royale; and was the most active Chenu in Louisbourg commerce. Pierre increasingly became rooted as a shipowner, outfitter, and merchant at St. Servan, while Claude was based in part at La Rochelle, handling affairs there; their vessels often made for La Rochelle during their homeward voyage, picking up salt for the fishery. Louis remained a captain-owner, and was a frequent visitor at Codroy and Cape Ray by the late 1730s and the early 1740s. Presumably he supervised family affairs there.

The exact location of the Chenu fishing station is not certain. The documents suggest that a few people lived at Cape Ray but that most resided at Port aux Basques and Codroy Island (see Figure 4). The island is small, barren and windswept, bleak in appearance and quite boggy in places; as a place of settlement, the more hospitable and fertile Codroy River valley just a few miles to the south seemed to make more sense. But Codroy Island was settled by fishermen attracted by a different kind of logic, one governed by the excellence of the local cod fishery and the particular qualities of the island that made it ideal for curing fish. According to James Cook, on its landward side was "a small snugg Harbour for Fishing Shallops, wherein is 12 or 14 Feet at high Water ...in this Harbour are...convenient places [for stages] with good Beaches for drying of Fish. In the Road of Cod Roy is very good Anchorage for Shipping." William Taverner claimed that the harbour provided good fishing for salmon and cod from April until June, while wood and wild geese were abundant nearby.[37] With easy access to additional salmon fishing, hunting, and good stands of timber in the nearby Codroy Valley, Codroy Island was a sensible place for fishermen to settle.

By the mid to late 1720s, Codroy had become more than just a seasonal fishing station supported in part by the Chenus. Women appeared early in the 1720s when Codroy was still a seasonal station. Jeanne Bourny, the sister of Basil and daughter of Jean Bourney and Marie Commaire of Grand Bank, must have spent considerable time there because several of the children by her first husband, Jean Sabot,

---

[37]Taunton, Admiralty Hydrographic Department (hereafter cited as AHD), C.54/5, James Cook, "A Chart of the Sea-Coast...between Cape Anguille and the Harbour of Great Jervis..." (1766). As early as 1714, William Taverner remarked that "the biscayers generally fish here, but their Ships ride under an Island, about two Leag^{s} to the S^{o} ward of the North Cape, where they generally anchor close to the maine." The "North Cape" was Cape Anguille, and the island was Codroy; see Captain Duhaldy's information in Taverner, "Second Report," PRO CO 194/6/240.

were born at Cape Ray: Antoine (born around 1723), Guillemette or Gilette (born about 1725), and Michelle (born about 1728).[38] By 1734 there were at least ten families living there.[39] Six years later, Louis Colas, a chaplain on a fishing vessel that put in at Port aux Basques, recorded the names of some forty individuals in the course of performing a number of baptisms and marriages; the people, wrote Colas, had not seen a priest in seven years. Nearly two dozen more names were recorded in 1741 when a visiting Recollet priest performed some more marriages and baptisms at Codroy Island.[40] Some of the witnesses belonged to the fishing and trading vessels then in port; one was Louis Chenu. Most, however, were permanent inhabitants, living in multi-generational family units. Many were former French Newfoundlanders who had drifted there from Ile Royale: names like Bourny, Commaire, Durand, and Vincent were conspicuous.[41] Living with them, and frequently related by marriage, were French fishermen who had either been *engagés* at Ile Royale or else arrived with the fishing vessels of St. Malo, Granville, and Bayonne. There was Jean Nicholas de Malvilain of St. Malo; several of his children by his marriage to Marie Magdelaine Durand were baptized at Port aux Basques in 1740. There was Guillaume le Marechal, a fisherman from Carolle on France's Cotentin Peninsula; the daughter by his marriage to Jeanne Sabot was similarly baptized at

---

[38]De la Roque Census, 66.

[39]Lord Muskerry's "Answers to Heads of Inquiry," 1734, PRO CO 194/9/259-v, especially Nos. 60-62.

[40]Louis Colas, "prestre au monier du navire Le Mars," "Extrait de registre de bapteme et de mariage de la poste du Petit Nord nommé Port au Basque," 18 May 1740, ANO G^1/410, No. 12; "Baptemes fait à lisle de Cadray," 12 July 1741, ANO G^1/407, Registre 1, fol. 76. Mass baptisms and marriages of this type were not uncommon in eighteenth-century Newfoundland, where appearances by the clergy were infrequent. See Handcock, *Origins*, 153.

[41]In 1740, Louis Colas performed a marriage between Jeanne Bourny, now widowed, and Pierre Berteau. Pierre was a native of French Newfoundland; his father was also Pierre Berteau and his mother was Renée Carmel. In 1752 Renée was still alive, though she was by then 102 years old and living with Pierre and Jeanne in Ance Daranbourg in Ile Royale; de la Roque Census, 65-66. Renée was the sister of Marie Carmel, who witnessed some of the marriages and baptisms at Cape Ray in 1740. At the same time that he married Pierre and Jeanne, Colas baptized Pierre, their first son, who was born in September 1739. Jeanne's brother, Charles, married Anne Vincent.

Port aux Basques. A significant proportion were not even French. About half were Irish who may have drifted west from Placentia, where a substantial influx of Irish labourers had occurred in the 1720s.[42]

The people supported themselves principally through the fishery, turning to trapping in the winter. They exchanged the fish and furs for supplies and provisions from passing ships. The Cabot Strait was a gateway for French shipping bound for Canada, the fishery of western Newfoundland, the Gulf of St. Lawrence, and the "Grand Bay" towards Labrador. Vessels put in at Port aux Basques and Codroy either to fish, to trade for fish from the inhabitants, or to trade with one another. It was this trade that kept the settlements alive. According to Taverner:

> ...their greatest Supply is from St. Malo and Rachael [La Rochelle], who Supply them with almost every thing Needfull, to carry on the Cod Fishery, Salmon-Fishery, Seal-Fishery, and Furring, nay even with green Men, which are Engaged for thirty Six Months, which the Masters in France pretends...Serve at Cape Breton.[43]

A French Minister of Marine later complained that two vessels from St. Malo and Granville "a donné du Secourse a des deserteurs françois et anglois qui se refugies au port des basques situé prée de l'Isle Royalle ayant fourny...des hommes et des Ustenciles malgré les deffensce faites tant par le Gouverneur de L'Isle Royale."[44] Clearly, the people of Port aux Basques and Codroy would not have survived had it not been for regular visits by metropolitan ships and vessels.

---

[42]Several children belonging to Daniel Rourque and his wife Anne Macnamara and to Francis O'Neill and Georgina Hill were baptized at Port aux Basques in 1740. Magdelaine Hill was married to Louis Thebaut; three of their children were baptized at Codroy in 1741. The son of Augustine Hill and Hélène Porré was baptized at Codroy in 1741. See ANO G^1/407, registre 1, fol. 76 and ANO G^1/410.

[43]Taverner to Board of Trade, 2 February 1734, PRO CO 194/23/180-182v.

[44]Maurepas to M. de la Fossingnant, the *commissaire-général de la marine* at St. Malo, 4 March 1738; AM Brest $1P^1$/2, 1738, 10/60. The vessels were *Le Mars* (St. Malo, 200 tons, 112 men), Captain Jean Baptiste Le Pelley, Sieur des Cerisiez, in concert with *Le Vandangeur* (Granville, eighty tons), Captain Olivier Grentel. *Le Mars* was also the ship on which the priest, Louis Colas, served when he visited Port aux Basques in 1740.

FIGURE 3:
SOUTHWESTERN NEWFOUNDLAND

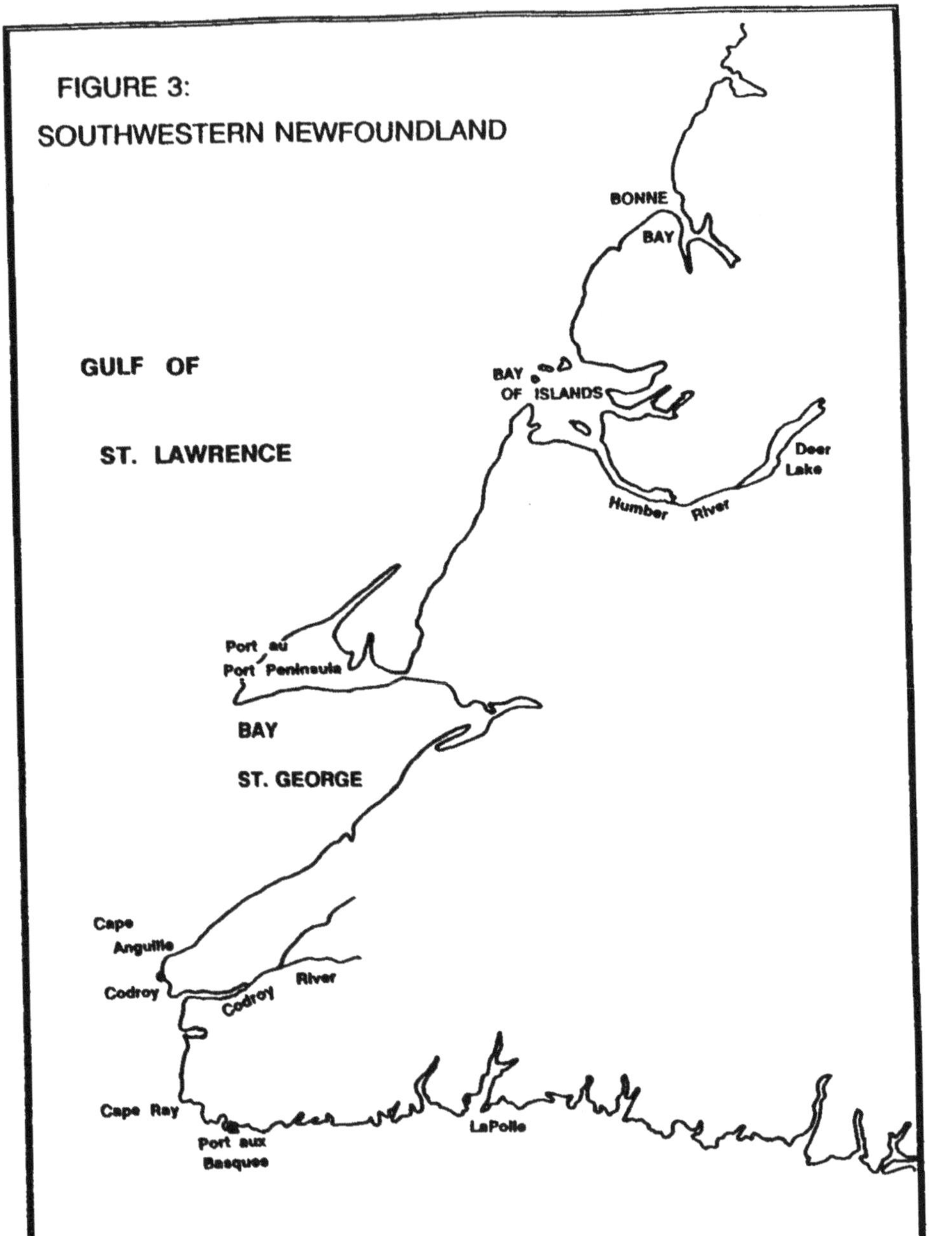

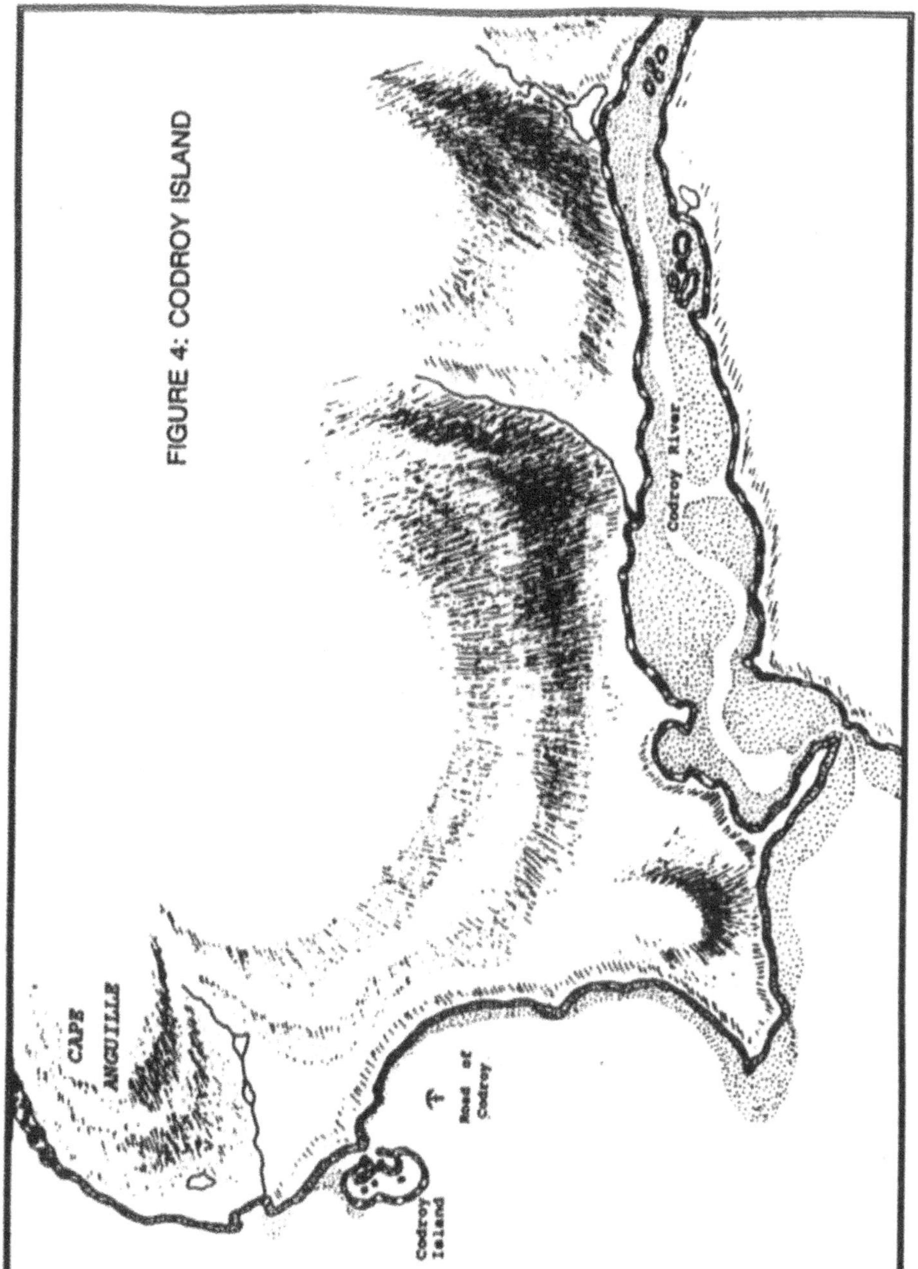

FIGURE 4: CODROY ISLAND

It was a situation quite characteristic of eighteenth-century Newfoundland, where "merchants...were the activating agents" of settlement.[45] In this particular instance, however, the activities of the merchants were neither approved nor desired by the authorities at Louisbourg. From the start, officials were concerned by the way in which the Newfoundland settlements allowed the fishermen and inhabitants of Ile Royale to abandon ("abandonner") Ile Royale.[46] As the settlements persisted, they acted as temptations to the *engagés* employed in Ile Royale to desert their employers and their contracts, in the process of which some also stole their employers' shallops and gear.[47] Saint-Ovide referred to Port aux Basques as a hideout or lair ("ce repaire") for those evading the law, and its inhabitants were variously described as "déserteurs" and "fripons" at best, and "brigands" and "bandits" at worst. What most disturbed officials was that in Newfoundland, unlike Ile Royale, the fishermen were free of restrictive and burdensome regulations, fees, and supervision. As Bigot succinctly explained, "c'est qu'ils y sont independans." Another official characterized the society of Port aux Basques and Codroy as "cette petite Republique."[48]

Of possibly equal or greater concern was the way in which the Cape Ray settlements developed into a centre of illicit trade, for not all the merchants who traded at Port aux Basques or Codroy were French. In 1732 Governor Saint-Ovide reported that Anglo-American as well as French vessels were supplying the people at Cape Ray with supplies and provisions in exchange for fish and oil; Anglo-American vessels were

---

[45]W. Gordon Handcock, "English Migration to Newfoundland," in Mannion (ed.), *Peopling of Newfoundland*, 24. John J. Mannion, "Settlers and Traders in Western Newfoundland," *ibid.*, 234, maintains that in Newfoundland, "Unlike so many parts of frontier North America, established trading patterns preceded permanent settlement..."

[46]Maurepas to Saint-Ovide, 26 June 1724, AN AC B/47(ii)/1260-1275.

[47]"...nombre de matelots et engagez y ont enlevé cette plusieurs chaloupes à leurs maistres et les ont emmené en l'Isle de terreneuve dont quelques unes ont esté reprises." Maurepas de le Normant de Mazy, AN AC B/52-2/607v-8.

[48]Bigot to Maurepas, 4 October 1742, AN AC C¹¹B/24/117v; Memorial enclosed in J. Burnaby (Paris) to John Courand, 2 March 1735 (N.S.), PRO SP 78/207/675.

found at Port aux Basques as early as the late 1720s.[49] For several years Jeanne Bourny's brother-in-law by her second marriage, Antoine Berteau, managed a fishing station at Port aux Basques for an unidentified English merchant.[50] In 1734, William Taverner complained that a French planter at Port aux Basques with the improbable name of Russell had died two years earlier still indebted to him, and "tho' the Man Dyed worth Money," the other residents conspired to prevent Taverner from collecting his debt.[51] What drew the New Englanders was not only the fishery and trade but also the opportunity to trade with French merchants without fear of supervision or interference by the authorities.[52] Yet these commercial activities were ultimately responsible for the continued survival of the Cape Ray communities. The French authorities recognized this fact and would use it in their attempts to bring settlement in southwestern Newfoundland to an end.

The ideal solution would have been to evict the inhabitants from Newfoundland altogether. Tempting though the idea was, France exercised no jurisdiction in Newfoundland because of the Treaty of Utrecht.[53]

---

[49]Saint-Ovide to Maurepas, 14 November 1732, AFL C[11]B/12/254-262. In 1727 a Boston vessel at Port aux Basques was attacked and seized by Micmac Indians from Cape Breton Island; Saint-Ovide to Maurepas, 13 September and 30 November 1727, AN AC C[11]B/9/50v-51, 64-70v.

[50]De la Roque Census, 44.

[51]Taverner to Board of Trade, 2 February 1734, PRO CO 194/23/180-182v.

[52]Maurepas to de la Bove, 27 April 1742, AFL AC B/75/84-84v.

[53]Saint-Ovide transmitted to Maurepas the suggestion of the British commander at Canso, Nova Scotia, to launch a joint Anglo-French expedition against Cape Ray. No immediate action was taken, Maurepas preferring to handle the question at that point through diplomatic channels; Saint-Ovide to Maurepas, 14 November 1732, AFL AC C[11]B/12/254-262. France eventually offered to organize such an expedition if the British were to grant permission; Memorial enclosed in J. Burnaby (Paris) to John Courand, 2 March 1735 (N.S.), PRO SP 78/207/675. By then, however, British concerns that the settlements at Codroy and Port aux Basques were French and therefore in violation of the Treaty of Utrecht had eased following a visit to Port aux Basques by Captain Crawford in HMS *Roebuck*. Crawford assured his superiors that the settlers had all sworn allegiance to England, and were subjects of the crown; Lord Muskerry, Answers to Heads of Inquiry, Nos. 60-62, 1734, PRO CO 194/9/259-259v. Any thought of allowing the French to evict British subjects from British soil was quickly dismissed.

Officials therefore tried to discourage the movement of people to Newfoundland at its source in Ile Royale. Numerous orders and proclamations were issued, demanding that the fishermen at Cape Ray return at once to French territory. At one point, officials even directed the priest at Niganiche to stop performing marriages between women of that outport and men from Cape Ray, out of recognition that the viability of the communities in Newfoundland depended less on the number of men who settled there than the number of women who joined them.[54] This, too, proved futile; in the absence of an effective enforcement mechanism, orders forbidding migration were difficult, if not impossible, to enforce.[55] Officials at Louisbourg then tried to interdict trade with Newfoundland, in the realization that commercial linkages with France and America were nurturing the settlements.[56] This strategy proved no more successful than the others--a confirmation, perhaps, that regulation and supervision of overseas commerce and possessions were more theoretical ideals than practical measures in the eighteenth century.

The fact was that French authorities lacked the means to investigate merchants suspected of illegal trade. There were few warships stationed at Louisbourg, and these were expected to patrol the fishing banks, not adjacent coastlines or in search of illicit trade.[57] To monitor and regulate trade, Paris relied on port officials in Normandy, Brittany, and the Basque country. However, to judge by the ineffectual efforts to

---

[54]Bigot to Maurepas, 4 October 1742, AN AC C[11]B/24/117-117v.

[55]See, for instance, the proclamation of Governor Saint-Ovide to the "habitans françois du port aux basques," 28 June 1734, AD C-M B-274.

[56]In 1733, the French government ordered a "Défense absolue" on all French merchantmen trading with Cape Ray, and declared its intention to punish those who had been doing so. Yet ships continued to go there. See Saint-Ovide to Maurepas, 14 November 1732, AFL C[11]B/12/254-262; Maurepas to Saint-Ovide and Le Normant de Mézy, 19 May 1733, AFL AC B/59-2/522-523v; and Saint-Ovide and Le Normant de Mézy to Maurepas, 13 October 1733, AFL C[11]B/14/43-50v.

[57]McNeill, *Atlantic Empires*, 92-93, 239n. F.J. Thorpe concedes that while Louisbourg was expected to play a significant role in Maurepas' efforts to restore the French navy after 1723, naval growth failed to keep up with the naval infrastructure established at Louisbourg; "The Cod Fishery in French American Strategy, 1660-1783" (paper presented at the Annual Meeting of the Canadian Historical Association, Québec, June 1989), 5-6.

stop trade with Newfoundland, this approach was simply not reliable. Louisbourg officials seemed to expect their counterparts in France to crack down on illicit trade with Newfoundland, while port officials like the *commissaire-général de la marine* at St. Malo, de la Fossingnant, seemed to perceive the problem more as a colonial than a metropolitan one. In any case, whatever their feelings about the affront to their authority that the "petite République" might represent, officials at Louisbourg or St. Malo adopted a fairly tolerant attitude towards illicit trade if it meant prosperity for their respective ports.[58] For this reason, by 1742 the *ordonnateur* at Louisbourg was claiming that more harm than good would ensue, should the communities at Codroy and Port aux Basques be eliminated.[59] Consequently, the French authorities seemingly could do little more than suspect and accuse merchants of illicit trade, to which the merchants responded either with excuses or assurances that any illicit activity would cease--but of course, it did not.

The family Chenu provided a striking demonstration of this practice. The men were flagrant participants in the trade at Codroy; certainly they attracted considerable attention, not to mention threats, from the authorities both in Louisbourg and Paris. Yet at no time was there any evidence that the Chenus came into serious difficulties because of their association with fishing settlements. Nor did the Chenus try very hard to disguise their activities. Cape Ray appeared in the port records of St. Malo as the intended destination of two of Jacques Chenu's vessels in 1743 and 1744, while Codroy was the intended destination of another in 1743; in that same year Claude Chenu was co-owner of a vessel destined for Cape Anguille, which looms over Codroy Island. Indeed, at one point they not only admitted that their ships were destined for Cape

---

[58]On illicit trade between Louisbourg and New England, A.H. Clark, *Acadia: The Geography of Early Nova Scotia to 1760* (Madison, WI, 1968), 319, remarked that "Not only did the Louisbourg officials wink at it, but at times they encouraged it, both because of the real need of the colony and because its extra-legal nature made it possible for the officials to profit from it..."

[59]Governor Duquesnel and *ordonnateur* Bigot to Maurepas, 17 October 1742, AFL C11B/24/28-30. By 1742 the fishery at Ile Royale was experiencing a fall in production; Bigot wanted permission to allow French ships to make up their cargoes with purchases of New England cod if necessary. Additional urgency was provided by the war between England and Spain; French merchants were scrambling to satisfy Spain's enormous demand for cod with the Spanish markets closed to English fish. See Janzen, "Bretons... sans scrupule," 193.

Ray but also argued that they should be permitted to maintain a fishing station there on the grounds that the fishery there was extremely productive; they responded to charges of trading at Cape Ray by insisting that any trade was with other French fishing vessels.[60] Nevertheless, there is much evidence that their activities in southwestern Newfoundland were being covered up. Louis Chenu spent some time at Codroy with his vessel, the *Légère*, in 1741; Chenu was both a godparent and a witness that July when a visiting Recollet priest performed some marriages and baptisms. Yet the voyage summary recorded upon his return to St. Malo in December gave no indication that there had been any ports of call between his departure from St. Malo on 3 June and his arrival at Laurembec on Ile Royale an otherwise unaccountable two months later. Other Chenu vessels made equally lengthy and suspicious ocean crossings, but cannot so easily be proven to have put in at one of the ports of southwestern Newfoundland.[61]

By 1743 even Maurepas was sceptical that trade with the Cape Ray settlements could successfully be interdicted, though he never gave up entirely on the idea. Success would come only with the cooperation and assistance of the English, who alone exercised sovereignty and therefore jurisdiction over southwestern Newfoundland.[62] The English, however, could never be roused to act vigorously against the settlements, even though the Board of Trade had been emphatic that "it was not for the Interest of the Fishery of Newfoundland to encourage Settlements there, even of His Majesty's Subjects."[63] This was not an age in which government was noted either for its familiarity with specific colonial

---

[60]Maurepas de M. de la Fossingnant (St. Malo), 31 March 1733, AM Brest 1P[1]/2, 1733, 19/67.

[61]*Hirondelle* (or *Irondelle*): AD I-et-V 9B/501, 13 March 1743, and 9B/420, 157, 21 March 1744; *Achille*: AD I-et-V 9B/171, 7 June 1743; *Saint-Ursin*: AD I-et-V 9B/171 and 9B/420, 22 May 1743; *Légère*: compare AD I-et-V 9B/501, 5 December 1741 with ANO G[1]/407, Registre 1, fol. 76, "Baptemes fait à lisle de Cadray 1741."

[62]Maurepas to Governor Duquesnel and Bigot, 30 June 1743, AFL AC B/76/508-509v.

[63]Board of Trade to Duke of Newcastle, 24 April 1734, CO 194/23/176.

possessions or for the vigour of its administration of empire.[64] When government could be roused to investigate reports of settlers at Port aux Basques or Codroy, officials were soon satisfied that neither British sovereignty nor the British fishery at Newfoundland were in jeopardy. It is ironic, then, that the first phase of settlement at Codroy came to an end, not because of government action, but through its inaction. When England and France went to war in 1744, the tiny fishing settlements in southwestern Newfoundland were utterly defenceless; the very ambiguity of authority that had left Louisbourg officials frustrated by their inability to bring these settlements to an end, and which had left the British indifferent to their presence, now left the inhabitants without protection against marauding privateers. Choosing discretion over valour, the residents, both French and Irish, withdrew to the seeming security of Ile Royale. Within a few months, their homes and properties had been destroyed by privateers.[65]

The Resumption of French Settlement in Newfoundland (c. 1748-1755)

The inhabitants who fled their homes in southwestern Newfoundland remained true to the independence of character which Bigot had found so lamentable. Those who can be identified by name tended to return to the outports of Ile Royale, especially Scatari, Niganiche, and Petit Bras d'Or. Some went to Louisbourg; of these, a few refused to join the general evacuation that followed the capture of the town in 1745. When the war ended in 1748, most appear to have remained in their new homes, rather than return to Newfoundland. Yet Codroy, Port aux Basques, and the other settlements in southwestern Newfoundland were reestablished by the early 1750s. Who settled there and in what numbers has not yet been determined; perhaps the question will never be answered. Yet by the time the next war flared in 1755, the population at

---

[64]James Henretta, *"Salutary Neglect": Colonial Administration Under the Duke of Newcastle* (Princeton, 1976), 31-33, 64-67, 104-105, 107, 266-267; Ronald Higham, "Imperial Interests and the Peace of Paris (1763)," in Ronald Hyam and Ged Martin (eds.), *Reappraisals in British Imperial History* (Toronto, 1975), 21-43.

[65]Governor Duchambon and Bigot to Maurepas, 4 November 1744, AFL AC C[11]B/26/32-36.

Codroy and its environs was substantial and gave every indication of once again filling the kind of role it had played in the 1730s and 1740s.

What little we know about the rebirth of these settlements comes from documents describing their destruction in 1755. Though France and England were not officially at war, their armies had already clashed deep within North America. In Nova Scotia, British civil, military, and naval authorities met to discuss what to do with the several thousand French-speaking Acadians who had been living under their jurisdiction since 1713 but had consistently refused to swear an oath of allegiance to the British crown. As a precaution against their giving assistance to France in the fast-approaching war, the authorities agreed to the controversial solution of expelling the entire Acadian population from the province. Lost in the enormity of this decision is the fact that those same authorities also decided to remove the hundred or so people living in south-western Newfoundland. Upon his arrival in Nova Scotia, Edward Boscawen, Vice-Admiral of the Blue, learned that French fishermen had settled once again at Port aux Basques.[66] As preparations for the Acadian deportation were begun, he ordered three ships to Newfoundland to deal with the situation.[67]

Commanding this expedition was John Rous, in the *Success* frigate; he was accompanied by *Arundel*, Captain Thomas Hankerson, and *Vulture*. Rous was an obvious choice for the job. As a New England privateering captain, he made extensive raids on French fishing fleets and harbours in the Petit Nord of Newfoundland in 1744. In July 1755, he participated in the decision to expel the Acadians from Nova Scotia; in October, he would be in charge of the convoy that removed the Acadians of the Chignecto Isthmus.[68] In effect, the operation in Newfoundland was a small dress rehearsal for the greater tragedy in Nova Scotia.

In company with *Arundel* and *Vulture*, Rous sailed from Halifax early in August; after a brief stop at St. Peter's, he arrived at "Cape Ray Road" (Codroy Road) on 21 August. While the other ships went off to cruise the adjacent trade lanes and to reconnoitre Port aux Basques, Rous proceeded to seize the Basque vessels he found at Codroy, together with

---

[66]W.A.B. Douglas, "Edward Boscawen," *DCB*, III, 70-71.

[67]Boscawen to Admiralty, 15 November 1755, PRO ADM 1/481/67-69v.

[68]W.A.B. Douglas, "John Rous," *DCB*, III, 572-574.

their fish, oil, and other marine products.[69] Assisting him were four English inhabitants of Port aux Basques (though whether they had been coerced is not clear). All the inhabitants at Codroy this time appear to have been French; many fled in shallops while one small vessel managed to slip its moorings before it could be seized. Nevertheless, at least sixty-seven inhabitants, mostly women and children, were taken. The crews of the Basque vessels were caught almost entirely unawares by this aggression and watched helplessly as their catches were seized, and the shore facilities, including cabins, stages, and shallops, put to the torch. Five harbours were devastated in total, their facilities and habitations destroyed, and four vessels taken (including at least two merchantman captured while making their way from Bordeaux to destinations in French Canada). Rous then delivered his prisoners to Ile Royale, where they were deposited unceremoniously on the beach at Gabarus Bay.

What little we can learn from these events about settlement in southwestern Newfoundland between 1748 and 1755 is instructive. Once again, several harbours, most notably Port aux Basques and Codroy, had attracted not only seasonal residents but also, to judge by the number of women and children, permanent inhabitants. Once again, the existence of these settled outposts depended not simply on the fishery but on metropolitan merchants and traders who maintained fishing stations and presumably included residents among their employees. There is a suggestion that Port aux Basques harboured more English-speaking residents while Codroy was predominantly French. Though we cannot attach a single name to any of these residents, the speed with which the

---

[69] Captain's log, *Success*, Captain Rous, PRO ADM 51/940, ii; Master's log, *Vulture*, Mr. Joseph Marriott, PRO ADM 52/1092, iii. The vessels seized were the *Ste. Catherine* (150 tons) of St. Jean de Luz, Captain Sansin Halsouet, and the *Deux Maries* (140 tons), Captain Jean Lafreche. *Vulture* later sailed north to Bay St. George where it took the *Saint-Jean*, Captain Marticot Hiriboure (*Vulture*'s log identifies it as the *St. Jean Baptiste*); to judge by the destruction ashore of "Tents & Craft," this was definitely a seasonal camp with no hint of permanence. Both *Saint-Jean* and *Deux Maries* were owned by Esteban Dargainarats of the Basque port of Ciboure. See statements of the captains of the fishing ships in ACCB I.2, Nos. 40, 41, 44, 46, 47, 48. All three ships had departed Socoa, near Ciboure, in February "pour aller au Cap de Ray en terre neuve faire la Pescherie et Sescherie de Morues." They had arrived early in April and had just begun loading the fish that their crews had made that season when they were seized. The *Notre Dame du Rozaire* of St. Malo managed to escape, but not without leaving sails, new cables, an anchor, several shallops, some fish, and "Tous les Coffres des equipages" behind.

communities were reestablished after peace was restored in 1748 suggests strongly that their inhabitants were the same people who had abandoned them in 1744 and were simply returning to their Newfoundland homes. Finally, and also once again, the remoteness which enabled the little society at Codroy to escape official notice and allowed it to grow in peacetime was its undoing in time of war. The second phase of French inhabitancy in southwestern Newfoundland had come to an even more abrupt and traumatic end than the first. As it turned out, 1755 also marked the end of the last phase of French residence. When Codroy again reappeared in the documentary record early in the 1760s, it would be as a British settlement.

The Final Phase of Inhabitancy (c. 1760-1783)

When the Seven Years' War came to an end in 1763, Newfoundland station ships began patrolling the west coast for the first time. In 1764, Governor Palliser became the first governor of Newfoundland to visit the area, bringing most of his ships in a deliberate assertion of British sovereignty. In 1766 and 1767 James Cook surveyed the coast for the British Admiralty. These various official visits were responses to French claims after 1763 that the fishing rights and privileges they enjoyed under the terms of the Treaty of Utrecht included the entire west coast of Newfoundland.[70] The British Board of Trade had quickly challenged this claim with some cartographic research, adding that "many of Your Majesty's Subjects have long been used to frequent and carry on a fishery in those Harbours, particularly that near Cape Ray and in the Bay of St. George."[71] This was indeed stretching the truth, for most of the "Subjects" of King George III in the region had been French until 1755.[72] It was to add weight to these conclusions that Hugh Palliser was

---

[70]Olaf Janzen, "Showing the Flag: Hugh Palliser in Western Newfoundland, 1764" (paper presented at the Annual Meeting of the Canadian Nautical Research Society, St. John's, Newfoundland, June 1992).

[71]Board of Trade to the King, 20 April 1764, PRO CO 195/9/330-356.

[72]The Board of Trade must have been quite aware of this fact. The *Lark*, Captain Samuel Thompson, had spent two months patrolling the coast between Port aux Basques and Port aux Choix in 1763; his report to his superiors indicated that Codroy had belonged to the French until "the beginning of the late Warr." Thompson's report to

directed to "visit all the Coasts and Harbours of the said Islands and Territories under Your Governm^t^," a directive which took Palliser and most of his ships to the Bay of Islands during the summer of 1764.[73] It was also largely for this reason that the authorities offered no objections and took no actions against the British merchants who began to nurture settlement on that coast, even though elsewhere in Newfoundland it was official policy to regard permanent settlement as a threat to the well-being of the migratory fishery and to discourage its spread.

When Captain Samuel Thompson of the warship *Lark* visited western Newfoundland in 1763, he found a substantial settlement on the old French site at Codroy Island. About a hundred people lived there in homes built directly on the island. This made Codroy a substantial settlement; it was also the only settlement on the west coast, and in contrast to the earlier communities, Codroy in 1763 did not yet include many women; Thompson counted only five families.[74] Nevertheless, most of the inhabitants stayed at Codroy year round, supporting themselves in a familiar pattern of fishing in the summer and trapping beaver, otter, marten, and fox during the off-season. Most of the fishing was conducted locally at Codroy, though some of the inhabitants fished at various locations as far north as the Bay of Islands.[75]

A significant number of the people were Irish, and many were former residents of St. Pierre until displaced by the British decision to

---

Admiralty Secretary, Philip Stephens, 12 March 1764, PRO ADM 1/2590, No. 4, Captain Thompson's Letters. The most detailed description of the Codroy settlement appears in his "Remarks" in Answers to Heads of Inquiry, 1763, Greenwich, National Maritime Museum (hereafter NMM), Graves Papers (hereafter GRV), item 105. Unless otherwise indicated, the descriptive details concerning the Codroy settlement after 1760 all come from Thompson's "Remarks" and "Answers."

[73]Board of Trade, draft of instructions for Hugh Palliser, No. 12, 10 April 1764, PRO CO 195/9/286-287.

[74]"Answers to Heads of Inquiry, 1763," especially "Remarks" and "Answers" of Captain Thompson, GRV/105, No. 46.

[75]In 1764, Governor Palliser would learn that some unidentified Englishmen had overwintered in the Bay of Islands in 1762; see his remarks in London, British Library, Additional Manuscripts (hereafter BL Add.) 17,693a, "A Plan of the Bay of Three Islands in Newfoundland...; taken on board HMS Guernsey, June 1764." Presumably these overwinterers were connected with the settlement at Codroy.

return that place to France in 1763; others were from various parts of Newfoundland. However, at least twenty-six servants were brought from Louisbourg and Halifax--it would be nice to think that some servants from Louisbourg had names like Sabot, Bourny, and Commaire, but thus far no records of names have been found. The willingness of metropolitan merchants to maintain a permanent fishing station through the employment of imported and residential labour had been essential for Codroy's survival in its earlier incarnations; this was also the case in 1763. The settlement's "principal inhabitant" was Jonathan Broom; during the 1750s, he had been linked with Bonavista on Newfoundland's east coast, but by the 1760s Broom was maintaining Codroy as a fishing station, like the Chenus and other predecessors. His employees could also be found at Bay St. George, the Bay of Islands, and possibly points beyond that.

Though there was clearly some commerce between St. Pierre and Codroy, Broom supplied most of the settlers' needs; he shipped in salt, clothing, and some bread and flour from England, pork and butter from Ireland, while most of the provisions, including pork, bread, flour, rum, and molasses, as well as tobacco, salt, and cordage, came from New England. Apart from the fishery, the attraction of this part of Newfoundland for Broom and the inhabitants, as it had been for their French predecessors, lay in its abundant resources. Mention has already been made of fur trapping, and visitors also remarked on the wealth of the salmon fishery and the quality of the timber. Captain Thompson observed that "in general the Coast is cover'd with large Trees fit for Ship Building, such as ye various Kinds of Birch, Juniper, Pines & Spruce fitt for masts;" in 1767 at least two vessels were built at Codroy.[76]

In 1783 the entire region fell under French control, following the re-definition of the French Shore. The eastern limits of the French Shore were moved west to Cape St. John, and a similar adjustment was made to its western limits, which now extended all the way to Cape Ray. Though their claims in 1763 to the west coast had not been pursued vigorously, the French had worked long and hard to settle the question of whether the fishery on the Treaty Shore was exclusively French or whether it had to be shared with the British--the Treaty of Utrecht had

---

[76]Thompson, "Remarks;" Head, *Eighteenth Century Newfoundland*, 165.

not made this clear. The French had failed to prevent the penetration of Notre Dame Bay during the 1720s and 1730s by British fishermen and settlers, and did not insist that their fishing privileges on the Treaty Shore were exclusive, rather than concurrent, until the 1760s. Since it was too late by then to remove the British from Notre Dame Bay, France chose to abandon it and to re-define the Treaty Shore to include the relatively empty west coast. In this way, the French hoped to acquire a second chance to develop their Treaty Shore fishery exclusively.[77]

As a result of this re-definition of the Treaty Shore and of government subsidies and bounties, the French fishing industry was quickly reestablished on the west coast. But this meant discouraging any English settlers found here, to forestall a repetition of what had happened in Notre Dame Bay. The settlements on the west coast therefore found themselves under pressure from the French to leave. In 1785 the French destroyed two salmon posts in Bay St. George, and tried to force settlers in the area to leave. Broom (or perhaps by then his son) re-located to the Burin Peninsula, though it is not clear what, if anything, happened to the people living at Codroy. French hostility to settlement in western Newfoundland was interrupted by the French Revolutionary and Napoleonic Wars after 1793, with the result that during the next twenty years the commercial and demographic growth in the region continued.[78] By the time the French returned after 1815, it was too late to reverse this growth. Thus, the single greatest contrast between the earlier French incarnations of Codroy and its eventual English one was in the effect that war had on the survival of settlement. Conditions of war had always forced the French inhabitants to abandon their homes, whereas wartime conditions allowed settlement to persist once Codroy's identity became English. Today, the French settlements at Codroy in the early eighteenth century are largely forgotten, except for the many French and Basque place-names that can still be found on the map.

---

[77]Brière, "Pêche et politique," 175-183; James K. Hiller, "The Newfoundland Fisheries Issue in Anglo-French Treaties, 1761-1783" (paper presented at the Ninth Atlantic Canada Studies Conference, St. John's, Newfoundland, May 1992), 10-11.

[78]The settlement history of western Newfoundland after 1783 is discussed in Mannion, "Settlers and Traders," in Mannion (ed.), *Peopling of Newfoundland*, 234-279.

Changes in Aleut Communities Following Russian Contact

Judith Ball Bruce

The year 1991 marked the two hundred fiftieth anniversary of the Russian discovery of the northwestern coast of North America by members of the Second Kamchatka Expedition. That discovery resulted in contact between the Russians and the inhabitants of the islands of the Aleutian archipelago. As in so many of the other early interactions between Europeans and indigenous groups, in the wake of Russian contact the Aleut population declined drastically and irreversible changes in indigenous patterns occurred. In spite of this, not all the consequences of contact with the Russians proved negative.

Many historians and anthropologists have painted a fairly simple picture of the Russian-Aleut relationship in which the latter were overwhelmed by the far greater strength of the former. This explanation, however, does not incorporate all relevant data and generalizes too broadly. Instead, neither Russian strengths nor Aleut weaknesses were as great as the traditional accounts suggest. For example, no Russian fur-hunting crew had more than sixty members, and they were customarily divided into three work groups. Twenty men, even with firearms, were not a particularly difficult challenge for the Aleuts. Moreover, the Aleuts had a tremendous advantage in that they knew the territory far better than the Russians. In short, many explanations of the Russian-Aleut relationship ignore several important elements which demonstrate that it was complex and far from static. This paper attempts to identify some of those operative factors and to suggest how they alter the more familiar accounts of the relationship between Russians and Aleuts.

One of the most important tasks of the Second Kamchatka Expedition, headed by Captain Vitus Bering and Alexei Chirikov, his second-in-command, was to determine conclusively whether the Asian land mass was connected to the *Bolshoi Zemlia* ("Great Land") to the east. One of the two vessels that sailed in search of this information was commanded by Bering, the other by Chirikov. After the two became

Research in Maritime History, No. 3 (December 1992), 35-46.

separated, Chirikov went on to make the first sighting of the north-western North American coast and then returned to Russia.[1]

Bering was less fortunate. He and his crew were shipwrecked near the island that now bears his name and forced to winter there. Although Bering and some of his men died before spring, the survivors were able to rebuild their vessel and sail back to Russia. At the time great numbers of marine mammals lived in the north Pacific; Bering's crew survived by hunting them for food and using their pelts for clothing, which they were wearing when they reached Kamchatka.

Eastward Expansion and the Fur Trade

Late in the sixteenth century Russia began a process of eastward expansion across northern Asia that continued across the northern Pacific into the New World territory eventually known as Russian America.[2] This expansion was important both politically and economically. The addition of vast new lands to the Russian state strengthened its early claims to great power status and later validated its right to empire. But the political aspect was a long-term consequence measurable only subjectively. The economic component was far more important in the short-term and could be gauged much more precisely through the revenues generated. To a great extent Russia's entire expansion was driven by demand, first in Europe and then in the Orient, for the fur which could be obtained from animals that lived in the harsh northern latitudes.[3]

The expansion of the fur trade across Siberia proceeded fairly evenly and predictably. Petty entrepreneurs, traders and trappers known collectively as *promyshlenniki* moved into a new area and began systematically to hunt its fur-bearing animals. They augmented their

---

[1]Raymond H. Fisher, *Bering's Voyages: Whither and Why* (Seattle, 1977), 120-151, discusses the reasons for both of Bering's expeditions, the plans for meeting the objectives, and the relevant historiography.

[2]George V. Lantzeff's work on Russian eastward expansion, completed by Richard A. Pierce after his death, is the most complete account of expansion to the Pacific. See *Eastward to Empire: Exploration and Conquest on the Russian Open Frontier to 1750* (Montréal, 1973), especially chapters 8 and 11.

[3]Raymond H. Fisher, *The Russian Fur Trade, 1550-1700* (Berkeley, 1973), remains the standard work on the Siberian fur trade.

efforts by trading with the indigenous people for pelts, by coercing the natives to hunt for them, or by some combination of the two. The government received tax from both *promyshlenniki* and natives on the value of furs taken. When the animal population was decimated, *promyshlenniki* moved into virgin territory and the cycle was repeated.

Late in the seventeenth century the Russians reached the Pacific. Fifty years later the Second Kamchatka Expedition formally established Russia's presence in the north Pacific. Yet it was only the return of the survivors from Bering's crew with their fur clothing that caused ordinary men to venture to sea from the relative safety of Siberia.[4] While generated by the same economic demands that impelled expansion across Siberia, the move from the Kamchatkan peninsula across the northern Pacific to the American mainland was significantly different. Most important was a fundamental transformation of the fur-gathering enterprise: the hunt moved from land to water.[5]

Fur-gathering in a marine environment required a drastic change not only in technique but also in auxiliary equipment. Land hunting required a minimum of equipment for which relatively small sums of money were needed. Boats and supplies for ocean travel, however, necessitated larger, longer-term capital investment. The change to a new hunting environment also had a secondary political dimension: movement from the northern Asian mainland, an area acknowledged as Russia's sphere of interest, to international waters, where the likelihood for conflict with other Europeans was almost certain.[6]

The *promyshlenniki* quickly mastered the requisite sailing and hunting skills for gathering the furs of the pelagic animals of the north Pacific and acquired large numbers of pelts. Accumulating the capital or

---

[4]Pavel Golovin's report to the Board of the Russian American Company, translated as *The End of Russian America* (Portland, 1979), traces the beginning of Russian America to the return of the survivors of Bering's crew.

[5]One of the most difficult obstacles in the transition from land to water was lack of expertise in the building of suitable sailing vessels. The early Russian *promyshlenniki* were forced to be shipbuilders as well as hunters, since there were few of these skilled craftsman either in Siberia or Russian America.

[6]In the classic Soviet work, *The Russian American Company* (Cambridge, Mass., 1951), S. B. Okun argues that the only effective protection against foreign interests in the region would have been permanent settlement.

securing the credit for boats and supplies, however, was far more difficult. Because voyages for fur usually lasted at least three years (sometimes as many as seven) and were considered extremely high-risk ventures, the pool of investors remained small.[7]

Risk was assessed based upon information accumulated from previous voyages.[8] Analysis showed the most accurate predictor of profitability for a given voyage to be its duration. Although a full hold of furs almost always guaranteed a profit, a number of other factors influenced the gross and net amounts. The most important was the condition of the pelts. Many furs taken in good condition were lost because of improper handling and preliminary processing. Shorter voyages helped to minimize damage and were also a boon for investors, who measured the success of an expedition partly by its turnaround time. Successful shorter voyages also meant greater tax revenues for the government.

The Escalation of Demand

The indigenous inhabitants of the islands of the northern Pacific archipelago lived by harvesting the pelagic mammals, the most important of which was the sea otter. The otter was most important to the Russians as well. By the early 1700s, although European demand for fur had flattened, Chinese demand was increasing rapidly. The economic objectives of the Russian hunters in the north Pacific were closely related to the demands of the Chinese market.[9] While the Russians became fairly proficient in hunting on the open sea, their skills were no match for the native hunters of the Aleutians. As the demand for furs and the pressure to shorten expeditions both increased, the *promyshlenniki* attempted in an *ad hoc* fashion to supplement their fur-gathering, as they

[7]V. N. Berkh, *Chronological History of the Discovery of the Aleutians* (St. Petersburg, 1823) is the most comprehensive record of the early voyages to the Aleutians and provides substantial financial information.

[8]*Ibid.*

[9]An early nineteenth-century appraisal of cargo from the north Pacific to Russia between 1743 and 1797 estimates the value of furs shipped at 8,000,000 rubles. See Basil Dmytryshyn, *Russian Penetration of the North Pacific, 1700-1797* (2 vols., Portland, 1988), II, xiii.

had in Siberia, by trading with the natives, by coercing them to hunt, or both.

No consensus toward the newcomers existed among the native inhabitants of the Aleutians. Some Aleut communities welcomed them, while others attempted to eliminate them. In fact, the relationship between the *promyshlenniki* and the indigenous inhabitants of the Aleutians was characterized at different times by varying degrees of willing association and brutal violence on both sides.

Russian sailors in the North Pacific faced an inhospitable marine environment in frail boats with primitive nautical equipment. Information that could help them sail safely and directly was critical. Maps were becoming more widely available, but they were not entirely reliable. Large areas of land and water remained uncharted, and the renderings of even many known areas were incomplete or inaccurate. Every Russian crew in search of furs needed specific information about local geography and navigation patterns, as well as fresh water, safe summer harbour and winter anchorage. The most certain source for all this was the Aleuts; the Russians, following the practices established in Siberia, used whatever help the native people could provide.[10]

The relationship that developed might have been almost entirely beneficial for both Russians and Aleuts, yet it was not. Every Russian expedition was under government injunction to observe and describe both the land and people encountered. The relationship with the Aleuts was expected to be governed by a combination of Christian charity and the same type of pragmatism that characterized Russian-indigene relations in Siberia.[11] Yet the record of such relationships in the Aleutians is mixed. Accounts of lay baptisms by Orthodox Russians alternate with accounts of some of the worst cases of Russian violence and brutality on record. This reflects the interaction of several factors. While the fur trade in Siberia was the foundation of Russia's eastward expansion, Siberia had other potentially attractive possibilities for development. As a result,

---

[10]The Russians also used native nomenclature in naming the individual islands of the Aleutian chain. See Lydia Black, *Atka: An Ethnohistory of the Western Aleutians* (Kingston, Ont., 1984), 48.

[11]That "charity" was often laced with prejudice. See William W. Fitzhugh and Aron Crowell, "Crossroads of Continents: *Beringian Oecumene*," in Fitzhugh and Crowell (eds.), *Crossroads of Continents* (Washington, D.C., 1988), 9-10. The authors quote Martin Sauer's report of the Billings Expedition, 1802.

government administrators, soldiers, and clergymen followed across the Eurasian plain on the heels of the *promyshlenniki*. While their presence did not prevent violence and brutality between fur hunters and natives, it seems to have curbed them significantly.

The situation in the north Pacific, however, was very different. Fur was the sole reason for continuing across the ocean. Due in large part to the perception that the area had a more limited potential, no institutional or administrative representative was sent during the first half-century of Russian presence in northwestern North America to regulate the activity of the *promyshlenniki*. The nature of the contacts between Russians and Aleuts was thus largely dependent upon the individuals involved. On balance, the contacts were positive more often than not. Although the records of the early voyages have not been comprehensively quantified, I believe on the basis of a preliminary examination that fewer than one-third of Russian-Aleut contacts involved violence of any kind.

Unquestionably, indigenous society in the Aleutians suffered as a result of contact with the Russians, yet it appears that Russian violence was not the sole cause. Other factors contributed to post-contact changes. Three that I would like to explore below are the nature of Aleut society; changes in the patterns of native pelagic fur-gathering; and the eventual presence of a large Creole population.

The Nature of Aleut Society

The modern designation of the archipelago that stretches from the tip of the Alaskan peninsula across the northern Pacific as the Aleutian Islands suggests a political and social unity that did not exist until the late nineteenth century. While the islands were named by the Russians, the origin of the term "Aleut" remains unclear and does not seem to have originated with the inhabitants. Both before and after Russian contact, the inhabitants identified themselves as members of small, immediate communities with no formal political or conscious cultural ties to their neighbours. Some of the largest communities numbered in the hundreds of people, but most Aleut groups comprised less than one hundred individuals.[12]

The Russians divided the Aleutians into groups of islands whose inhabitants were relatively familiar with their neighbours and among which regular trade relationships existed. But even in these smaller arrays, no sense of political, social or cultural unity existed beyond the immediate community. Moreover, the Aleuts, never a non-violent people, were often hostile to each other. Tremendous variation existed among the native societies that inhabited the American territories eventually under Russian control. While it is true that there were societies, such as the Tlingit and the Chugach, which were more "warlike" than the Aleuts, it is also the case that the latter waged fierce war against each other and sometimes sailed to distant regions for trade and warfare, obtaining slaves in the process.[13]

A major difficulty experienced by many Aleuts in their contact with the Russians was their own limited concept of population source and supply. Male members of the relatively small Aleut communities hunted and fought together. When Aleut warriors faced their opponents, they could be certain that all able-bodied men of the enemy community were present. Countless references detail the depopulation of islands that resulted from the victory of one group over another. Many Aleuts who attempted to rid themselves of the Russian newcomers believed that the problem could be solved simply by eliminating those immediately present. They did not understand that destroying isolated groups of newcomers would not stop the Russians, but would only increase the likelihood of more violent encounters in the future.[14]

---

[12]See the "Report of the Sea Voyage Performed in 1768 and 69 by Captain Krenitsin and Lt. Levashev from Kamchatka to the Newly-Discovered Islands," in Peter Simon Pallas, *Bering's Successors, 1745-1780: Contributions of Peter Simon Pallas to the History of Russian Exploration toward Alaska* (Seattle, 1948) 58, as well as Pallas' 1777 comments on p. 43.

[13]Slaves were also used for sacrifice. See Lydia Black and R. G. Liapunov, "Aleut Islanders of the North Pacific," in Fitzhugh and Crowell (eds.), *Crossroads*, 53.

[14]In *Russian America* (New York, 1965), 37-38, Hector Chevigny describes a well-known incident in which the Aleuts attacked five Russian ships, destroying four. The retribution was the systematic destruction of eighteen villages on Unalaska, all the villages on Unmak and Four Mountains, and several on Unimak.

Many other Aleuts, however, found contact with the Russians useful. They had discovered small pieces of iron which had washed ashore from shipwrecks and had perfected a method of cold-forging to produce weapons. Trade with the Russians provided a steady, if limited, source of iron and metal tools.[15]

Russian attitudes toward the Aleuts were varied. While some of the *promyshlenniki* were notoriously cruel, others were apparently devoted Orthodox laymen who took seriously their responsibility to spread the Gospel in the absence of official representatives of the church. The Russian Orthodox Church permitted lay baptism in extenuating circumstances, and the first conversions to Christianity and baptisms in the Aleutians were made not by missionaries but by lay Christians.[16]

Changes in Patterns of Pelagic Fur-Gathering

Since the Aleutian Islands sustained only limited vegetation and could not support agriculture, human settlement was contingent upon the sea's resources. While fish were important, marine mammals, especially the sea otter, provided food, clothing, shelter and transportation for the inhabitants.[17] Because hunting was so critical, it was the community's most pressing concern. Hunting organization followed the same pattern of small-group organization that characterized Aleut communities. At the same time, however, it was ritualized and elevated to a status far more important than mere "task."

No tradition of accumulating and gathering food existed. Women gathered whatever roots and berries were found on a particular island, but these minimal resources were used only to supplement the diet. The primary responsibility for providing food was left to the male hunters,

---

[15]From the account of Totma merchant Stepan Cherepanov during his stay in the Aleutians, 1759-1762, Tsentral'nyi Gosudarstvennyi Archiv Drevnikh Aktov (Central State Archives of Ancient Arts), Moscow, portfolio No. 532, chapter 1, 21-27.

[16]See "The Russian Orthodox Church: Contributor to Policy-Making in Alaska," in O.W. Frost (ed.), *Bering and Chirikov: The American Voyages and Their Impact* (Anchorage, 1992), 355-365.

[17]The relationship between Aleut and otter verged on the sacred. The Aleut hunter, who called the otter his brother, dressed in special clothing and then asked the otter to give up its life for the sustenance of the Aleuts.

who traveled miles into the open ocean in small boats known as *baidarkas*, light, kayak-type craft made of skins stretched over a wooden frame. Usually designed for one person, *baidarkas* were precisely crafted and perfectly balanced, ideally suited to the stance Aleut hunters took to throw their darts.[18]

Aleut hunting skills, enhanced by their *baidarkas*, darts and throwing boards, astounded the Russians, whose hunting techniques were far less sophisticated. Pressure to accumulate furs more quickly and thereby shorten the duration of fur-gathering voyages made the employment of Aleut hunters for Russian fur-hunting seem only logical. As long as the animal population remained relatively constant, this arrangement posed no problems for the inhabitants. Yet within less than twenty years the marine mammal population had been decimated in parts of the Aleutians and the food supply of many communities was endangered. At the same time Chinese demand for furs continued to grow and the high prices made the greater risk and higher cost of longer expeditions acceptable. Hence the Russians and their Aleut hunters followed the populations of pelagic mammals to the east.[19]

The absence of hunters from their local communities for long periods had untoward consequences. Although more vulnerable to attack from other native groups, their most difficult problem during the long-distance hunting expeditions was an irregular food supply. The sources make almost no reference to the consequences of this problem, but the missionary priests who worked among the Aleuts years later recorded native accounts of great hunger, disease, and death.[20]

Early Russian fur-hunting expeditions, loosely organized and financed by small groups of hunter-businessmen, many of whom participated directly in the expeditions, were of relatively little consequence for the Aleuts. Beginning in the last third of the eighteenth century, however, determined efforts to change the fundamental nature of fur-gathering began. Continuing success in the north Pacific attracted the

---

[18]George Dyson, *Baidarka* (Edmonds, Wash., 1986) explains the construction of this craft. Chapter 1 provides a history.

[19]Pallas, *Bering's Successors*, 30; Dmytryshyn, *Russian Penetration*, II, xxxi-xxxii.

[20]Ivan Veniaminov was a missionary priest who lived for a decade among the Aleuts and first recorded their stories and oral history. His *Zapiski* (St. Petersburg, 1840), contains a vast amount of information on Aleut social organization and custom.

attention of a number of merchants, each of whom wanted to establish a monopoly over the trade and to exploit it more systematically. The competition among these men was a key factor in the over-hunting of marine mammals. More damning, their competition seems to have been one of the most significant factors in changing the relationship between Russian and Aleut hunters, which degenerated to the virtual enslavement of the latter and threatened the survival of hundreds of Aleut communities.

The Creole Population

Grigorii Shelikhov and his partner, Ivan Golikov, stubbornly persisted and were finally successful in obtaining a monopoly from Catherine II.[21] The company they formed later became the nucleus of the quasi-official Russian American Company, chartered in 1799. Meanwhile, Shelikhov established the first administrative structure in Russian America, and local officials answered to company officers not only in Siberia but eventually even in St. Petersburg.[22] As the new, more formally structured business and the company that succeeded it began to expand and diversify, a larger pool of skilled labour became necessary. Since government policies regarding colonization generally sought to preserve serfdom and to protect the interest of the owners, free movement of the Empire's population was banned. Thus, permanent Russian colonization of Russian America was never a real possibility. Nevertheless, the demand for educated and skilled labour remained pressing.

The sexual mores of the people of the Aleutians differed radically from the Christian sexual ideal to which the Russians, at least in theory, subscribed. Polygamy was practised and it was customary for Aleut men to share their wives with visitors. Their Orthodox standard to the contrary, Russian men began almost immediately after contact to cohabit with available Aleut women, the majority of whom apparently were

---

[21]Hector Chevigny, *Lord of Alaska: Baranov and the Russian Adventure* (Portland, 1951), 24-25, discusses the methods employed in pursuit of the monopoly.

[22]When the Russian American Company was chartered after Shelikov's death, control became centered in the Russian capital.

unopposed to the arrangement.[23] In time, these relationships posed serious problems for the administrators of Russian America. Many Russian men wanted to marry their Aleut wives (who were not allowed to go to Russia) and remain with them permanently, thus violating the limitation on length of service abroad. Another problem was the status of children that resulted from these unions.

Though a number of proposals were suggested, the first problem was never successfully resolved. The latter dilemma was simpler because of the precedent set in Siberia, where the offspring of Russian fathers and indigenous mothers were considered wholly Russian with full rights as citizens of the Empire. Yet the Aleuts, whose fondness for children is often mentioned in travelers' accounts, considered these mixed children as Aleut, with full rights and responsibilities in *their* society.[24]

Ultimately this particular double standard was a boon to the colonial society. The officials in Russian America who needed skilled labour successfully lobbied for priests and educators to teach their youthful Creole citizens. And as these children matured, they largely answered the labour shortage. Beyond this, however, the many children of Russian fathers and Aleut mothers cemented a bond between the two peoples that makes this case of European-indigene contact unique.

Conclusion

Long before Alaska was sold to the United States, Russians and Aleuts for all practical purposes had formed a single society. No similar bonds were formed between the Russians and any of the other indigenous groups (including Tlingit, Koniag, and Chugach) with whom they had contact. Neither the instances of violent confrontation that occurred periodically in the first decades after contact nor the coercion that resulted from the rapacious practices of businessmen were sufficient to destroy the bonds that developed.

---

[23]See Chevigny, *Lord of Alaska*, for an account of these relationships and the response of the company manager. But these practices were not confined to the Aleuts; see Kyrill Timofeevich Khlebnikov, *Colonial Russian America: Kyrill T. Khlebnikov's Reports, 1817-1832* (Portland, 1979), 28.

[24]Lydia Black, "The Story of Russian America," in Fitzhugh and Crowell (eds.), *Crossroads*, 80, traces this development.

Although this relationship is imperfectly understood, its continued existence is incontrovertible. In response to the systematic efforts made by the United States government early in this century to Americanize Alaska's natives, the Aleuts discovered a sense of unity and social cohesion where once there was none. What made the Aleuts truly a "people" were the bonds created through the history they shared with the Russians who came to America. The most important part of the legacy from that period is the Russian Orthodox faith, now the bedrock of Aleut cultural indivisibility.

Five Years Before the Mast: Observations on the Conditions of Maritime Labour in Finland and Elsewhere

Yrjö Kaukiainen

I

The grim living conditions of ordinary sailors, and the despotic discipline to which they were subjected, were integral parts of the Western maritime past. These unpleasant realities came to wide public notice for the first time in 1840 when Richard Henry Dana published his famous *Two Years before the Mast.*[1] This book, which was followed by other more or less authentic descriptions, inaugurated a literary tradition that later included writers such as Herman Melville and Jack London. Although such books only seldom embodied true "voices from the forecastle," they still comprise an extremely valuable stock of knowledge on which many scholars have relied. Recently, however, authentic documentary sources increasingly have been exploited to gain an even more accurate comprehension of living conditions before the mast.[2]

---

[1]See, for example, the introduction by Thomas Philbrick to the 1981 Penguin edition. Of course, Dana's book was not the first realistic description of maritime life; authentic accounts from the life in the Royal Navy in particular exist at least from the late eighteenth century. See Henry Baynham, *From the Lower Deck. The Navy 1780-1840* (London, 1969).

[2]See, for example, Lewis R. Fischer, "A Dereliction of Duty: The Problem of Desertion on Nineteenth-Century Sailing Vessels," in Rosemary Ommer and Gerald Panting (eds.), *Working Men Who Got Wet* (St. John's, 1980), 51-70; Eric W. Sager, *Maritime Labour: The Merchant Marine of Atlantic Canada, 1820-1914* (Montréal, 1989); Marcus Rediker, *Between the Devil and the Deep Blue Sea: Merchant Seamen, Pirates and the Anglo-American Maritime World, 1700-1750* (New York, 1987).

Research in Maritime History, No. 3 (December 1992), 47-62.

Although the cruelty of maritime discipline sometimes closely resembled some of the features of slavery, it was not not always this way. Medieval maritime codes, such as the well-known *Rôles d'Oleron*, did not vest all power in the master; on the contrary, collegial rather than hierarchical relations were most typical. Common sailors had the right to express their opinions on important decisions and often their consent was required before the master could act. In coasting, deep-sea fishing and other traditional maritime trades egalitarianism and patriarchal rather than despotic discipline prevailed. It thus seems that masters with absolute power prepared to exercise "naval" discipline were a product of the early modern period, and that they only became the norm after a fairly protracted process of diffusion.

Marcus Rediker contended that the new system was quite fully developed at the end of the seventeenth century. Eric W. Sager, on the other hand, seems to believe that in Canada the transition occurred during the early nineteenth century (although he connected it with industrialization). It is certainly reasonable to presume that it may have started at the centre of the early modern maritime world and spread only gradually to more peripheral countries. Thus far, however, there seems little real evidence, apart from some general statements in older textbooks, on the origins of the new system, nor is it clear how uniform it was--in fact, it is difficult even to define its elements. While it seems logical to assume that the semi-military character of early voyages of discovery and the development of early modern navies established models adapted by the merchant marines, the very process of diffusion in different trades and sections of the maritime world--such as the role of navies and East Indian companies in the education of masters--is not fully understood. Even the function of the transition--whether it was an autonomous cultural phenomenon or an inseparable element of economic change--has not really been discussed.

In this essay, I begin with the hypothesis that there actually was a change in which a new system replaced, or at least challenged, an older practice. I will test the relevance of this proposition by examining whether such a transition occurred in a remote corner of Europe, Finland, and to what extent the traditional system continued to co-exist. To present a complete picture, however, is not easy. As elsewhere, legal documents and business records seldom reflect the opinions and emotions of ordinary sailors. It is quite clear that since the new laws shifted the balance of power to the side of the master, many acts which in the forecastle were regarded as unreasonable or harsh never received any notice or provoked legal actions. As sailors seldom were able to present their experiences in writing, much has been lost forever. Moreover, in Finland the literary tradition represented by Dana was very weak. This means that conclusions must be inferred from indirect and often ambiguous evidence. Much of what will be discussed below should therefore be regarded as tentative and preliminary rather than conclusive or empirical.

II

That what we think of as the "naval" command system prevailed in the Finnish merchant marine is beyond doubt. In the late nineteenth century in particular, the evidence is sufficient to demonstrate that on practically all Finnish bluewater vessels the power of the master was as absolute as anywhere else in the north Atlantic maritime world. There are even a few examples of genuine "voices from the forecastle" which suggest that the type of cruel scenes depicted by Anglo-American writers were not uncommon in ships from Oulu, Vaasa, Turku or other distant Baltic ports. As an appendix I have included a translation of what I regard as the best Finnish document on this subject. It is a song which describes some events aboard the ship *Toivo* (Hope) of Oulu during her five-year maiden voyage (October 1871-August 1876), which took her three times to the Far East and once to the Gulf of Mexico. The author (or rather the originator, for an amateur Finnish poet living in New York was involved) of these verses seems to have been a sailor who served as second mate aboard the vessel between October 1874 and October 1875. As far as existing documents enable us to verify his descriptions, the story is quite accurate.[3] In fact, here we have a case with all the classical ingredients of maritime cruelty; it would certainly have furnished Jack London with splendid material for another *Sea Wolf*.

The case of the *Toivo* is also a good example of another dimension of maritime life. The song is an adaptation of the well-known contemporary song "Marching through Georgia," which comes not from Finland but from the U.S. Civil War. While the master may have

[3]For more details on the song and its presumed author, see Yrjö Kaukiainen, "'Laiva *Toivo*, Oulu'–en röst från skansen," *Historisk Tidskrift för Finland*, No. 3 (1988), 465-488.

accepted the values of the upper-class, the crew wholeheartedly adopted the values of popular Atlantic maritime culture.

How typical was the case of the *Toivo*? First, it is clear that the master was a product of his times who came of age imbued with a tradition of harsh "naval" discipline; in this regard he appears unexceptional. On the other hand, he had graduated from the local navigation school with top marks and was a fairly successful master. That he was well above average is demonstrated among other things by his ability to write immaculate English. As the son of a wealthy merchant and shipowner--Johan Wilhelm Snellman G:son (the cousin and namesake of the famous senator and nationalistic philosopher)--he certainly was in a privileged position. In fact, his only obvious weakness was a strong fondness for liquor, and many of the incidents described in the song seem to have been inspired by heavy drinking. What happened aboard the *Toivo*, however, was never so unusual that newspapers wrote about it, despite the fact that they occurred at a time in which there was some public discussion in Finland concerning the conditions of common seamen. Only once was the master summoned to court--for not allowing a man who was dismissed to take his belongings with him--but this was a civil rather than a criminal case.[4]

Between 1860 and 1880 Finnish newspapers exposed a number of cases involving cruel masters who carried their disciplinary powers beyond what was regarded as acceptable. Young boys acting as cooks or master's servants were beaten or punished by sending them to the top for hours; whole crews were imprisoned in foreign ports because of what the master interpreted as mutiny; provisions for long voyages were so scanty that most of the crew were hospitalized; and so on.[5] While such cases were exceptional in that they often involved gross incompetence or criminal action, they were the "tips of the iceberg," indicating that a large number of minor violations occurred and that the general principles of maritime discipline were similar to those practised by the master of the brig *Pilgrim*, whom Dana had immortalized. For example, it was not

---

[4]A copy of the court decision is to be found among the papers concerning *Toivo*'s crew in the archives of the Snellman trading house, C I, 88, Oulu Provincial Archives.

[5]See, for example, *Åbo Underrättelser*, 1865: nos. 81, 88, 124, 132, 147; 1866: no. 18; 1879: no. 282; *Helsingfors Dagblad*, 1872: nos. 188, 189; 1881: nos. 185, 276. See also Oscar Nikula, *Åbo sjöfarts historia II.2: Segelsjöfarten 1856-1926* (Åbo, 1930), 172-177.

regarded as too stern for a master to ban his men from going ashore in port if he suspected they might desert. To enforce their discipline, Finnish masters were commonly equipped with revolvers and handcuffs.

High desertion rates were an integral part of this labour system, as the events on the *Toivo* demonstrated. While her full complement of crew excluding the master was nineteen, her crew lists during the nearly five-year voyage included no fewer than ninety-six different names, or an average of five men for each position; even the two mate's posts were filled by eleven different officers.[6] Although the sources are incomplete, it seems that between 1856 and 1860 at least 500 men, or one hundred per annum, deserted from Finnish ships. By 1872-1875 the correspon-ding figure was over 800, or 200 per year.[7] The latter figure represents an annual desertion rate of about ten percent of the seamen serving in the Finnish bluewater fleet, and since Finnish tonnage was much reduced after the Crimean War, the figure for the late 1850s was in fact of the same magnitude. Whether this was high by international standards is difficult to determine because comparable figures are unavailable. In the Canadian fleet, sample decadal desertion rates ranged between sixteen and twenty-two percent of all seamen entering service in the 1860s, 1870s and 1880s. It seems probable that comparative Finnish rates exceeded twenty percent in the 1860s and 1870s.[8]

There were at least two unique reasons for high Finnish desertion rates. First, the wages paid to Finnish seamen were so low relative to levels elsewhere in the north Atlantic that the temptation to decamp in

---

[6]Kaukiainen, "'Laiva, *Toivo*, Oulu,'" 482-483. It is clear that while the song exaggerated the number of sailors, its depiction of the number of mates was close to reality.

[7]Kustaa Hautala, "Merimiesten karkaaminen suomalaisilta laivoilta 1800-luvulla," in Sven-Erik Åstrom, Yrjö Blomstedt and Ilkka Hakalehto (eds.), *Näkökulmia menneisyy-teen. Eino Jutikkalan juhlakirja* (Porvoo, 1967). The figures for 1872-1875 lack data for a few towns, but by extrapolation a sum between 800 and 900 seems probable.

[8]The total number of Finnish seamen is derived from Yrjö Kaukiainen, "Från jungman Jansson till Kalle Aaltonen. Sjömän i Finlands handelsflotta 1860-1914—en kvantitativ översikt," *Historisk Tidskrift för Finland*, III (1988), 356. Canadian desertion rates come from Fischer, "A Dereliction of Duty," 56. Assuming that even thirty percent of non-deserters only remained for one voyage, the total number of entrances in the Finnish deep-sea merchant fleet in 1871-1875 was close to 4500 men, of which about 1000 deserted.

search of better pay must have been high.[9] Second, while in most other countries labour contracts only covered a single voyage or a clearly defined sequence of passages, Finnish sailors were always hired for a entire round-trip back to the home port. Since many vessels, like the *Toivo*, engaged in a lengthy series of foreign "cross-trading" voyages before returning home, the contract in reality might span four or five years. It is clear that such long terms of service tended to increase desertions. Only in 1873 was the law amended to enable a seamen to obtain a legal discharge after two years' service.[10] While even this failed to halt the behaviour, it did lead to a decrease: desertions declined during the late 1870s and were only a third of the level of the early 1870s in the next decade.[11] But before giving total credit for this improvement to the new law, it is well to remember that the decrease in desertions was related to a dramatic downturn in the shipping industry. In the 1880s Finnish deep-sea tonnage declined, thus diminishing the demand for seamen and the opportunities to desert.

Desertion rates should not be interpreted as direct reflections of conditions onboard; many other factors also motivated seamen to jump ship.[12] What is perhaps most important is that they highlight one typical feature of the early modern maritime labour system--the short terms of service and the lack of any real attachment to a particular vessel. This is in sharp contrast to the traditional system, which was characterized by long-term service and loyalty not only to the ship but also to the people who served onboard.

III

The late nineteenth century in many respects represented the apex of the early modern maritime labour system. But to what extent did the traditional system survive? In the Finnish merchant marine, coastal and Baltic

---

[9]Yrjö Kaukiainen, *Sailing into Twilight. Finnish Shipping in an Age of Transport Revolution, 1860-1914* (Jyväskylä, 1991), 111-113, 120.

[10]The law is in the new Finnish maritime code of 9.6.1873.

[11]Hautala, "Merimiesten karkaaminen," 106. In the comparison only seaports with continuous data have been included.

[12]See especially Fischer, "A Dereliction of Duty."

shipping was fairly extensive, employing at least as many seamen as long-distance trade. Moreover, most coastal tonnage, and even an unusually high proportion of large vessels, was owned by peasants and other non-urban coastal inhabitants, the bulk of whom must have continued to adopt a more traditional approach in their economic transactions than urban burghers. It is on such vessels that the traditional system continued to survive.

A small sailing vessel, with a total crew of two, three or four men, carrying firewood or other primary products to Stockholm or St. Petersburg, must have remained a traditional workplace. Often all the men were family members. Masters were not required to pass formal examinations; their posts were earned through seniority and a good knowledge of local waters and trading customs. There was no absolute command or despotism, but instead a patriarchal system in which each man's position depended upon his skills. In such a system it was impossible for a master to choose isolatation in his cabin. A rather good symbol of such a "preindustrial" shipboard community is reflected in an 1871 painting called "Ace of Clubs" by K.E. Jansson of the Åland Islands. In it the entire crew, including the boy, are sitting together playing cards. The familial atmosphere makes it difficult to select the master (although it is likely that he was the oldest man onboard). Labour conditions aboard coasters persisted for decades, as we know from descriptions of conditions on small sailing vessels and auxiliaries even in the 1930s and 1940s.[13] And this was not solely characteristic of Finland; similar fraternal relations were also the norm elsewhere, as Tristan Jones's autobiography *A Steady Trade* vividly demonstrates.[14]

Finnish peasant shipping expanded greatly after the Crimean War and owners, especially from the Åland Islands, southwestern Finland and the Carelian Isthmus started building vessels for the Baltic, North Sea and long-distance trades. Unfortunately, because of a lack for relevant sources it is difficult to make an overall assessment of working conditions aboard these vessels. Still, it seems that as long as crews were hired principally from local communities, masters did not possess quite as

---

[13]See, for example, Yrjö Kaukiainen, *Koiviston merenkulun historia* (Lahti, 1975), 297-298. The author's family in the 1930s owned a coastal steamer, on which one of his uncles was master and another was the chief engineer. Two other relatives were hired as additional hands.

[14]Tristan Jones, *A Steady Trade* (London, 1984).

much absolute authority or follow "naval" practices as frequently as their urban colleagues. Nonetheless, there are stories of peasant masters who did not fit this generalization, sometimes even resorting to revolvers to enforce discipline.[15] While "naval" behavior never became the norm, this may have reflected the fact that voyages were short and family (or community) relationships reinforced acceptable modes of behaviour.

It is also worth remembering that even though the worst abuses were uncommon aboard peasant craft, the largest hardly constituted democratic workplaces. As crews of ten to twenty men could not usually be recruited from among family members or close neighbours, the social differences between owners and workers were accentuated. The lot of the common sailor increasingly fell to the poor, while the sons of owners, even while continuing to serve for several years before the mast, sooner or later established themselves as mates and masters, or left shipboard life altogether. The grim realities of the Åland maritime community, with its lack of equal opportunity, are impressively described by the great local writer Sally Salminen.[16] Her novels are excellent antidotes to the common tendency to idealize traditional societies.

If medium-to-large peasant vessels seem to have been borderline cases, so too were urban coasters and Baltic tonnage. Unfortunately, very little relevant data can be found about such craft. On the one hand, it is clear that the smaller the crew the more difficult it was to maintain a strict division of labour and military-style discipline. Yet it seems that at least as far as the permanency of labour contracts was concerned, typical Baltic vessels followed urban rather than rural models: short-term wage labour prevailed. In places like Rauma and Uusikaupunki, men were typically hired for a single voyage, often being shipped only after the vessel was fully-loaded and dismissed the same day it returned. While summer-long labour contracts were not uncommon, long-term family or

---

[15]One such case was Eerikki Klami, who was even elected a peasant representative to the 1863 Diet. See H. Malmi, "Klamit merenkulkijoina," *Klamin suvun vaiheita. Historiaa, tutkielmia ja kuvasatoa* (Lahti, 1968).

[16]Above all, her first work, *Katrina* (1936), is a semi-authentic description of the leading rural shipping community on Åland, Wårdö, with mighty and wealthy shipowners and masters and poor crofters and sailors.

neighbourhood crews were rare. Accordingly, masters seem normally to have had sole decision-making power.[17]

IV

It is useful to remember that such ideal types as "new" or "traditional" labour systems are really simplifications which are not easy to find in real life. Moreover, the master's personality was of such decisive importance that it might make all the difference between a happy vessel and a "hell-ship." It would be hopeless therefore to attempt even crude estimates of the quantitative prevalence of each system. Nor do I believe that this is the most relevant problem. Far more important is to determine how and when the "new" system arrived and why it was able to displace traditional structures.

Once more, it must be stressed that there are substantial source barriers to answering this question. The farther one tries to go before the mid-nineteenth century, the thinner the evidence. One logical starting point, however, is the fact that there were few Finnish long-distance traders before the 1720s (or the 1690s at the earliest). The real take-off in deep-sea shipping only occurred after the 1740s, but even this concerned merely the few so-called staple towns; in Ostrobothnia, for example, such trading was prohibited until 1766.

Examples of harsh discipline and desertions were in fact found in the first half of the eighteenth century. In Turku (Åbo), which was then the leading seaport in the country, these conducts were regarded as problems in the 1740s and 1750s. As early as the 1730s an attempted mutiny was experienced aboard the *Södra Finlands Wapn*, most likely in response to a despotic master. From the same decade there were two other cases in which the crew complained of harsh treatment by the master. In one, the men deserted because the master regularly beat, kicked and abused them. Even mates were not immune to such brutality, as was the case with one who deserted in Plymouth in 1763. That masters also thought it advisable to enforce the separation of officers and

---

[17]These conclusions are based on a rather large sample of logbooks of Baltic vessels from Rauma and Uusikaupunki in the Archives of the *sjömanshus* of Rauma and Uusikaupunki, Turku Provincial Archives.

crew can be seen from a 1749 document in which a mate was blamed for being too sociable with ordinary seamen.[18]

It is quite obvious that at least in Turku, despotic masters and "naval" discipline dated from the 1730s. That the crews of three long-distance traders (of a total of only five owned in the town) engaged in mutinous behaviour would seem to indicate that they were still used to different labour conditions. On the other hand, it is not clear that there was a total transformation. As late as the 1750s, two Turku masters were forced to change their plans because crews regarded conditions to be too risky to sail.[19] Nonetheless, cases of sailors clinging to medieval rights were obviously rare, and became practically nonexistent in the nineteenth century.

How the new labour system was established aboard Turku vessels is not difficult to ascertain. Since the town's deep-sea shipping had been extremely modest during the seventeenth century and was totally blocked during the Great Nordic War, there were no competent local masters. As a result, shipowners had to hire foreign officers to re-establish the trade. In the beginning they used Dutch and Danish masters, and even a few former Swedish naval officers; later, men from Stockholm became more common. Only gradually did locally-born men gain sufficient experience to command vessels sailing to Spain and the Mediterranean.[20]

It seems evident that these foreign masters introduced the new "naval" system to Turku merchantmen. The same phenomenon probably occurred in the easternmost staple town, Hamina (Fredrikshamn), where practically all long-distance traders in the 1730s were Dutch-owned "ships of convenience." It is even probable that some direct Dutch and German influence reached the Ostrobothnian seaports--where some merchants from these regions had become established--but since they in effect were in the hinterland of Stockholm, the capital must have been the prime origin of innovations.

Whether the new systems came from Stockholm or directly from abroad, they had common origins. The Netherlands was not only the leading seventeenth-century sea power but also in the vanguard of

---

[18]All the examples are from Carl-Erik Olin, *Åbo sjöfarts historia I. Intill branden 1827* (Åbo, 1927), 211-225.

[19]*Ibid.*, 222-223.

[20]*Ibid.*, 194-196.

maritime technology.[21] Dutch customs, shipbuilders and masters were diffused throughout the Baltic world. At the end of the seventeenth century, perhaps sixty percent of Stockholm merchant tonnage was owned by Dutch immigrants or absentee investors, and it is clear that they preferred Dutch masters and techniques for managing their vessels. Moreover, many Scandinavian sailors served on Dutch ships in both the seventeenth and eighteenth centuries: Swedish sailors were so common in Amsterdam that in 1735 the Dutchman Tersmeden was able to hire more than one hundred in almost no time.[22] How profound the Dutch influence was is clear from the fact that a major portion of Swedish shipboard and maritime terminology is of Dutch origin. Even the titles for certified masters, *coopwaerdi-skeppare* and *coopwaerdi-capitan* (later *kofferdiskeppare*, etc.) were similarly borrowed from the Dutch.

The question of whether the "new labour system" originated in the Netherlands or was a common western European development falls outside the scope of this paper. It does seem, however, that the tradition of concentrating power in the hands of the master did not develop in Spain or Portugal. On Iberian ocean-going vessels the master shared his authority with a pilot, who was responsible for navigation, and a captain, who commanded the soldiers onboard.[23] On seventeenth-century Dutch East Indiamen, on the other hand, masters were both commanders of the sailors and navigators. This created a much greater concentration of power than in either the Iberian or traditional systems, both of which were characterized by not only division of labour but also separation of responsibility. This concentration may even have created new ways of exerting authority. Some descriptions of Dutch East India ships from the end of the seventeenth century claim that masters behaved quite harsh-

---

[21]See, for example, C.A. David, "The Transfer of Technology between Britain and the Netherlands 1700-1850," in J.R. Bruijn and W.F.J. Mörzer-Bruyns (eds.), *Anglo-Dutch Mercantile Marine Relations 1700-1850* (Amsterdam, 1991), 11-13.

[22]Eirik Hornborg, *Segelsjöfartens historia* (2nd ed., Helsingfors, 1948), 386.

[23]*Ibid.*, 247-248.

ly.[24] This was, of course, not unique--what we know of contemporary English masters suggest no significant differences.[25]

That the "new system" diffused relatively rapidly must have been a function of certain changes in shipping which made the new behaviour highly practical. In this respect harsh discipline was not the most relevant feature but only an expression of a system which made sternness possible or even useful. Perhaps the essence of the change was that pure wage labour and short-term contracts replaced "traditional" labour relations, which had been ensured by the fact that many sailors owned shares in vessels or received a proportion of profits as salary. It is quite clear that such a transformation also changed the methods of leadership.

The growth in both vessel size and total merchant tonnage, as well as the lengthening of voyages, rapidly increased the demand for capital and labour. Compared with North Sea or Baltic vessels, the new ocean-going ships were so expensive that new forms of ownership developed, with wealthy merchants playing the most prominent roles. While masters and even seamen in coastal service frequently owned large shares of their vessels well into the twentieth century, this was rare in ocean trades. Thus, it seems that if the classical separation of capital and labour did not develop in shipping before the early modern period, it at least made major advances during this era.

At the same time, the increasing demand for labour could not be satisfied using traditional methods of recruitment or by hiring experienced maritime "craftsmen" with long family traditions in shipping. But it is also easy to understand that the lot of waged sailors did not appeal to coastal fishermen or seamen with experience on traditional small craft. On the one hand, there continued to be demand for coastal shipping; on the other, the most skilful found new possibilities in the expanding shipbuilding industry. The net result was that the expanding shipping industry had to rely increasingly on an urban proletariat to satisfy the demand for labour. Quite a similar situation occurred in eighteenth-century Finland when long-distance shipping began to expand. Thus, the adoption of a new labour system was not just a mechanical imitation of

---

[24]*Ibid.*, 389.

[25]Rediker, *Between the Devil and the Deep Blue Sea*, contains a number of relevant examples.

foreign examples, but rather a functional process, vital for the growth of shipping.

The other side of the coin was that the new generation of sailors, particularly if they originated from large urban centres in western Europe, were not always easy to lead. Many likely shared a loathing for order and authority which was common among the lowest urban classes (it was, in fact, a tradition with medieval roots). The copious use of spirits, which was equally common aboard as ashore, did little to make them more manageable. Moreover, men on long ocean voyages were detached from the normal restraints of law and social order. The same problems were faced by western European navies, although it did not present an unsurmountable barrier because there already was a strong tradition of using military disciple to control heterogeneous crews. This naval example (as well perhaps as the example of Mediterranean galleys) came in handy on deep-sea merchantmen as well.

Although it is very difficult to define the precise characteristics of the "new" maritime labour system, it still seems that enough changes occurred during the early modern period to make it meaningful to speak of a transformation. It also seems reasonable to conclude that this shift was an integral part of what we now call merchant capitalism. While it is true that the "system" continued to develop during the eighteenth and nineteenth centuries, it is questionable whether the subsequent changes were so great that some new, "industrial," system emerged.[26] In fact, while foreign trade and shipping comprised the core of merchant capitalism, they were quite peripheral in the development of modern industrialization. Not surprisingly, the transformation of maritime working conditions lagged substantially behind corresponding developments in manufacturing and related industries. In most developed countries it was only in the 1930s, 1940s and 1950s that sailors managed to negotiate wages, working conditions and other social benefits similar to those enjoyed by their more fortunate landward colleagues.

---

[26]In principle, I agree with those critics of Sager's *Seafaring Labour* who doubted the relevance of industrial revolutions to the change in Canadian maritime labour relations; see "Roundtable," *International Journal of Maritime History*, II, No. 1 (June 1990), 227-258.

Appendix I

The Song of the Ship *Toivo* from Oulu

(In) eighteen hundred and seventy nine
the master tried to sailors hire.
He hired one Sunday, and another, and still a third[1]
For the ship *Toivo* from Oulu.
Hurrah, hurrah for its owners,
hurrah, hurrah for its officers.
The fame of *Toivo*'s master will sound everywhere,
and the name of *Toivo* from Oulu.

But not was he able to keep the lads aboard for long,
when they came to England they said him goodbye.
They left Mr. Skipper and Mr. Laiberg,[2]
in the ship *Toivo* from Oulu.
Hurrah, hurrah...

Mr. Skipper's mother said they were pure rascals,
as they so deserted from our young Skipper.[3]
But mother could not see what the life was to be
aboard the ship *Toivo* from Oulu.
Hurrah, hurrah...

To recount all his mischiefs would make a too long song,
but I'll try to tell the most remarkable of them,
which sailors use to recite of their voyages
aboard the ship *Toivo* from Oulu.
Hurrah, hurrah...

Once Mr. Skipper called a group of friends aboard
to pass some happy hours in his ship the *Toivo*.
But suddenly they heard a report from a gun
aboard the ship *Toivo* from Oulu.
Hurrah, hurrah...

---

[1]The crew list shows that men were in fact hired on three successive Sundays.

[2]Laiberg was the chief mate during the first voyage.

[3]The master, Henrik Wilhelm Snellman, was at that time only twenty-three years old.

All the folks aboard then rushed to the deck,
forgetting the pleasures they tried to get ashore.
But Mr. Skipper just was playing with his gun
aboard the ship *Toivo* from Oulu.
Hurrah, hurrah...

He pressed his revolver on the chest of a mate[4]
who happened to be standing in front of him.
But the powder was wet and no shot was heard
aboard the ship *Toivo* from Oulu.
Hurrah, hurrah...

He then sprang to his cabin and took another gun
shouting when returning, I'll find you anyway.
He fired and the bullet hit a backstay
aboard the ship *Toivo* from Oulu.
Hurrah, hurrah...

Then he let all his folk to be taken to the jail,
but when he became sober he begged them all:
Come on boys, let us live in peace from now
aboard the ship *Toivo* from Oulu.
Hurrah, hurrah...

When they tried to find the bullets from the gun,
they found the one buried in the backstay wire,
and that was witnessed by all the hands and mates
aboard the ship *Toivo* from Oulu.
Hurrah, hurrah...

Once Mr. Willy made some folly with the watchman,
asking him to fix three brooms to one single stick.
As he could not do so he was made to crawl
aboard the ship *Toivo* from Oulu.
Hurrah, hurrah...

Once Mr. Willy was shooting in his berth,
the bullets pierced the ceiling of a passenger's cabin,
but paying hundreds dollars he made good for that
aboard the ship *Toivo* from Oulu.
Hurrah, hurrah...

---

[4]A subnote in the manuscript even gives the name of this (second) mate.

They flogged the poor cook like crazy savages
until the cook was fed up with such miserable life,
they sought to kill him, so he jumped overboard[5]
from the ship *Toivo* from Oulu.
Hurrah, hurrah...

So much did they shed blood from good sailors
that the deck was often red like a butcher's bench.
The mate flogged them together with the Skipper
from the ship *Toivo* from Oulu.
Hurrah, hurrah...

Thirteen mates during all the five years
did Mr. Skipper ship aboard his ship,
but they all were fed up with their job
aboard the ship *Toivo* from Oulu.
Hurrah, hurrah...

Two hundred and fifty sailors did Mr. Skipper ship
to his vessel when making four voyages,
but the most of them did part on their own will
from the ship *Toivo* from Oulu.
Hurrah, hurrah...

Had he not been a rich man's son by birth
no law would have allowed him to command a ship,
but since the father was the supervisor of insurances[6]
for the ship *Toivo* from Oulu.
Hurrah, hurrah...

So the son thinks that he is a real gentleman
boasting to other skippers: this is my own ship,
but all the folk know well that it's a lie
of the ship *Toivo* from Oulu.
Hurrah, hurrah...

Source: Translated from the original manuscript in the Finnish Folklore Archives, Haataja, Jaakko.

---

[5]This episode is fully verified by both the crew accounts and the master's letter to his father. It took place on 12 November 1873, when approaching Hong Kong.

[6]J.W. Snellman G:son was one of the supervisors (or councillors) for the Finnish Mutual Insurance Association. The Association was active in controlling not only the quality of ships but also of masters; in at least one case, it refused to insure a vessel unless a new master was appointed.

Expressions of Longing, Sources of Anxiety? The Significance of Contacts with Home for Finnish Sailors in London and Hull in the Late Nineteenth Century[1]

Merja-Liisa Hinkkanen

"Klingar icke modersmålet skönast, Binder ej ditt hem med dubbla garn, Lyser icke själva gräset grönast På den tuva där du lekt som barn?"	Is not your mother tongue the sweetest, Does not your home with double ties you tie, And surely grass must shine the greenest on the fields you walked in days gone by?

The text above was embroidered by a young girl from the Åland Islands in 1906 on a wall tapestry for her fiancee and accompanied the seaman (later captain) for the next thirty years as a reminder of home and those who awaited his return.[2] This story neatly summarizes an established, if somewhat idyllic, view of the emotional bonds between seaman and home: that at the bottom of the itinerant mariner's heart was a constant longing for hearth and kin.[3] While this perception has some foundation, merchant seafaring not only made it difficult to have a permanent abode but also loosened or severed the seaman's ties with his birthplace. A good indication of the scale of this problem is an 1886 estimate that one-third of the seamen entering London lacked a real home.[4]

[1]I am grateful to Professor Heikki Mannila for comments on an earlier draft of this paper.

[2]Christina Remmer, *Listersby* (Mariehamn, 1989), 7.

[3]See, for instance, Erkki Kansanaho, *Kirkko ja merenkulkijat. Sata vuotta Suomen merimieslähetysseuran työtä* (Saarijärvi, 1983), 14.

[4]Sarah Palmer, "Seamen Ashore in Late Nineteenth Century London: Protection from the Crimps" in Paul Adam (ed.), *Seamen in Society* (Bucharest, 1980), 55.

Research in Maritime History, No. 3 (December 1992), 63-79.

Among these homeless mariners were a great many Finns who in the late nineteenth century served on foreign vessels. They decided on this path in search of higher pay, because they were deserters, or because they preferred employment abroad.[5] In the case of deserters, the prescribed punishment must have further deterred returning.[6] As a consequence these men became itinerant and internationalized. Perhaps as many as 6000 sailed the oceans in 1881, or about as many as served in the Finnish merchant marine.[7] Whether their work experiences differed substantially is unknown,[8] but the intensity and level of contact with home certainly differentiated the two groups.

Finnish seamen serving on domestic vessels, whether on regular routes or longer voyages, had an automatic opportunity to return home that the itinerants lacked. But perhaps as important, Finns on domestically-owned craft in a very real sense never left home: they served mostly with other Finns and shared a language (and perhaps even memories). On the other hand, those on international vessels tended to become alienated from their home and past. For these men, the best site

---

[5]Yrjö Kaukiainen, *Sailing into Twilight: Finnish Shipping in an Age of Transport Revolution, 1860-1914* (Jyväskylä, 1991), 119-122. It has been estimated that six to eight percent of men serving in the Finnish merchant fleet (500 in all) deserted in the years 1856-1860; see Kustaa Hautala, "Merimiesten karkaaminen suomalaisilta laivoilta 1800-luvulla," in *Näkökulmia menneisyyteen: Eino Jutikkalan juhlakirja* (Porvoo, 1967), 102-106; see also Lewis R. Fischer, "A Dereliction of Duty: The Problem of Desertion on Nineteenth Century Sailing Vessels," in Rosemary Ommer and Gerald Panting (eds.), *Working Men Who Got Wet* (St. John's, 1980), 63.

[6]Reino Kero, "Sjömän från Finland som emigranter i Amerika under 1800-talet," *Historisk Tidskrift för Finland*, No. 3 (1988), 397; Hautala, "Merimiesten karkaaminen," 111-113.

[7]The figure for Finns sailing on domestic ships excludes coastal vessels; Yrjö Kaukiainen, "Från jungman Jansson till Kalle Aaltonen: Sjömän i Finlands handelsflotta 1860-1914--en kvantitativ översikt," *Historisk Tidskrift för Finland*, No. 3 (1988), 356, 364. The contemporary estimate of 6000 tallies rather well with the finding that between 1863 and 1913, 5600 seamen in the Canadian merchant fleet have been identified as Finnish; Lewis R. Fischer and Helge W. Nordvik, "Finländare i den kanadensiska handelsflottan 1863-1913," *ibid.*, 377.

[8]Fischer and Nordvik, "Finländare i den kanadensiska handelsflottan," 392-393. They conclude that Finns in the Canadian merchant fleet did not on the whole differ much from other seamen.

from which to have contact with their homeland was not the ship but the port, where they could meet countrymen and post or receive mail. Paradoxically, a major foreign port was one place where the distant home country could once again become tangible to the itinerant sailor.

From 1880 a major change occurred in the way such seamen could have contact with their native culture. In that year the Finnish Seamen's Mission began its work in Britain, establishing churches in London and Hull, with occasional pastoral visits to Liverpool.[9] For itinerants, this provided increased opportunities to get in touch with Finland. The first pastors attempted to make the mission known in the maritime community. To the surprised seamen lured away from pubs and invited to worship in their mother tongue, these clerics represented more than religion and church. Having in many cases sailed for decades on foreign ships with little contact with Finland, the mariners may well have interpreted their presence as a sign that their homeland was reaching out to them.

How and why did the homeland reach out to seamen and *vice versa*? What was the nature of these contacts, and what kinds of emotions did they arouse in itinerant Finnish seamen? This essay seeks to shed some light on these questions. The period examined extends from the beginning of the Mission to the early 1890s, when the demise of homeward-bound crimping and the fierce labour conflicts of 1892-1893 closed the pages on an era of British sailortown life.[10] The primary material comes largely from the records of the Seamen's Mission and its publication, *Merimiehen Ystävä* (*Sailor's Friend*). It is well to keep in mind the probable biases of these sources when considering the examples below.

While the ministers of the Seamen's Church understood and sympathized with the harsh lot of seamen, they also perceived them within a clearly delineated framework. Like many contemporaries, they saw seamen in foreign ports as helpless figures, lonely, gullible and

---

[9] Kansanaho, *Kirkko ja merenkulkijat*, 52-90.

[10] Palmer, "Seamen Ashore," 62; Conrad Dixon, "The Rise and Fall of the Crimp, 1840-1914," in Stephen Fisher (ed.), *British Shipping and Seamen, 1630-1960: Some Studies* (Exeter, 1984), 59-61.

carefree to the point of recklessness.[11] Lack of support and guidance in their eyes made the sailor easy prey for the temptations and predators of sailortown. As the pastor in Hull wrote in 1888,

> let us remember that a sailor, when sailing into a foreign port after a long and difficult voyage, cannot be welcomed by his nearest and dearest, that there is no loving home waiting for him, that his friends are not there to keep him pleasant company. Instead, he is all alone, and therefore it is all the more difficult for him to resist the temptations of the Devil's emissaries, those who for their own gain seek to offer the sailor respite in their detestable dens, pubs, dancing places and brothels where the sailor will be destroyed body and soul.[12]

Not surprisingly, the priests decided that one of their most important tasks was to re-establish the tenuous connections between the itinerant Finn and home; virtually everything they did was guided by a wish to enhance the itinerants' "Finnish identity."[13] One method was to collate and transmit to Finland information on individual seamen; another was to act as intermediaries to forward mail. The data they collected was published in *Sailor's Friend* and mostly comprised greetings and snippets of information about the recent whereabouts of seamen.[14] Often the

---

[11]Judith Fingard, "'Those Crimps of Hell and Goblins Damned': The Image and Reality of Quebec's Sailortown Bosses," in Ommer and Panting (eds.), *Working Men Who Got Wet*, 327; Kansanaho, *Kirkko ja merenkulkijat*, 53-54.

[12]L. Oscar Kjäldström, "Tee-juhlista merimiehillemme," *Merimiehen ystävä* (henceforth cited as *MY*), No. 6 (1888), 136. See also "Muutama sana Suomen merimieslähetyksen toimesta sekä suuremman kannatuksen ja avun antamisen tarpeellisuudesta," *MY*, No. 8 (1885), 127.

[13]David Kirby, "One Hundred Years of the Finnish Seamen's Mission in London," in Erkki Arni, *et al.* (eds.), *100 vuotta: 100 Years of the Finnish Seamen's Mission in London* (Kajaani, 1982), 46; Ludvig Enkvist, "Suomen Merimieslähetys-Seuran Toimikunta 1893. Vuosikertomus. Lontoo 12.5.1893," *MY*, No. 9 (1893), 136-137.

[14]See Kero, "Sjömän från Finland som emigranter," 397, 406-409, for an example of what can be gleaned from this information about Finnish seamen in American ports during the nineteenth century.

messages amounted to miniature biographies which though brief are rather moving.

Take the case, for instance, of Karl Törnrot, aged sixty-two and lying ill in 1883 in the Seamen's Hospital in Greenwich. He had lived abroad for decades and married in London; his wife was now dead, and about his relatives in Finland he knew nothing--not even whether they were still alive. Karl Törnrot's Finnish still seemed intact, however, and he was glad to receive from the pastor a Finnish bible--the first that Törnrot had seen since leaving Uusikaupunki on the west coast of Finland thirty-five years earlier.[15] Or consider Frans Vesander, known in London by his English name Frank Sanders, resident in the Greenwich Union Workhouse in the autumn of 1882 and badly ill. "Once a month he is allowed to go to town," wrote the minister, "and, despite being paralysed, he tries to get himself down by the riverside to see the ships. Greetings to his mother and sisters and brothers in the homeland!"[16]

To judge from the numerous letters that arrived on clerics' desks from relatives anxious to receive information about missing seamen, the material must have been valuable. It was also revolutionary in that it afforded a reasonably easy channel for seamen and relatives to establish contact, often after silences of a decade or more. But the Mission also increased contact with the homeland in other ways. For example, reading rooms housed a wide selection of Finnish papers as well as letter-writing facilities. At Christmas, the aroma of home was particularly strong. Indeed, Christmas was the zenith for the churches, an occasion to think about home and relatives. Presents made by Finnish women were distributed and the Christmas tree was normally brought by a visiting Finnish ship. During the 1884 London celebrations, H.H. Snellman prayed that although his congregants were abroad, they might still

> experience a loving breeze from home, because it was those at home who offered seamen this celebration. From home were the Christmas presents, from home came the money to pay for the expenses, from home

---

[15]H.H. Snellman, "Sanomia ja tervehdyksiä," *MY*, No. 8 (1883), 92.

[16]"Sanomia ja tervehdyksiä," *MY*, No. 11 (1882), 92.

were greetings and prayers that this might be a true Christmas celebration.[17]

In this way Finland, through the Seamen's Mission, reached out to its sons in the wider world. But it was not only feelings of love and gratitude toward the homeland that the church hoped to inculcate in the sailors' breasts.[18] Its expectations for its itinerant sons were much greater, and the needs of seamen's relatives both pressing and concrete. In short, Finland was also rather interested in the seamen's pay-packets.

Among the reasons Finnish men went to sea in the nineteenth century, perhaps the most important was to earn money.[19] When a Finnish seaman served on a domestic vessel, his relatives could draw some of his pay directly from the owner and thus achieve a modicum of financial security.[20] But if the man deserted--or preferred to work on non-Finnish craft--there was no equally convenient method for the family to share his wages. The seaman could send his pay home via Russian consulates--a route which for most was barred by language--or use the

---

[17]H.H. Snellman, "Kirje Englannista, helmikuu 1885," *MY*, No. 6 (1885), 89-90; Emil Panelius, "Työalaltamme. Juolujuhlat [sic] Hullissa ja Liverpoolissa," *MY*, No. 2 (1887), 29-34.

[18]Ludvig Enkvist, "Kirje Lontoosta 4.1.1895," *MY*, No. 1 (1895), 5-6. See also Enkvist, "Suomen Merimieslähetys-Seuran," 136-137.

[19]While we do not know how many Finnish seamen were married, had families or supported relatives, we do have information on particular areas. The overwhelming majority of seamen from the islands of Houtskär and Korpo were unmarried in 1895; see Beatrice Moring, "Sjömans och båtmansfamiljernas livsvillkor i sydvästra Finlands skärgård under 1700- och 1800-talen" (Unpublished paper presented to the Sixth Bottnisk Kontakt, Gävle, February 1992). On the other hand, we know from a Norwegian study that while the maritime labour force was predominantly young, this did not necessarily mean that seamen were unmarried. See Helge W. Nordvik and Jan Oldervoll, "Seafarer and Community in Norway: An Analysis based on the 1801 Census," in Adam (ed.), *Seamen in Society*, 81-83. For Finnish seamen's family relations, see Christian Ahlström, "Sjömän i Helsingfors 1819-1849: Iakttagelser om levnadsvillkor och arbetsförhållanden," *Historisk tidskrift för Finland*, No. 3 (1988), 521; and Jari Lybeck, "Sjöfolket i Raumo under sjöfartens expansionsår 1840-1870," *ibid.*, 538-539, 546-548.

[20]Sjöhistoriska museet vid Åbo Akademi, Folkbok för Skeppet *Atka* 1865, file 221.

services offered by the sailors' homes.[21] With the arrival of the seamen's church, however, another possibility was at hand. The priests, who perceived in seamen careless attitudes toward money and wanted relatives to receive a share of wages, began to offer various financial services.[22] The pastors could take the money for safe keeping, deposit it in a bank, or even send some of it to Finland. Of these, the most important--both quantitatively and in terms of its emotional significance to seamen--seems to have been the forwarding of money to Finland.

The sums involved varied widely and could be anything from about £5 and up. The aggregate, however, was considerable. A very crude calculation for 1882-1892 suggests that an annual average of 26,200 Finnish marks (£1040) was sent to Finland through the churches in London and Hull.[23] To put this in perspective, an able-bodied seaman on Finnish foreign-going sailing vessels in the 1880s earned forty-five to sixty marks per month, which means that the total transmitted over the period represents one year's earnings for 416 ABs at average wages.[24] We might also compare the total with a seaman's average monthly wage of £3.3 in Britain in 1870,[25] or gain a sense of the commitment of some individuals by noting that the largest lump sum sent to Finland by the

---

[21]For the monetary services of the Sailors' Home towards the mid-nineteenth century, see David M. Williams, "Henry Mayhew and the British Seaman," in Stephen Fisher (ed.), *Lisbon as a Port Town, The British Seaman and Other Maritime Themes* (Exeter, 1988), 120-121. The Sailors' Home was used as a pay office by some shipowners, and also served as a savings bank for seamen.

[22]H.H. Snellman, "Lontoon asemalta," *MY* No. 7 (1887), 151.

[23]No allowance has been made for variations in monetary value, exchange rates or levels of pay.The figures are derived from the Annual Reports of the Seamen's Mission published in *Merimiehen Ystävä*.

[24]Kaukiainen, *Sailing into Twilight*, 111-122, particularly 112. To facilitate matters, I have assumed average pay to have been 52.5 marks per month.

[25]Kaukiainen, "Från jungman Jansson till Kalle Aaltonen," 351, note 12.

London pastor in 1886-1887 was £135 saved by a "hard-working AB leading a regular life" during a four-year voyage to Australia.[26]

These comparisons aside, the remittances must have represented welcome additions to the relatives' incomes. In the mid-nineteenth century, sailors' spouses and children figured prominently in poor law statistics and as recipients of charity.[27] On the other hand, it is clear that only a fraction of the seamen sailing on foreign ships sent money through the Seamen's church[28]--the number of sailors involved, when it is mentioned, seems to have varied between fifty and seventy per year. It is not, however, the precise sums that interest us here. Instead, it is that sending money home seems to have been emotionally significant to many seamen, and that the way in which they came to send money home can reveal something of their feelings. Money formed an important emotional bond between the itinerant seaman and his family. To see more clearly the issues involved, we must examine in some detail how the contact between the seaman and his homeland was established and maintained.

---

[26]See the Mission's annual report, "Vuosikertomus, annettu 'Yhdistyksen sielunhoidon hankkimista varten Suomen merimiehille ulkomaan satamissa' Johtokunnalta vuosikokouksessa 9 p. Kesäkuuta 1887," *MY*, No. 7 (1887), 152.

[27]In Kristiinankaupunki, for instance, child mortality rates in seamen's families were high at the end of the 1850s. This was assumed to be a consequence of mothers having to go out to work soon after giving birth; Oiva Turpeinen, "Lastensuojelu ja väestönkehitys: Lastensuojelun lääkinnöllinen ja sosiaalinen kehitys Suomessa," in Panu Pulma and Oiva Turpeinen, *Suomen lastensuojelun historia* (Kouvola, 1987), 316. In Helsinki during the 1850s and 1860s, the most common profession of fathers whose children received assistance from ladies' charitable organizations was seamen; Alexandra Ramsay, *Huvudstadens hjärta. Två fruntimmersföreningars roll i filantropi och social förändring i Helsingfors, 1848-1865* (forthcoming).

[28]We cannot estimate with any certainty how much of the money sent by Finnish sailors abroad was forwarded through the Seamen's Mission. According to the pastor in London in 1887, the church's share represented about a quarter of the total, the rest being remitted through the Russian consulate or the bigger seamen's homes; H.H. Snellman, "Työstä ulkomailla. (Vuosikertomuksesta) Lontoo," *MY*, No. 7 (1889), 57. Three years later the same pastor thought, however, that the importance of the Consulate had greatly declined; the annual sums, he suggested, were £57 and £1513 for the Consulate and the church respectively. H.H. Snellman, "Työ ulkomailla. Lontoo," *MY*, No. 10 (1892), 148.

The pastors offered their financial services during regular rounds of the notorious sailortowns of London and Hull where the clerics, following the well-established practices of British seamen's missions,[29] frequented boardinghouses and pubs in an effort to prise away Finnish sailors. As there were many adversaries for the money that seamen returning from long voyages had at their disposal, the pastors had to work hard to stave off keen competition from crimps, runners, boarding-house masters and publicans. Indeed, some Finnish seamen seem to have responded to the pastor's pleas for relatives at home with a blank refusal, replying that they wished to have some fun in port after an arduous voyage.[30] But even in these cases the pastor might still succeed if he were persistent. As an example, we can follow pastor Oscar Kjäldström one evening in 1888 as he made the rounds in Hull looking for a Finnish carpenter about whose discharge earlier that day from a Scottish ship with an unusually large amount of money he had heard.

The pastor found the man in one of the Finnish boardinghouses, where he was told that the wages in question were about £103 (2600 Finnish marks) and that the carpenter intended to go back to Finland after twenty years at sea because of ill health. Although chagrined to learn that none of the money remained, Kjäldström remained unruffled and eventually learned that the man had bought a ticket to Göteborg and deposited £75 at the Wilson steamer office, giving the receipt to the boardinghouse master who accompanied him. The minister then searched for the latter, who was found, half-drunk, asleep on the floor of an upstairs room. With some difficulty, the cleric divested him of the receipt, took it to Wilson's office, and collected the £75. In the process, he learned the fate of the remaining £28. The carpenter had spent £16 on clothes, paid the driver and bearer a pound each, and stood drinks in the boardinghouse. Finally, his purse, containing the remaining £8, had been stolen. To pursue the last point, Kjäldström called at the police station, but to no avail--the suspected culprit, the bearer, was released for lack of evidence. There thus remained £75 of the man's pay, most of which the pastor sent to Finland for the carpenter the next morning.

---

[29]Alston Kennerley, "British Seamen's Missions in the Nineteenth Century," in Lewis R. Fischer, *et al.* (eds.), *The North Sea: Twelve Essays on Social History of Maritime Labour* (Stavanger, 1992), 81.

[30]H.H. Snellman, "Kirje Englannista 1.10.1883," *MY*, No. 10 (1883), 112-113.

At this point, the carpenter grew restless and declared that he wanted the remaining £10 for himself. The reason, though repeated, seemed suspect to the priest--surely it could not cost all that much to travel from Göteborg to the carpenter's home. When the pastor remained unconvinced, the carpenter resorted to modest bribery, promising to donate some funds to the Mission if the cleric would only let him handle his own money. By now Kjäldström had taken as much as he could bear. With mild force--he was a heavily-built man well-equipped to deal with such emergencies--he dragged the carpenter to the Wilson office and paid for the journey from Göteborg to Finland out of the remaining £10. Moreover, he arranged for the carpenter to be met at each stop by one of his friends, who was instructed to pay for the man's meals and accommodation. The logistics of the journey resolved, it still remained to settle the bill with the boardinghouse keeper and to pay for the drinks the carpenter had allegedly consumed in the neighbouring pub. The police were called to settle the last point, but with no positive outcome--the pub bills had to be paid as well, with the carpenter urging the pastor repeatedly to "pay them all, pay them all. I am an honest man." After all was done, the carpenter was finally dispatched on his homeward journey, with a few shillings as pocket money.[31]

While this case was perhaps extreme, it was unusual only in the degree of control the pastor exercised. Other features correlate well with the general practices of crimping,[32] except that here it was the priest who acted as "runner," accompanying the sailor and supervising his financial affairs. Had Kjäldström been less persistent, the seaman's money might have been dissipated totally before he left Hull.[33] This is precisely what happened to an elderly sailor whose wife had written to the minister in Hull in 1891 requesting him to ensure that her husband

---

[31]L.O.K. [presumably L. Oscar Kjäldström], "Merimiehemme ulkomaiden satama-kaupungeissa, Hull 2.8.1888," *MY*, No. 8 (1888), 175-181.

[32]For crimping practices in British ports, see Dixon, "Rise and Fall of the Crimp," 52-55. It is also interesting that the pastor's offer to send the seaman's wages home was very similar to the so-called "Midge Scheme" in Britain under which the Board of Trade sought to curb crimping by offering to forward the sailors' pay to the Mercantile Marine Office nearest their home. Palmer, "Seamen Ashore," 62; Dixon, "Rise and Fall of the Crimp," 59-61.

[33]Enkvist, "Suomen Merimieslähetys-Seuran," 136-137.

sent his wages home directly upon receipt. Otherwise, the wife feared, the man might in his usual way spend the money on drink. The priest managed to snare his quarry even before the ship docked. While at first the man appeared glad to see the cleric and enlisted his help to forward his wages, £17 6s (about 650 Finnish marks), to his wife, when after a few days he received his pay, his mood changed. Now before giving the pastor the money he first wanted to have a few drinks with his friends--not to get drunk, of course, but simply to celebrate the completion of a long journey. Could the priest, he asked, come around the next day? "And I went the next day," wrote the slightly exasperated cleric,

> and the next day after that, and on a couple of other "next days" as well, warning and admonishing the man--but despite all his promises and my warnings the man carried, shilling by shilling, to a pub all the money that should have gone towards the upkeep of his wife and children.

After a few weeks the seaman, again destitute, took a berth in a foreign ship, while his wife and children, according to the pastor, had

> nothing but tears to garnish their rough bit of bread with somewhere up the Finnish Gulf in Ostrobothnia. Do make the man repent, O God, and wipe away tears from the wife's eyes so that they would not water the roots of bitterness and help to raise a crop of hatred in a heart cruelly deceived![34]

These stories, with both comical and tragic twists, allow us to sample some of the flavour of life in British sailortowns. But bearing in mind the sources from which these stories come, can we use them to gain any insight into how the seamen perceived life in port and the emotional import that contacts with home held for them? In trying to answer this question, we must remember that reports written by pastors are likely to have concentrated on the seedier sides of maritime existence--the sinfulness of life in ports was, after all, a legitimation of the priests' own work. Although the reports tend to portray seamen as heavy

---

[34]Ludvig Enkvist, "Kirje Hull'sta, 30.10.1891," *MY*, No. 11 (1891), 243-244.

drinkers--and although this undoubtedly was part of many seamen's lives--we should not consider this view as the whole (or sole) truth. Heavy drinking or ribald activity was not endemic among all Finnish seamen working on foreign ships.[35] Nor need all contacts with home have been quite as complicated as in the cases we have considered here.

The issue of representativeness is a problem which cannot really be resolved. We cannot say with any certainty how "typical" the seamen referred to by pastors were of Finnish seamen abroad. Nevertheless, leaving this issue aside and examining only the seamen about whom the pastors wrote, it is possible to glean much about their attitudes toward home. We can see this by considering several cases in which reluctance to remit money was based on considerations other than short-term gratification. These show that seamen sometimes purposefully set out to waste their funds as a kind of revenge on their relatives for emotional hurt.

In 1882, for example, a sailor's wife contacted the London pastor to ask for information about her husband, who had not written for some time despite several letters from her. The wife wrote that she and her children were suffering. When found, the seaman claimed that although he had been in London for some time awaiting a letter from home, he had received none. In consequence, he had become angry and in retaliation had spent almost all the money intended for his family.[36]

In another revealing case, involving the elderly Oulu sailor Jaakko Vanhala, a similar emotional response to contacts with home more or less determined the course of much of his life. Lying on his death bed in the Greenwich Seamen's Hospital, he told a Finnish pastor his life story. As a young man, he had sailed mainly on shorter voyages and always returned to Finland. There he had married, spent a couple of happy years at home, and then decided to take one more short trip. When his ship was sold in Lübeck, he joined another vessel and stayed away for longer than intended, mainly on short voyages. He did not

---

[35]Some pastors admitted that many of the sailors on foreign ships were decent men who had not fallen prey to crimps or drunkenness, but lived in decent sailors' homes and sent their savings to their families. See, for example, "Karanneitten merimiestemme elämästä II," *MY*, No. 8 (1882), 63-64; H.H. Snellman, "Kirje Lontoosta lokakuussa, 1888," *MY*, No. 11 (1888), 254-255.

[36]In this case, the wife's letters seem to have been lost in the post because the sailor had given her a phonetic spelling of his London address. "Eikö kirjettä?," *MY*, No. 11 (1882), 90.

manage to save much, since it was expensive to live in port while changing ships. Letters from his wife had assured him, however, that everything was fine at home. Finally, he took a berth for a year, during which he amassed a stake of 300 dollars. But just as he planned to return home permanently, he got an angry letter from his wife accusing him, based on reports from other seamen in his home town, of living a "fast life" in the port towns of the world. She reprimanded him for never sending any money and demanded to know where all his earnings went. At this point Vanhala decided that if this was what his wife believed, he might as well give her some reason to do so. Thus began what he called a "wild life;" for twenty-five years he lived abroad, not answering letters and not saving any money. Finally he fell ill in the Mediterranean, left his ship, used his last money to buy a ticket to England, and entered the Greenwich hospital, poor and fatally ill.[37]

It is of course difficult to know whether Jaakko Vanhala's dying confessional is entirely truthful or whether he was searching for a scapegoat to justify the life he had chosen. What is evident, however, is that stories like this are suggestive of complex relationships between an itinerant living abroad and his distant family. It could not have been easy for either party; as one pastor observed, "the sailor has little chance of enjoying the pleasures of home-life, yet he has to shoulder his responsibilities for his home."[38] For some seamen the emotional ties with home had in fact been weakened to the point that they even refused to give any personal information for publication in the *Sailor's Friend*.

Nonetheless, it is clear that home still mattered to all the seamen whose lives we have described here. It meant enough to lead to oft-expressed plans to send savings home, even if the wishes often went unfulfilled. And it mattered sufficiently to be used to explain the type of life the seaman was living, as in the case of Jaakko Vanhala. Many itinerant seamen still maintained emotional ties to their homes. The act of sending money to relatives, whether through the seamen's church or other channels, must also in its way have been satisfying to seamen--it was, after all, what they had set out to do. There could be emotional

---

[37]G.E.B., "Erään merimiehen elämästä," *MY*, No. 9 (1882), 70-72.

[38]H.H. Snellman, "Kirje Merimiehen Ystävälle, Kemi 14.9.1885," *MY*, No.10 (1885), 154.

dividends as well, such as when the family, on receiving money after a long silence, poured out heartfelt thanks in a letter.[39]

The importance of home can also be seen from diametrically opposite cases, in which it was not the seaman but the home folk who failed to maintain communication. Some cases involved a regular flow of savings from the seamen but no letters in return. When this occurred, it invariably seemed to weigh heavily on the man.[40] It was a shock that an unwritten contract, in which money was exchanged for letters, could be broken by the other party.

On the other hand it is also clear that contacts with home could be far from idyllic; indeed, in most cases we have considered they appear to have filled the seamen with conflicting and ambiguous emotions. There may have been a wish to send money home, but instead it was spent on something else and tender feelings toward family are transformed into resentment by rebukes in letters. Why, then, was it that affection and longing for one's relatives were intertwined with more complex emotions? It seems evident that the ambiguity must have arisen from conflict, either endogenous or exogenous, in which a certain amount of emotional conflict was inherent. For many seamen, it may have been a combination of the two.

The exact nature of these conflicts can only be surmised. While this is a complex issue for which it is impossible to provide conclusive answers, we can surmise that two kinds of related conflicts in particular might have been central to the itinerant seaman's experiences. First, let us consider the conflict between the sort of life a seaman could live in a foreign port and his obligations as a breadwinner.

For a seaman, time in port was both an antidote and a response to his experiences at sea.[41] The understandable need for some comfort after an arduous voyage presumably made the seaman more appreciative of the pleasures sailortown could offer, and an uproarious spree must

---

[39]"Suomen merimieslähetys," *MY*, No. 4 (1895), 53.

[40]Enkvist, "Kirje Hull'sta," 244-245.

[41]Merja-Liisa Hinkkanen, "A Survey of the Mentality of Finnish Merchant Sailors at the Turn of the Century," *Scandinavian Journal of History*, XIV (1989), 306-307; Hinkkanen, "'En sjöman älskar havets våg': Sjömännens upplevelse- och erfarenhetsvärld som exempel på mentalitetshistorisk metodologi," *Historisk Tidskrift för Finland*, No. 3 (1988), 449.

have been a welcome relief from the many constraints--from strict hierarchy and hard discipline to cramped living conditions--that he endured at sea. Shipboard pressures could only be released in port.[42] This was exacerbated by the crimping system, which tied him to a lifestyle in which premiums were placed upon drinking and dissolution. But if a seaman behaved this way ashore, the corollary was that it made it difficult to send home any money. To complicate the seaman's financial dilemma, he was frequently bilked; an estimate for 1870 suggested that seamen in British ports received value from crimps for only about one-third of their money.[43]

The conflict may also have been internal, growing out of a divergence between the norms of sailortown life and those with which he had been reared. This friction must have been underscored sharply by the pastors who sought to reimpose the homeland's values on itinerant Finns who were "wasting their wages in sin and disgrace" in foreign ports.[44] "If your fathers, mothers or relatives at home could see the way you are spending the sabbath day, what would they think about it?"--thus rang the parting shot from a minister to a couple of young Finnish seamen spotted in 1882 in the company of women of questionable morals on the disreputable Ratcliffe Highway in Shadwell.[45] Possibly combined with the seaman's own nagging conscience, the priest's reminder of what those at home expected of him sometimes inspired the result the cleric desired. At other times, however, the result was more equivocal. To see

---

[42]Judith Fingard, *Jack in Port: Sailortowns of Eastern Canada* (Toronto, 1982), 139. See also Williams, "Henry Mayhew," 119.

[43]Dixon, "Rise and Fall of the Crimp," 52-55.

[44]L.O. Kjäldström, "Merimiehemme ulkomaiden satamakaupungeissa III, Hull, 1.12.1888," *MY*, No. 12 (1888), 278. In particular, those sailors who served on foreign ships were considered hardened in the ways of sin. See Emil Panelius, "Työalaltamme, 15.11.1886 Hull," *MY*, No. 12 (1886), 189; and the annual report of the Mission, "Vuosikertomus, annettu 'Yhdistyksen sielunhoidon hankkimista varten Suomen merimiehille ulkomaan satamissa' Johtokunnalta vuosikokouksessa 9 p. Kesäkuuta 1887," *MY*, No. 7 (1887), 156.

[45]Elis Bergroth, "Kirje Englannista 30.11.1882," *MY*, No. 12 (1882), 92, 96. See also Ludvig Enkvist, "Kirje Lontoosta, 4.1. 1895," *MY*, No. 1 (1895), 5-6; Kirby, "One Hundred Years," 49.

this we can examine the case of Simon Bris (a fictional name used by the pastor) in 1888 which in many ways epitomizes this conflict.

Bris, who had a history of heavy drinking, sailed on foreign vessels and featured on the ministers' list of missing seamen for years. His wife and four children lived in poverty in Finland and were unsuccessful at contacting him. Apparently of his own volition Bris suddenly wrote home, telling his wife that he was bound for Britain and even providing a contact address. Ill and unable to feed her family, she wrote to the priest in Hull asking for his help in persuading her husband to send some money home. With considerable effort, the pastor managed to find Bris and managed to convince him to send her some money. Things began to go less smoothly, however, when Bris, in accordance with the wishes of his wife and the minister, promised to return home after one more short journey. For a time he remained sober, frequenting services in the Finnish church and using the reading room. His wife even wrote him a grateful letter after receiving the money. But when the crunch came, Simon Bris was unable to face it. Instead, he spent his remaining money on drink and got into such a state that his master was unwilling to accept him on board. After the cleric convinced the master to relent, Bris deserted and the pastor lost track of him.[46]

Simon Bris, to judge from the story, was likely to have been an alcoholic whose behaviour can perhaps be explained in terms of a chronic alcoholic's inability to cope with the demands of sobriety. Yet his behaviour also suggests strains that must have been shared by many of his countrymen abroad, irrespective of their drinking habits. The conflict between the life of an itinerant seaman and the norms of a sedentary existence is clear--for a time, Bris sought to accommodate his family's expectations and returned to the fold of the church. While the nation temporarily regained a lost son, eventually the conflict became too great and Bris tried to escape. It is likely that contact with his family was again severed, perhaps permanently.

To conclude, I would like to advance a few thoughts on some of the issues raised by this paper and what they suggest about the relationships between itinerant Finnish sailors and their homeland. By examining seamen's behaviour we have learned that for many the relationship with home was far from arcadian. Instead, complex and even

---

[46]L.O.K., "Merimiehemme ulkomaiden satamakaupungeissa II," *MY*, No. 10 (1888), 217-226.

conflicting emotions seem to have been involved. Although we have concentrated on the "home" that the seaman left behind in Finland, the concept is perhaps not quite as straightforward as we have tended to assume. What is a home for a seaman, and where is it? In terms of emotional contacts or place of refreshment, the boardinghouses, for instance, might have represented far more important anchors for itinerant seamen than the abodes of their memories in Finland.[47]

Moreover, the same question may be asked in a wider context: how "Finnish" did the seamen living abroad feel? To what extent did something distinctively Finnish remain part of their identity? Seamen's pastors, strongly nationalistic, naturally tended to emphasize this concept.[48] While we should not accept their views uncritically, and while it is doubtless true that regardless of nationality mariners tended to identify themselves as sailors,[49] we might still ponder the extent to which "Finnishness" remained part of their mental construct. That their contacts with home so often were laden with conflicting emotions seem to provide good grounds for posing the question.

For now, however, these queries must remain unanswered. Instead, we can make one more general observation--that even when studying Finnish seamen in the world's ports or at sea, the way in which their past and homeland featured in their lives must be considered. If we think of the Finnish seaman living abroad as an itinerant *gastarbeiter*, this is obvious. A sailor, however mobile, could not completely escape from his homeland while he was still bound to it by responsibilities, education and mentality.

---

[47]Dixon, "Rise and Fall of the Crimp," 55.

[48]Kirby, "One Hundred Years," 46, 74-75.

[49]Kaukiainen, "Från jungman Jansson till Kalle Aaltonen," 364; Marika Ramström, "Sjömannens verklighetsuppfattning: En kulturanalys av fartygssamhället på långfartsskutorna under den finländska segelssjöfartens sista era, 1920-1940-talen" (unpublished M.A. thesis, Åbo Akademi, 1992), 4-5.

Death of a Merchant

Ian G. Layton

At the production end of the many chains of maritime contact between the peripheral north and the populous core of western Europe during the pre-industrial era, seaport merchants played key roles in co-ordinating the supply and transport of staples. Unfortunately, most of the business records of eighteenth and early nineteenth-century merchants in the port of Luleå in northern Sweden have been misplaced or destroyed. Alternatives must therefore be employed to investigate the patterns and organisation of trade in the Lule River valley.[1] In the Regional Archives at Härnösand, estate inventories are preserved for a number of Luleå's wealthier citizens; this is a useful beginning for a study of the role of the merchant in the utilisation of resources in the town's extensive hinterland. One such inventory is analyzed here to illustrate its scholarly value. Furthermore, an attempt is made "to see the universe in the locality" by drawing some general conclusions from the study of an individual.[2]

Abraham Stenholm, a Luleå merchant, died of dropsy (a rich man's disease) on 7 May 1821.[3] According to his inventory, he left a

[1]This paper is a revised and extended version of a short article previously published in Swedish as "En handelsmans död," in Ingvar Jonsson (ed.), *Geografi och samhälls planering: Studier tillägnade Erik Bylund* (Umeå, 1982). The material and context largely derive from the author's research within the interdisciplinary Lule Valley Project (*Luleälvsprojektet*), financed by the Bank of Sweden Tercentenary Foundation. The final results are shortly to be published in a comprehensive monograph entitled "Economic Change in the Lule Valley: An Historical Geography of Trade and Resource Utilization c. 1550-1900."

[2]O. Wärneryd, "Att se det stora i det lilla," *Svensk Geografisk Årsbok*, LVII (1981), 246-254. The notion owes much to the creative thinking of the Lund geographer Torsten Hägerstrand.

[3]Luleå stads journaler öfwer döde och begrafne 1810-1833, Regional Archives at Härnösand (hereafter HLA).

Research in Maritime History, No. 3 (December 1992), 81-98.

widow, Elisabeth, and three young children--Adam, Carl Frederic, and Frederica Elisabeth--for whom the alderman Abraham Ruth and the merchant Anders Magnus Söderholm were appointed guardians.[4] The fact that the children were still minors suggests that their father was not particularly old; indeed, the parish catechetical registers show that Abraham was born on 4 December 1773 and was therefore only forty-seven at the time of his death.[5] The same sources also reveal that the surname "Stenholm" did not figure among Luleå's merchants until 1806. Having moved to town from the neighbouring rural parish of Råneå in 1790, Abraham Stenholm was first recorded as an assistant living in the household of the young merchant Abraham Ruth, who was only eight years his senior. There were several branches of Ruths living in town, and the family had mercantile traditions pre-dating the establishment of Luleå in 1621. During the following two centuries the family name also featured prominently among the town's aldermen and mayors.[6]

Stenholm's somewhat more humble roots can be traced in Råneå's catechetical registers, which show that he was the sixth child and fourth son of the parish clerk Hans Stenholm (b. 1726) and his wife Beata (b. 1735),[7] a younger sister of Abraham Ruth's father, the merchant Anders Ruth, who died in 1790 at the age of fifty-seven. The two Abrahams were therefore first cousins and Stenholm's move to Luleå coincided with the death of his uncle and Abraham Ruth's assumption, at the age of only twenty-five, of the family business in Skeppsbrogatan (no. 13; see Figure 1). These kinship connections must have helped Abraham Stenholm considerably in making the difficult social and economic adjustment from a mere assistant to the secure position of an

---

[4]Bouppteckningar 1817-1831, no. 33, Luleå stads arkiv, HLA.

[5]Luleå stads husförhörslängderna 1778-1800, 1801-1818, 1819-1827, HLA.

[6]A. Nordberg, "Något om de tidiga borgarna i Luleå, deras handel och vandel," *Norrbotten* (1949), 22-25.

[7]Råneå sockens husförhörslängderna 1770-1798, HLA. Hans Stenholm had long been the assistant clerk but obtained the post of parish clerk in 1763, retaining it until his death in 1797 (E. Byström, *Råneå socken 1654-1954* [Luleå, 1955], 102). Another of his sons, Anders (one year older than Abraham), moved to Luleå in 1788, where he became a master tailor, married a merchant's daughter (Ulrica Stare) in 1800, had three daughters, and died in 1824.

independent and outwardly successful merchant.[8] By 1795 he had apparently taken new employment as an assistant to a wealthy merchant and alderman, Jöns Ekman (property no. 97, Figure 1).[9] One can surmise that Ekman gave him far more responsibility, thereby broadening his experience and personal contacts, for his employer was also engaged in the town's judicial affairs. This arrangement may have been only temporary, for in 1800 and 1805 Stenholm was still listed in the Ruth household, first as Ruth's assistant and then as his bookkeeper. This progression suggests a formal system of merchant apprenticeship.

Abraham Stenholm was first recorded as a head of household in 1806, when he moved to a property on Köpmangatan. This was listed in the registers as no. 37, but the church numbering system bore no relationship to available maps; it was almost certainly identical with no. 48, his residence at his death. Figure 1 shows it as a corner property between Köpmangatan and Rådstugatan, near the town hall square. The site was fairly central and the house was probably one of Luleå's best. His wife Elisabeth (Lisa) was born in 1778, the daughter of Eric Sandberg.[10] She was also a newcomer, having moved from Kalix parish in 1798 to enter service as a maid in the Ruth household. After his brief period with Ekman, Stenholm was again living with the Ruths and must have had daily contact with his future wife. They were married eight years later (16 January 1806) and set up house at no. 48. Here their first three children were born--Adam in 1809, Carl Fredric in 1811, and Anna Maria in 1814. The latter died only a few months after birth; it was another little girl, Fredrica Elisabeth (b. 1818), who appears in the 1821 inventory. At the time of Abraham's untimely death the surviving children were therefore only twelve, nine, and not quite three years-old.

---

[8]The question of whether he was his cousin's employee, apprentice or partner remains unanswered.

[9]According to Luleå town's *mantalslängder* for 1795, Jöns Ekman's inventory confirms that at the time of his death in 1817 he owned the land and buildings referred to as house/property (*gård*) nos. 97 and 96. These numbers evidently relate to those on Boström's town map of 1819. An earlier map registering land ownership shows that Ekman already owned the same property by 1790; once established, fully-fledged merchants and craftsmen rarely changed residence within the town.

[10]Sandberg has not been traced thus far, but he may have still been living in the more northerly parish of Kalix.

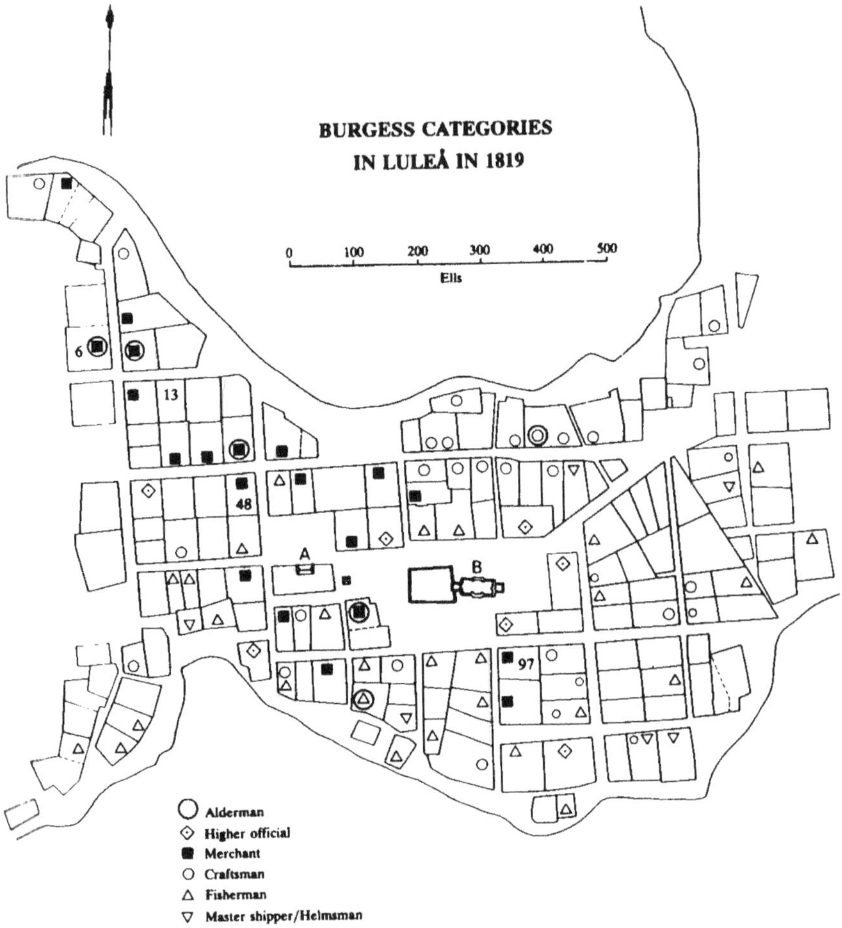

Figure 1: The distribution of burgess categories in Luleå in 1819 reveals early socio-economic segregation. Merchants and higher officials retained ownership of the oldest parts of the town, near the main harbour in the north and around the town hall (A) and church (B); craftsmen were concentrated in the northeast but were also dispersed among the fishermen and seamen in the newer eastern area and around the southern harbour. Abraham Stenholm lived first with the Ruths at no. 13, worked briefly at no. 97, and finally moved to no. 48. His cousin Abraham Ruth built a new home at no. 6, letting no. 13 to several less prosperous households.

Source: Based on M. Boström's map of 1819 (showing property numbers), together with contemporary taxation rolls and catechetical records.

Table 1
Abraham Stenholm's Property, Assets and Liabilities
According to his Estate Inventory of 1821

Property	*Rdr.*	*Sk.*	*Rst.*						
Real estate	900	-	-						
Other buildings	78	-	-						
Land	373	41	-						
Silver(ware)	87	9	-						
Tin	6	-	-						
Copper	80	32	-						
Brass	4	16	-						
Other alloys	2	-	-						
Iron implements	98	2	-						
Glass and porcelain	58	16	-						
Pewter articles	5	6	-						
Bedding and linen clothing	247	32	-						
Diverse household utensils	231	6	-						
Sea and fishing equipment	86	-	-						
Transport and farming equipment	102	12	-						
Livestock	60	-	-						
Merchandise	1288	16	-						
Cash at home	44	32	-						
Total inventory	3753	28	-	3753	28	-			
Credits									
Secured credits	2981	28	8						
Unsecured credits	2098	34	8						
(of which one half is taken to be secured)	1049	17	4						
Total credits	4030	46	-	4030	46	-			
Total assets				7784	26	-	7784	26	-
Debits									
Magistrate's one percent	77	40	-						
Town poor's 1/8th percent	9	35	-						
Fee for the second copy of the estate inventory deed	21	39	-	109	18	-			
Debts				10827	42	8			
Total debits				10937	12	8	10937	12	8
Deficit							3152	34	8

Notes: Rdr. = *riksdaler* banknotes; Sk. = *skillingar* (shillings); Rst. = *runstycken*. 1 rdr. = 48 sk.; 1 sk. = 12 rst.

Source: Abraham Stenholm's estate inventory deed of 1821, no. 33, Bouppteckningar 1817-1831, Luleå stadsarkiv, HLA.

With these fundamental biographical facts in mind, we can now turn to Stenholm's estate inventory with a good deal more insight. Unlike a will, an inventory is posthumous and therefore a precise record of wealth at the time of death. Abraham's inventory was compiled by his widow, witnessed by two aldermen (Abraham Ruth and Johan Nordström), and submitted to the Luleå magistrates' court on 27 August 1821, sixteen weeks after his demise. The document details his possessions, credits and debts, concluding with a balance sheet depicting his finances on the day he died (see Table 1). A number of the items tell us much about his various means of livelihood. The list begins with a description of his real estate, which comprised far more than his town house and outbuildings. He also owned a drying house (for grain and meat) and two piers (one with two warehouses) in the northern town harbour. At "Fisket" in Nederkalix, at "Holmen" in Råneå and in Jokkmokk, he owned "market houses," as well as a hut or store in Gällivare (all located in the inset to Figure 3). His commercial activities are clearly evident, for his town property also included an office in the main house, a large warehouse, a salt store and packing warehouse (for fish), a spice store, and overnight shelter for visiting *Saamis* and farmers.[11]

Apart from the usual outside toilet and woodshed, his main property contained other buildings suggesting an additional occupation: farming. These comprised a barn with two stalls and a hayloft, a cattle shed, a hay barn, and sheds for implements and winter sledges. In addition he owned 5.24 hectares of land (about thirteen acres), specified as arable and meadow--in ley, newly-tilled, and burn-beaten land. This must have provided summer grazing and winter fodder for his livestock, which consisted of one eleven year-old brown horse, six cows and a heifer. The horse clearly earned its keep, for the list of transport and farm equipment was extensive, including a chaise, three farm carts, six sleighs and seven working sledges, a plough and a harrow, together with all the necessary harness and tackle. Hand implements included a pitchfork and nine rakes, while the list of iron goods and tools included eleven old horseshoes, nine scythes, three spades, one shovel, one pickaxe, three sledge-hammers, and four crowbars. Many of the iron implements must have been manufactured locally, either at the neighbouring ironworks at Selet or even at Melderstein in the Råneälv valley;

---

[11]The terms *Saami* and *Saamish* are generally used today rather than the more well-known Lapp and Lappish, which the *Saami* feel have somewhat derogative implications.

alternatively, there were blacksmiths in the town, who probably used bar iron from one of these early industries.[12]

Two maritime activities are suggested by the items under marine and fishing equipment. Abraham was presumably engaged in fishing not only commercially but also for his household. Nets, yarn and lines were mentioned and he owned two small boats, one specifically for herring fishing. The major item was his half-share in a cargo ship. This is consistent with his role as a merchant, for he would have required a larger sailing vessel to collect bulky commodities such as tar and timber from coastal villages, like Råneå and Nederkalix, and from Heden, just below the first falls about thirty-five kilometres up the Lule River. The value of this half-share was only fifty *riksdaler*, suggesting that the vessel was not particularly large. It was probably a *stor-båt*, an open sailing boat of fifteen to thirty net registered tons (nrt).[13] While it was unlikely to have traded with Stockholm,[14] small vessels of this type plied the Gulf of Bothnia and Abraham likely sailed to Uleåborg and Brahestad in Finland, where his debts show he had trade connections. Commercial contacts between coastal Västerbotten and Österbotten had existed for centuries; despite Sweden's loss of the latter in 1809, socio-economic ties were apparently maintained, with or without official sanction.

In the lists of ships' manifests for 1805 Abraham Stenholm was named as master (*skeppare*) of the barque *Enigheten* and apparently sold goods in Stockholm for the first time on his own account (see Table 2). *Enigheten* was a vessel of 105 *svåra läster* (c. 190 nrt), launched from nearby Sävast in 1805.[15] As the owner was Abraham Ruth, it is clear

---

[12]Most output from Melderstein and Selet was exported as bar iron. It was mainly sent to Stockholm for re-export but some went directly abroad after the Bothnian trade restraints were relaxed in 1767 and finally removed in 1812. Nevertheless, manufacturing at these ironworks was at least in part geared to the needs of shipbuilding (anchors, chains, etc.) and the local community. P. Norberg, *Forna tiders järnbruk i Norr- och Västerbotten* (Uppsala, 1958), 110 and 131.

[13]A.A. Hülphers, *Samlingar til en Beskrifning öfwer Norrland. II: Om Westerbottens städer* (Westerås, 1797), 90.

[14]I.G. Layton, *The Evolution of Upper Norrland's Ports and Loading Places 1750-1976* (Umeå, 1981), 253.

[15]A. Moberg, *Sjöstad: skeppsbyggnad och sjöfart i Luleå under 350 år* (Luleå, 1971), 64.

that Stenholm was still working with his cousin the year before he married. Manifests for the following years show that the "merchant" Abraham Stenholm sent his goods to Stockholm on larger commercial vessels owned by his fellow townsmen. In particular, his cousins, Adam and Abraham Ruth, owned the greater part of Luleå's merchant shipping, with vessels plying regularly between Luleå and Stockholm as well as engaging often in lengthier voyages abroad.[16] Moreover, according to the custom records for 1820, the two Ruths accounted for 15.6% and 14.8% of Luleå's exports, respectively, and ranked first and second among the town's merchants. Abraham Stenholm's 5.3% placed him seventh out of twenty-nine names mentioned, clearly indicating that he held a leading position in Luleå's commercial and social life.

With their trade and shipping interests, the two main branches of Ruths illustrate the diversification and vertical integration of the early nineteenth-century Norrland coastal economy. Yet no direct financial connections with shipyards or sawmills have been traced to complete the picture of proto-industrialization, in which traditional merchant activities were often combined with entrepreneurship.[17] While Stenholm seems to have lacked the necessary capital to purchase a vessel on his own, in 1814 his name was again coupled with Jöns Ekman, the town's leading merchant, in an order for the 348-ton frigate *Prins Oscar*. Launched from a yard near Råbäcken, it was sold the following year to a Stockholm merchant.[18] In 1816 Abraham represented another Stockholm firm--C. and G. Hambré--in the purchase of the 130-ton brig *Mariana Henriette* from the stocks at Vibbonäset.[19] Shipbuilding was undoubtedly an important part of the local pre-industrial economy.[20]

---

[16]*Ibid.*, 64-75.

[17]Layton, *The Evolution*, 193.

[18]Carl E. Zandelin was the purchaser, according to Moberg, *Sjöstad*, 65.

[19]*Ibid.*, 69.

[20]Hülphers, *Samlingar*, 91, noted that Luleå shipbuilding grew during the American Revolution. Many vessels were sold to Stockholm and elsewhere, often with cargoes of local produce. Moreover, the Napoleonic wars increased demand; between 1792 and 1816 Luleå built 123 craft, an average of eight per year. M. Nyström, *Norrlands ekonomi i stöpsleven. Ekonomisk expansion, stapelvaruproduktion och maritima näringar 1760-1812* (Umeå, 1982), Table 1, Appendix J, 263-264; Moberg, *Sjöstad*, 64-76.

Table 2
Abraham Stenholm's Shipments of Goods from Luleå for Selected Years

Product	1805	1807	1808	1810	1811	1815	1819	1820	1821	1823	1824	unit
Tar	55	256	676	410	156	632	629	525	150	408	190	barrel
Butter	14	69	258	86	33	128	215	222	-	86	117	lispd.
Salt beef	-	1	-	-	½	-	1	1	-	-	-	barrel
Tallow	-	-	5	-	-	-	-	-	-	-	-	lispd.
Cow/calfskins	-	24	53	82	108	20	130	139	8	50	270	no.
Ox hides	-	-	-	-	-	-	-	-	1	-	-	no.
Sheepskins	-	-	19	-	-	-	-	-	3	-	-	no.
Sheepskin coats	-	-	-	-	2	-	-	-	-	-	-	no.
Goatskins	-	-	-	-	-	-	-	-	1	-	-	no.
Birchwood	-	2	2	6	3	9	-	-	-	-	-	lass
Birch firewood	-	-	2	-	-	4	-	-	-	-	-	famn
Sawn boards	-	-	-	-	100	-	170	-	15	-	-	dozen
Cloudberries	-	18	-	-	-	-	-	-	-	-	11	kanna
Lingonberries	-	¼	-	¼	-	-	¼	1	-	-	-	barrel
Field raspberries	-	-	-	-	-	-	-	3	-	-	-	skålpd
Seal blubber	-	-	-	-	-	-	½	½	-	-	¼	barrel
Sealskins	-	-	-	-	-	-	-	-	1	-	-	no.
Salt salmon	-	4	10	1	12	1	28	9	1	6	8	barrel
Salt pike	-	2	-	¼	-	9	3	-	½	-	1	barrel
Salt fish	-	3	-	5	3	2	-	11	½	3	2	barrel
Salt Baltic herring	-	-	-	-	66	49	56	-	-	-	-	barrel
Sea trout	-	-	-	1	-	¼	-	-	-	-	-	barrel
Dried pike	-	7	-	20	5	9	10	21	2	4	1	lispd.
Smoked salmon	-	-	44	2	-	-	56	36	-	-	-	no.
Smoked trout	-	-	68	12	-	-	70	30	-	-	-	no.

Product	1805	1807	1808	1810	1811	1815	1819	1820	1821	1823	1824	unit
Reindeer hides	-	25	73	30	21	25	25	25	3	37	166	no.
Reindeer cow skins	-	189	606	230	160	-	147	92	160	-	-	no.
Reindeer calf skins	-	40	390	-	-	-	118	-	28	-	-	no.
Horn glue	-	35	67	27	70	22	52	46	33	18	8	lispd.
Reindeer horn	-	-	-	-	-	-	-	-	-	15	-	lispd.
Saamish shoes	-	80	165	-	60	-	-	-	-	-	-	pair
Saamish gloves	-	-	-	-	-	-	-	-	39	-	-	pair
Reindeer tongues	-	-	-	-	-	-	-	50	-	-	-	no.
Hare skins	-	-	21	3	4	-	63	-	-	-	50	no.
Bear skins	-	1	-	-	-	-	2	1	1	-	-	no.
Wolf skins	-	-	-	-	-	-	1	-	1	-	-	no.
Marten skins	-	-	10	-	-	-	1	1	-	-	-	no.
Fox skins	-	-	1	-	2	-	2	-	1	-	-	no.
Wolverine skins	-	-	2	3	1	-	1	1	-	-	-	no.
Winter squirrel skins	-	-	2200	520	240	-	1152	-	600	240	-	no.
Winter stoat (ermine)	-	-	-	-	-	-	5	-	-	-	-	no.
Swan skins	-	-	-	-	-	-	-	-	-	1	-	no.
Feathers (down)	-	-	-	-	-	9	11	-	-	-	-	lispd.
Value									1288			rdr

Notes: 1 barrel = 140 kg. (tar), 136 kg. (salt fish), 102 kg. (blubber), 125.6 litres (cranberries); 1 ***kanna*** (can) = 2.617 litres; 1 *lispund* = 8.5 kg; 1 *skålpund* = 0.425 kg; 1 *famn* (armful) = 3.14 m^3; *lass* = waggon-load. For practical reasons fractions are only shown where there are no whole numbers. For additional information, see S. O. Jansson, *Måttordbok–Svenska måttstermer före metersystemet* (Stockholm, 1950).

Sources: Birullor, 1805, 1807-1808, 1810-1811; Sammandrag av birullor och tolagsräkenskaper, 1815, 1819-1820, 1823-1824, Luleå stads enskilda räkenskaper, HLA; Abraham Stenholm's estate inventory deed, 1821.

At the end of the list of possessions, Stenholm's inventory specifies in great detail his stock of merchandise, appraised at local market rates and equivalent to the value of his real estate, or one-third of his total assets. There is no clear order to this list; the traditional products destined for Stockholm (Table 2) are intermingled with a wide variety of manufactured goods and luxury items, mostly from the capital and derived from other parts of the world (e.g., salt, tobacco, spices, small wares and textiles). The exports indicate his role as a wholesaler, while the imports imply his retail function. Unfortunately, the 1821 custom records are missing and, as the inventory only gives a static picture of his estate at the time of his death, we have no means of estimating how successful his widow was in reducing the large deficit.

Table 2 shows that the volume of export products from Lappmark in 1821 was fairly consistent with previous years. We can deduce that the hides and furs had been delivered to town by the *Saamis* in the traditional manner--using reindeer-drawn sleighs after the February markets in Jokkmokk and Gällivare.[21] The paucity of products from the coastal parishes is to be expected since shipping and full-scale fishing had not yet begun for the year--but the 150 barrels of tar, some odd hides and skins, and fifteen dozen sawn boards pose interpretative problems. Was the inventory based on Stenholm's accounts on the day he died (7 May) or on the state of the business when it was compiled (27 August)? In the first case, these goods could either represent stock left over from late deliveries after the end of the previous year's shipping season or goods brought to Luleå during the winter by local farmers. In the second case, the tar and timber might have arrived after Abraham's death and might partly account for his debts in villages such as Pålänge and Bredåker. Yet certain facts conflict with this latter notion of "business as usual." If the inventory had recorded goods brought to Luleå by sea after his death, would not others have been shipped out and thus omitted? Why, then, were the *Saamish* products still recorded in full? Obviously they had arrived during the period of snow-cover before he died, and they would normally have been among the first consignments sent to Stockholm when the new shipping season began. It seems most likely, therefore, that the inventory recorded the actual state of affairs at the time of Abraham's death.

---

[21]Hülphers, *Samlingar*, 86.

Despite a number of missing years and incomplete data on foreign trade, Table 2 shows certain variations in types and quantities of goods which, even at this micro-level, can be broadly related to fluctuations in external demand caused by political and economic changes. The whole of the period 1792-1815 was a time of war and trade upheavals in Europe, as France attempted to exclude Britain from commerce with the continent. Abraham Stenholm began trading on his own in 1805, when he shipped tar and butter to Stockholm, and he rapidly expanded the range and volume to an absolute peak in 1808. That same year marked the outbreak of hostilities between Sweden and Russia; the trade booms in tar (for the navy), reindeer hides (for clothing the army), and butter are clearly apparent. The loss of Finland in 1809 was presumably reflected in the low trade figures for 1811; however, at the end of the Napoleonic wars commerce revived under the "Pax Britannica."[22] After Abraham's death his widow continued the business for a few years, but she apparently ceased trading by 1825. Fluctuations in the volume of individual products may have been due partly to natural causes, such as climate and biology, but they must also reflect the flexibility of merchant activity in which the dearth of one commodity could be compensated by more of another. The previous year's prices probably affected the farmers' choice of alternative sources of income at this time.

In his quinquennial report for 1817-1821, the County Governor of Norrbotten described Luleå's trade as based on surpluses from the rural parishes of Luleå, Råneå, Överkalix and Nederkalix, and from the "Lappmarks" of Jokkmokk and Gällivare. At these markets town merchants purchased tar, timber, butter, fish, furs, reindeer meat, hides, glue and other related commodities, often by previous agreement with farmers and *Saamis*.[23] Stenholm's ownership of market houses and stores indicates his active interest in these parishes. Figure 2 illustrates the normal sequence of market visits by Luleå's merchants, together with the main periods of goods transport to and from the town.[24]

---

[22]Layton, *The Evolution*, 80.

[23]*Kongl. Maj:ts befallningshafvande i Norrbottens Län, till Kongl. Maj:t afgifne Fem-års Berättelse år 1822* (Stockholm, 1823).

[24]R. Bergling, *Kyrkstäder i övre Norrland* (Umeå, 1964), 239-242; A.A. Hülphers, *Samlingar til en Beskrifning öfwer Norrland. V.3: Om Lappmarken* (1790 manuscript; first published, Stockholm, 1922), 89 and 92.

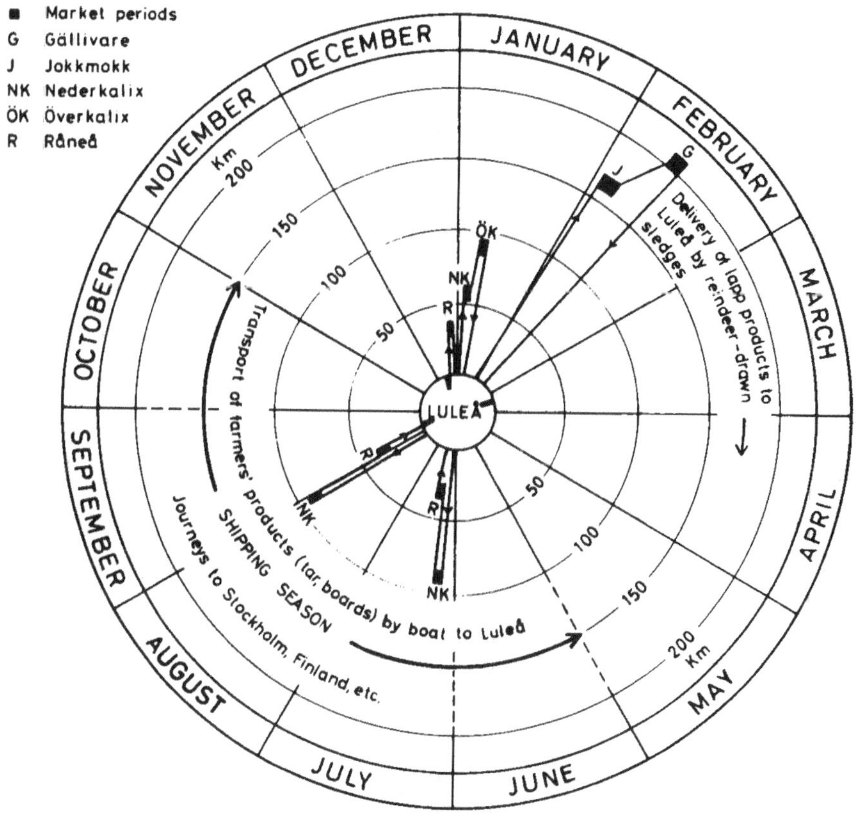

Figure 2: The seasonal round for a Luleå merchant in the early nineteenth century.

Sources: Market dates according to official ordinances (landshövdingen af Donners allmänna kungörelse ang. frimarknader i Västerbottens län, 17 December 1794. Handel och näringar 1794-1911, Kronofogdens i Torneå fogderi arkiv, HLA).

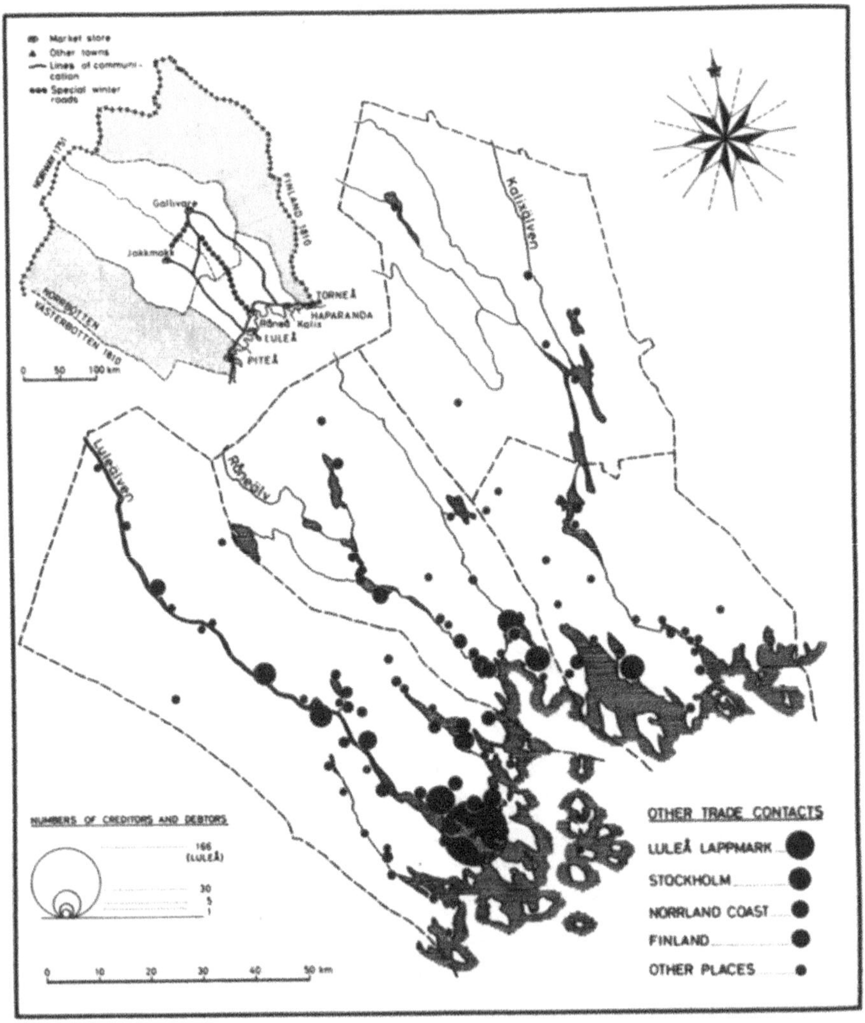

Figure 3: Abraham Stenholm's business contact field in 1821. The unshaded area on the inset map shows the extent of Luleå's traditional trade monopoly (the former *handelsgebiet*), together with the main lines of communication and Abraham's market houses.

Source: Based on the lists of cash credits and debts in his estate inventory.

One of the few commercial differences between the eighteenth-century and the 1820s was the increased freedom to trade at times other than fixed market periods. Other trips to Lapland and villages in the coastal parishes were probably made and it is also likely that such visits were extended to include calls elsewhere. The main lines of overland communication are shown on the inset map in Figure 3; to a large extent, they followed the valleys of Luleälven, Råneälven and Kalixälven. Gunnar Hoppe has calculated some average journey times for the early nineteenth century. In summer, by horse and boat, it took about five days to reach Jokkmokk and over six to Gällivare--but only three days for the return trip. In the winter, using reindeer and *pulkas* (*Saamish* sleighs) it normally took less than three days to Jokkmokk and just over three to Gällivare. By the coast road, about one and one-and-a-half days, respectively, were required to travel to Råneå and Kalix, but most trips used more direct routes over the ice or (especially for the transport of bulky goods such as tar) by sea.[25]

Over half of Abraham's forty-page inventory was comprised of detailed lists of credits and debts. The economic system appears similar to that described by Hülphers in 1797 in which the country people, instead of having their capital tied up with merchants, increasingly required credit; the result was that merchants often had large outstanding claims in the coastal and Lapland parishes. According to the accounts, Abraham's 532 secured and unsecured credits totalled 5,080 *riksdaler*; with a handful of exceptions, these were mostly for small sums and averaged less than ten *riksdaler*. Of these minor items, 380 were owed by country folk living within Luleå's sphere of influence and the remaining 152 by residents of Luleå.[26]

On the other hand, Abraham's own debts were mostly to people of another category and status. The largest of his ninety-nine debts (totalling 10,827 *riksdaler*) was for 1810 *riksdaler* to Banco Disconto Wärket, a Stockholm bank; it would be interesting to know more about

---

[25]G. Hoppe, *Vägarna inom Norrbottens län* (Uppsala, 1945), 234-236.

[26]The population of Luleå had increased by thirty-five percent during the three decades or so of Stenholm's residence (from 759 in 1793 to 1026 in 1819). The number of households (*matlag*) in 1793 was 144, and a proportional increase suggests that there were no more than 200 at the time of his death. Hence, it appears that three-quarters of these families were indebted to Stenholm and that some part of his retail trade probably served the whole town in one way or another.

the circumstances of this loan.[27] It is tempting to suppose that it was somehow related to the acquisition of his town property, market houses and farmland, which he must have purchased from a mercantile family in 1805/1806. At the time of his death his real property was conservatively valued at 1351 *riksdaler*, and Table 1 reveals that he had a similar sum (1288 *riksdaler*) tied up in trading goods. This bank loan might well have provided much of his initial capital, since his paternal ancestors were not merchants. When his uncle died in 1790, his cousin took over the family business and Abraham was unlikely to have inherited any major sums of money, despite his Ruth connections.

Abraham Stenholm's mean debt to sixteen Stockholm merchants was 278 *riksdaler* and he owed an average of 252 *riksdaler* to seven Finnish merchants in Uleåborg and Brahestād.[28] The remainder of his debts averaged only thirty-eight *riksdaler*, mostly to townspeople in Luleå and wealthy farmers in villages like Bredåker and Pålänge. The financial links revealed by these accounts demonstrate the chain of credit that was typical of a pre-industrial economy in which rural people were given credit by merchants who in turn obtained credit from larger houses in Stockholm and (in this case) Finland. Yet the chain did not stop here, for Stockholm's merchants also depended upon capital and credit from the leading merchants in great commercial cities such as London and Amsterdam, rivals within the European "world-economy."[29]

The contact field shown in these accounts is mapped in Figure 3. The majority of his business contacts lived within the coastal parishes of Luleå, Råneå, Överkalix and Nederkalix, and their numbers vary inversely with distance from the town. The spatial pattern broadly reflects the distribution of population in villages along the coast and river valleys where the best farmland, fishing waters, and lines of communica-

---

[27]This bank was presumably a kind of commercial credit institution. See Eli Heckscher, *An Economic History of Sweden* (Cambridge, Mass., 1954), 249.

[28]When Sweden's loss of Finland in 1809 released the Österbotten towns from Stockholm's dominance, Finnish merchants became increasingly involved in direct foreign trade. It has not been clearly established to what degree this political change affected social and economic contacts across the Gulf of Bothnia. The case study of Abraham Stenholm does not help, since there is no way to ascertain whether his debts were the result of recent commercial activity or were pre-war in origin.

[29]Fernand Braudel, *Kapitalismens dynamik* (Värnamo, 1988), 68-73.

tion were to be found. Only thirty names seem to come from the Lapland parishes of Jokkmokk and Gällivare, as there were few debts still outstanding after the February markets and the subsequent delivery of *Saamish* products to Stenholm's warehouses in town. Thus, by 1821 the areal extent of Luleå's hinterland appears to have been much the same as when the town was first granted its *handelsgebiet* two centuries earlier.[30] Since the main communication lines were developed primarily to serve these early patterns of economic and social contact, Luleå was firmly established as the principal regional gateway and entrepôt.[31]

In summing up Abraham Stenholm's significance, it would be unfair to pass judgement on his mercantile success based solely upon the balance sheet at the time of his death. It has already been noted that his merchandise was only valued at local market rates, so that clear profits from their eventual sale in Stockholm could be expected. It is uncertain whether all of the outstanding loans and debts had to be settled immediately, for his widow continued to run the business. Repayments of his unsecured credits may well have yielded more than the standard one-half accredited to his estate. Furthermore, it is conceivable that he may have had unlisted assets aboard such vessels as Abraham Ruth's *Enigheten*, which had been on an extended voyage outside the Baltic since 1818. Certainly he had been remarkably successful in progressing from the status of employee and "poor relation" to the position of an outwardly prosperous and respected merchant, which he must have been to be admitted to membership in the town's merchant society or guild. In his multiple roles of merchant, shipper, farmer and fisherman, Stenholm merely copied his contemporaries in following the traditions of seventeenth and eighteenth-century town merchants. The multiple sources of

---

[30]The *handelsgebiet* system ended in 1779, but the social and economic patterns that it spawned continued relatively unchanged for many decades thereafter. See Hülphers, *Samlingar*, 84; B. Steckzén, "Handel, sjöfart och annan näring," in B. Steckzén and H. Wennerström, *Luleå stads historia 1621-1921* (Uppsala, 1921), 212 and 216.

[31]A.F. Burghardt, "A Hypothesis about Gateway Cities," *Annals of the Association of American Geographers*, LXI (1971), 269-285. The growth of the port-town of Luleå and the economic development of its hinterland closely fit Vance's mercantile model of settlement based on exogenous forces; see J.E. Vance, *The Merchant's World: The Geography of Wholesaling* (Englewood Cliffs, N.J., 1970), 150-155. Particularly during the pre-industrial period, northern Sweden's commercial and economic relationships with Stockholm exhibited many of the characteristics of an "overseas" colony subordinated to a core region of capital and consumption.

livelihood contrast with the specialization that followed in the nineteenth century, when the wholesale trade, especially in timber, was increasingly usurped by new industrial entrepreneurs and companies.

How typical was Abraham Stenholm? Was his apparent lack of success at the time of his death merely the reflection of a general conjunctural decline, or had ill-health had a negative effect on his activities over a crucial period in the commercial round? What were his business relationships with Ruth before and after branching out on his own? What was the precise nature of his debts? How great were his annual profits? These and numerous other questions are raised by this brief analysis of one inventory; they can be answered, if at all, only through a painstaking scrutiny of a wide variety of other sources. Interdisciplinary studies of other contemporary inventory deeds seem to be required, while the investigation of similar material for more established families over extended periods might reveal much about the processes of change in commercial activity and organization, as well as in the utilization of resources in the Lule River valley.

Naturally, such micro-level studies run the risk of examining exceptional rather than typical cases. Nevertheless, detailed investigations bring the researcher into close contact with the realities of the past; when related to macro-studies, they should lead to generalizations based on fact rather than pure theory. "To see the universe in the locality" clearly has important implications, not only for historical geographers but also for maritime and other historians.

St. Petersburg's Bills of Exchange in the Russian Economy of the Eighteenth Century[1]

George E. Munro

In April 1991, one of the first issues of the new Leningrad newspaper *Stockowner* contained a curious article entitled "Prospects for the Circulation of Promissory Notes in the USSR."[2] It proposed that an instrument entirely new to the Soviet Union's domestic economy, the negotiable note, be introduced to ease the settling of business accounts. For a handful of readers, this was not so much something new as a return to an instrument that had helped to animate Russia's commercial economy in the eighteenth century. The terminology employed to explain the function of the promissory note, as well as the organization of the explication, echoed similar explanations in eighteenth-century legislation and academic lectures designed to educate the commercial public about the benefits and advantages of using the promissory note.

As uninformed as contemporary Russians may be about the mechanics of the negotiable instrument in today's business world, historians of the eighteenth-century Russian economy are generally only slightly more knowledgeable about its role then. There is an explanation for our ignorance. It begins with a short discourse into economic history.

Background

Throughout the eighteenth century, the economy of the Russian Empire became more fully integrated, largely as a result of policies and technological improvements undertaken early in the century. For

[1]Much of the research for this paper was made possible by grants from the International Research and Exchanges Board and by the Faculty Grants-in-Aid program of Virginia Commonwealth University.

[2]D. Pechalov, "Perspektivy veksel'nogo obrashcheniia v SSSR," *Aktsioner. Informatsionnyi ekonomicheskii vestnik*, No. 3 (1991).

Research in Maritime History, No. 3 (December 1992), 99-113.

example, the canal projects begun under Emperor Peter I and expanded under subsequent monarchs were largely completed by mid-century, opening water access to the Baltic for wares produced or mined as far away as the western slopes of the Ural Mountains in the east and Persia in the south.[3] Landlords began to become aware of the possibilities for profit represented by their estates, and printed works started to appear advising landowners on how to achieve more efficient production.[4]

The men who formulated government policy sought to encourage growth, if only to facilitate the collection of more revenue and to permit Russia to become a more powerful state. It was not easy, however, to determine what that policy should be. Not only were there competing patronage networks in the government, frequently espousing contending views, but also there were larger social groupings at odds over the best way to enrich Russia, because they saw differing possibilities for themselves. The most obvious (and persistent) difference of opinion was the well-known conflict between the nobility and the merchants that surfaced in the commission called in 1767 to draft a new legal code.[5] In addition to competing interest groups there was the weight of inertia represented by the outmoded but hardy system of serfdom that permeated virtually every economic, political, and social issue in the country.

Policy at times responded to the vast economic changes already taking place in Russia; more rarely it attempted to shape those transformations. Empress Elizabeth's decrees in 1754-1755 to end duties on trade between Russia and the Ukraine are an example of the latter type of policy. It fell to Catherine II, though, to address economic issues (as opposed to strictly fiscal questions) more broadly than her predecessors. Catherine read widely in economic theory. She has been identified with the cameralists, a group of theorists and policy-makers in the smaller

---

[3]See Robert E. Jones, "Getting the Goods to St. Petersburg: Water Transport from the Interior 1703-1811," *Slavic Review*, XLIII, No. 3 (Fall 1984), 413-433.

[4]The *Works* (*Trudy*) of the Free Economic Society, published annually from 1765, had this as their central purpose. See John H. Brown, "The Publication and Distribution of the *Trudy* of the Free Economic Society, 1765-1796," *Russian Review*, XXXVI, No. 3 (1977), 341-350.

[5]On the commission, see Paul Dukes, *Catherine the Great and the Russian Nobility: A Study Based on the Materials of the Legislative Commission of 1767* (Cambridge, 1967).

German states who took a rather narrow approach to issues bridging policy and the economy, developing theories of the well-regulated state.[6] But she also was familiar with the free-market principles of Adam Smith and incorporated some of his ideas in various projects and laws.[7]

One of the most vexing economic issues of Catherine's reign was the absence of a system of exchange. The problem had two parts. First, there were no means to provide credit within the "privatized" (*partikuliarnyi*) sector of the economy. Simple banking procedures to extend credit, refined in the Italian city-states during the Renaissance, had yet to take root in Russia. The problem was not that the country lacked specie[8]; what had failed to develop was a sizeable liquidity that could be provided reliably and at relatively low cost from non-governmental sources to entrepreneurs needing infusions of cash for varying periods of time. The related aspect is that there were no means in Russia to transfer accounts without moving large quantities of coin or bullion.Both facets of this issue were first addressed in the Statute on Bills of Exchange of 1729,[9] which gave formal legal recognition not only to governmental paper, enabling the state to transfer accounts throughout the Empire, but also to commercial bills of exchange, including the promissory note. Previously, the promissory note had no legal status in Russia.

The promissory note served several functions. First, it enabled a merchant to delay payment for goods. This was generally done formulaically, not uncommonly on pre-printed forms, with payment due in forty-five, sixty, ninety, or some other predetermined number of days, except for rare cases when it was stipulated to "pay to the bearer on demand." Second, the promissory note permitted funds to be remitted from city to city, in general through a firm with which either the payer or the receiver (or both) had an account. It was far safer to remit a note,

---

[6]See Marc Raeff, *The Well Ordered Police State: Social and Institutional Change Through Law in the Germanies and Russia, 1600-1800* (New Haven, 1983).

[7]Isabel de Madariaga, *Russia in the Age of Catherine the Great* (New Haven, 1981), 152-153.

[8]See Ian Blanchard, *Russia's "Age of Silver:" Precious-Metal Production and Economic Growth in the Eighteenth Century* (London, 1989), particularly chapter 4.

[9]*Polnoe sobranie zakonov Rossiiskoi imperii s 1649 goda*, Series I (48 vols., St. Petersburg, 1830-1835), VIII (May 16, 1729), 147-189.

with the appropriate accounts being debited or credited, than to ship coin or bullion. Third, the promissory note facilitated the exchange of one currency for another. Payment, coming at a later time in another place, could be stipulated in any currency; the note usually specified the rate of exchange relative to the currencies of the country where it was written and where it was to be paid. As all three functions demonstrate, the trade in negotiable bills served as a non-institutional form of banking. Their use seemed to cry out for a network of banks to undergird, discount, and regulate their operation, but banking failed to develop in Russia, a matter of some consequence for the trade in negotiable notes.

Russia's experience with banks was painful. There were, of course, no private banks. Empresses Elizabeth in 1754 and Catherine in 1769 and 1786 established lending banks capitalized at several million rubles, but they functioned principally as dispensers of largesse to the nobility. There is little evidence of anyone being forced to repay loans; when a bank's capital was exhausted, which invariably happened quickly, either more funds were infused or it was permitted to decay.[10]

The lack of banks made negotiable notes important as lubricants of the commercial economy. To judge from the number of laws dealing with promissory notes promulgated during the half-century after 1729, these negotiable instruments must have come into increasingly wide use. Because they were documents with extremely short-term utility, however, it is difficult to know just how widespread they became; presumably they were destroyed after payment was received. Only a few have survived, scattered among the papers of various historical personages, remarked upon in memoirs and diaries, or as exhibits and appendices in legal cases involving indebtedness or contested wills. Yet there is indirect testimony to their widespread use. The 1729 statute forbade peasants to be signatories to transactions in promissory notes, whether as drawer, drawee, claimant, or acceptant. One mark of the frequency with which peasants violated this prohibition is that at least eight laws were passed between 1729 and the early 1770s reiterating the ban. It may well have been the transitory nature of the instrument that encouraged peasants to violate the law with impunity: if all went well, after a short time the note would be redeemed and the peasant's role would go undetected.

---

[10]See the discussion of credit and banking in Arcadius Kahan, *The Plow, the Hammer and the Knout: An Economic History of Eighteenth-Century Russia* (Chicago, 1986), 311-313.

While the promissory note was used extensively in the leading mercantile countries at the time, in Russia it came to be more than simply an instrument of exchange. It augmented the amount of coin in circulation for the first three-quarters of the century, when Russia was a net importer of precious metals. Long before Catherine II created paper money by establishing the St. Petersburg and Moscow Assignat Banks in 1769,[11] the promissory note served as a form of paper money. It also reached into corners of the economy where silver coin was unlikely to be found. Even after Russian mines began to produce tons of silver annually, merchants continued to settle accounts with paper transfers as much as possible.

In the 1780s the extensive use of the promissory note drew the attention of Philipp Heinrich Dilthey, professor of jurisprudence at the University of Moscow, who developed a course of lectures on the history and law in Russia relating to the negotiable note, publishing it as a volume that quickly went through four editions, with an appeal to both foreign and Russian merchants.[12] It is valuable not only because it interpreted the law on negotiable notes but also because it identified those instances in which practical experience differed from legal prescription. It also catalogued situations in which practices were not standardized, such as the cost of writing a note. Although Dilthey taught in Moscow, many of his examples were set in St. Petersburg, often posited as contracts between its merchants and colleagues in a western city like Amsterdam. Clearly the promissory note was considered an important component of the international commercial economy.

The modern researcher would have no way of knowing how the promissory note worked in practice were it not for a document preserved in the Central State Archive of Old Charters in Moscow. This is a list of the 4035 promissory notes protested in 1773 in St. Petersburg.[13] A

---

[11]The law was published in *Polnoe sobranie zakonov Rossiiskoi imperii*, Series I, XVIII (December 29, 1768), 787-793.

[12]Philipp Heinrich Dilthey, *Nachal'nye osnovaniia veksel'nago prava, a osoblivo Rossiiskago kupno i Shvedskago*... (Moscow, 1772).

[13]Tsentral'nyi gosudarstvennyi arkhiv drevnikh aktov, fond 16, delo 497, listy 12-225: "Skol'ko imianno sego 1773-go godu genvaria 1-go dekabria po 13-e chislo publichnykh natariusov vekselei v proteste sostoialo i ot kogo i komu onye i v kolikoi summe o tom znachit nizhe sego." See also George Munro, "The Role of the *Veksel'*

protest was the first legal step against someone who refused to honour a note upon legitimate presentation. Had this kind of list survived for some other city in the Russian Empire, it would have meant something different. But such a list surviving for St. Petersburg has much to tell us about the dynamics of Russia's involvement in maritime trade in northern Europe, in terms not of the types and quantities of goods, but rather of the people involved and the mechanisms of paying for that trade.

St. Petersburg and the Baltic

The Russian Empire's internal water routes favoured St. Petersburg over older coastal towns such as Arkhangel'sk, Riga or Reval (Tallin) as the principal port for exporting agricultural, forest, and mining products from the interior. Arkhangel'sk had sustained Russia's maritime trade with Europe during the pre-Petrine period, but for geographic and economic reasons, not to mention the intrusion of the Imperial will, was unsuited as a truly large entrepôt. Riga and Reval, on the other hand, while boasting long commercial traditions, were ports newly joined to the Empire and Germanic in their customs and practices; Russians would have felt uncomfortable using them as the principal ports of the Empire even if they had been located on the major river systems to the interior. St. Petersburg was created precisely because its site was the best Russia could find for building a port.

For the duration of the eighteenth century St. Petersburg remained Russia's principal port. The long-sought southern access to European markets, through the straits into the Mediterranean, was not opened diplomatically until the mid-1770s. More importantly perhaps, it was not opened technologically until well into the nineteenth century, when the rapids on the lower Dnepr River were either bypassed with canals or blown up. The absence of easy water transport to the Black Sea explains why Empress Elizabeth's abolition of internal tolls between the Ukraine and Russia in the mid-1750s did little to stimulate commerce between those two parts of the Empire. St. Petersburg served as the exit and port of entry for much of the Empire, but seldom for the Ukraine.

---

in Russian Capital Formation: A Preliminary Inquiry," in R. P. Bartlett, A. G. Cross, and Karen Rasmussen (eds.), *Russia and the World of the Eighteenth Century* (Columbus, Ohio, 1988), 551-564.

Table 1
Occupational Distribution of Protested Notes, 1773

Holders	Payers: Unknown	Mer-chant	Mili-tary	Guards	Artisan	Civil Svce	Court Svce	Peasant	Noble	Other	Totals
Unknown	38	73	17	2	5	11	1		3	10	160
Merchant	180	1698	290	113	112	323	52	3	64	227	3062
Military	7	66	17	3	6	10	3		1	11	124
Guards		4	3			1				3	11
Artisans	7	17	21	2	19	13	4		6	18	107
Civil Service	8	140	24	5	5	34	1		3	11	231
Court Service	5	9	3	5	3	8			8	1	42
Peasant	5	64	3		1	1		1	1	1	77
Noble		1	10	8		4				4	27
Other	21	91	20	2	13	14	2		4	27	194
Totals	272	2171	406	132	168	415	64	4	94	309	4035

Source: See text.

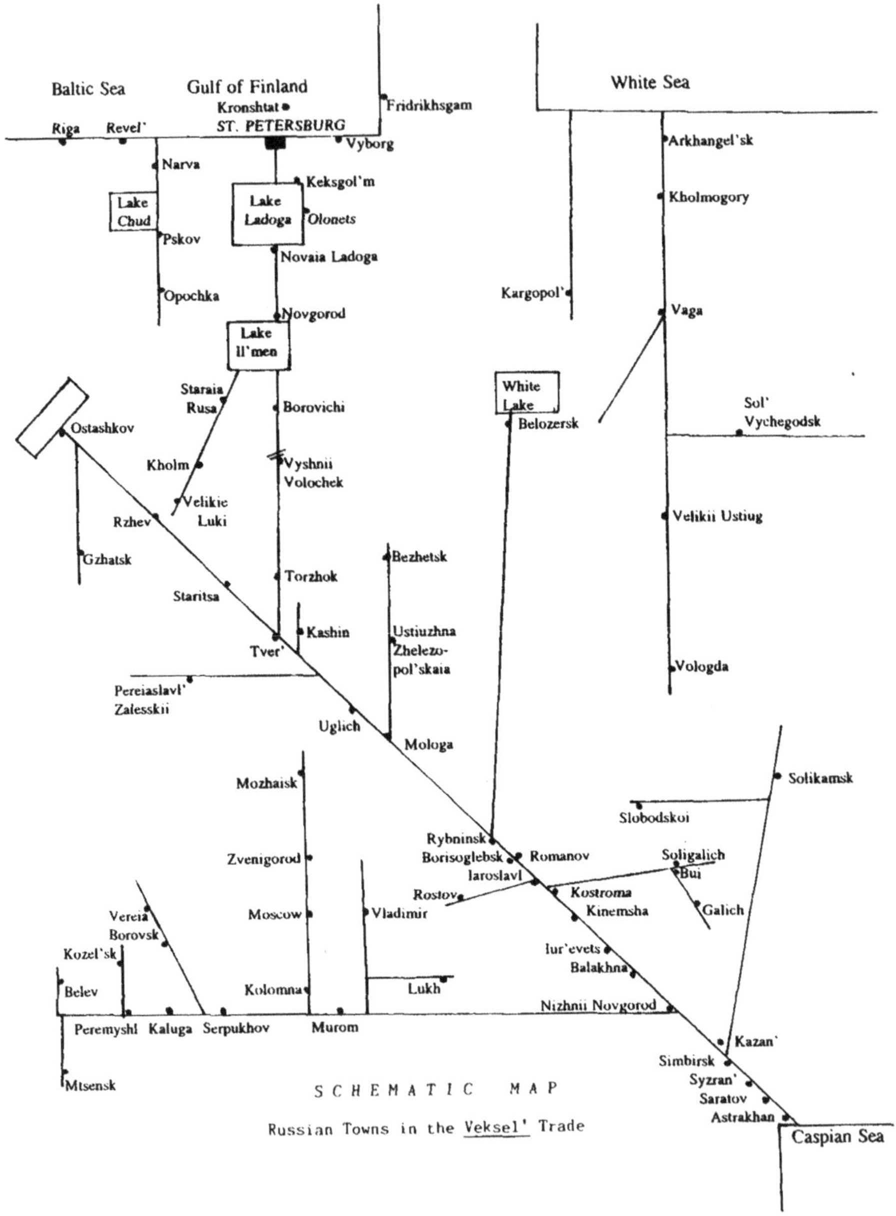

Figure 1: Russian Towns in the *Veksel'* Trade, 1773.

Source: See text.

Protested Promissory Notes

Because it was customary to identify the parties in a protested note--the one filing the protest and the one against whom he brought charges--we know who was using promissory notes in St. Petersburg in 1773. While the tens of thousands of notes that presumably were settled on time and without difficulties have escaped our attention, we can use what we have as a reasonable surrogate. Table 1 shows the number of protests involving each of several categories of people in that year. In more than seventy-five percent of the cases, it was a merchant who brought the protest (75.9%); in something over half of these, he protested against another merchant (55.5%). But only 53.8% of the protests were brought against merchants. St. Petersburg had a large military population and a growing number of civil servants, so it should not be a surprise that each group accounted for more than ten percent of those not paying or accepting notes when presented (military including guard regiments, 13.3%; civil servants including court officials, 11.9%).

Before turning to two questions regarding the participation of merchants in protested notes, attention should be drawn to the one group surprisingly under-represented in protests: the artisans (*remeslenniki*). One would have thought that they would have paid for their necessary inputs with negotiable notes. While they may well have done so, it is unknown to us. As far as protested notes were concerned, they brought fewer cases than men serving in the military (2.7% as against 3.1%) and were the objects of protests in only 4.2% of all cases. It is far more likely that artisans bought raw materials only in small quantities, using cash on hand, or that they utilized cutomers' deposits to purchase the necessary materials. If the latter were common, it suggests that St. Petersburg's artisans did not produce for a market but according to orders placed with them.

As for the merchants, it is clear that the commerce in promissory notes touched men from a number of different Russian towns. Of the 198 towns then existing in the Russian Empire, 112 were represented on the list. A schematic map (Figure 1) reveals that the vast majority were river towns in direct communication with St. Petersburg. Five others lay on the nearby Baltic coast or, as was the case with Kronshtat, on an island in the Gulf of Finland. The long diagonal line in Figure 1 represents the Volga River; the lines branching from it are its tributaries. Each of the towns was the home of at least one merchant involved in a protest in St. Petersburg in 1773. The appearance of a second major river system in

Figure 1, the Northern Dvina flowing past Arkhangel'sk into the White Sea, demonstrates the role of St. Petersburg in unifying the economy of northern and northeastern Russia with that of the centre and northwest. Significantly, a number of the foreign merchants who protested the non-payment of notes in St. Petersburg represented firms with Russian bases in Arkhangel'sk rather than St. Petersburg.

Three Commercial Zones

Three types of merchants were involved in protested notes: Russians from the interior, Russian merchants registered in St. Petersburg, and foreigners who lived and worked in St. Petersburg. The Russians from the interior have been identified in brief. The foreigners represented a variety of countries. The notaries who provided their identity in the 1773 list were not overly careful to maintain accuracy; during my study of these people in archives in Germany, the Netherlands, and England I have turned up a number of errors. Sometimes a merchant identified as a foreigner was a third-generation resident of St. Petersburg (for example, Login Boehtlingk, whose grandfather came from Lübeck). For the notaries, a merchant with a foreign name was a foreigner, and more may have been consigned to the catch-all categories of German or English than was warranted. (It was not too long before this that *nemets* meant any foreigner, not just a German.) Taking into consideration that errors exist, Table 2 nonetheless provides a breakdown of the foreign merchants by place of origin. Not surprisingly, the English (British would be more accurate, since some were Scots) predominated, followed by the Dutch. They far outpaced the activities of merchants from any of the nearer Baltic states--the commercial cities of Lübeck, Hamburg, and Danzig, or the kingdoms of Denmark, Prussia, and Sweden.

Because the value of each protested note is known, it is possible to construct a table showing the monetary worth of the notes signed by each of the three categories of merchants. Knowing this information sheds light on the economic roles each of the groups played. Table 2 distinguishes the value of protested notes, permitting comparison among merchant groups and between merchants and three other groups (military officers, civil servants, and peasants). As one might expect, the size of a note signed by a foreign merchant was larger on average than one signed by a Russian merchant. Foreign merchants tended to be whole-salers in the import-export business. Their contracts with St. Petersburg merchants were slightly larger than with merchants from the interior.

Table 2
Foreign Merchant's Participation in Protests of Notes

	Holders		Payers	
Country or city	No. of firms or individuals	No. of notes	No. of firms or individuals	No. of notes
England	42	157	3	5
Holland	17	105	5	19
France	19	49	9	15
Lübeck	10	35		
Austria	4	32		
Switzerland	8	23	2	2
Hamburg	5	15		
Armenia	6	8	3	4
Danzig	1	5		
Italy	1	6	1	3
Germany	2	5	4	14
Nuremberg	1	4		
Denmark	1	4	1	1
Prussia	1	1	2	3
Spain	1	1		
Sweden	1	1		
Unidentified	110	244	23	54
Total	230	694	53	120

Source: See text.

What is most striking in these comparisons is that St. Petersburg merchants seem to have had virtually the same commercial role as merchants from the interior, if we can judge solely from the value of protested notes (see Table 3). While one might have anticipated that the scale of operations would have been larger in St. Petersburg than in smaller towns, if anything the opposite was true. Russian merchants not registered in St. Petersburg held slightly larger notes, although the pattern was reversed when they were the subjects of a protest.

It is difficult to determine whether many notes represented actual commerce or were loans. The participation of officers and civil servants as holders suggests the latter. While it is unlikely that these men were trading in large amounts of goods, they undoubtedly made loans and were compelled, when payment was not forthcoming, to file protests.

Table 3
Distribution of Protested Notes By Value, 1773

Group	Holders					Payers				
	10,000	1000-9999	100-999	10-99	1-9	10,000	1000-9999	100-999	10-99	1-9
SPb merchants		84	524	624	52	2	124	550	320	20
%		6.5	40.8	48.6	4.0	0.2	12.2	54.1	31.5	2.0
Foreign merchants	7	159	414	123	1		33	68	19	
%	1.0	22.6	58.8	17.5	0.1		27.5	56.7	15.8	
SPb merchants	2	65	167	34						
%	0.7	24.3	62.3	12.7						
Russian merchants		93	466	435	41	4	122	490	366	34
%		9.0	45.0	42.0	4.0	0.4	12.0	48.2	36.0	3.3
Military officers		13	54	31	1	1	43	150	154	3
%		13.1	54.5	31.3	1.0	0.3	12.3	42.7	43.9	0.9
Civil servants	1	49	115	59	7		35	105	236	39
%	0.4	21.2	49.8	25.5	3.0		8.4	25.3	56.9	9.4
Peasants		4	33	38	2					
%		5.2	42.9	49.4	2.6					

Source: See text.

There is one other way to examine the notes signed by merchants to try to determine their purpose. The specific monetary figure indicated in a protest may be a clue. If the amount were uneven--that is, if it ended in an odd number of kopecks--the note likely covered a consignment of goods or payment for wares. On the other hand, a transfer of funds, similar to a bank transfer, or a monetary loan were more likely to be expressed in round sums. It is quite possible, of course, that notes covering the cost of wares were rounded to the nearest whole number, but as "neat" figures were expressed in larger denominations (from tens to hundreds to thousands), the distinction becomes clearer. An application of this hypothesis to the notes protested by foreign merchants demonstrates its significance. Just over half the notes protested by Dutch merchants involved "rough" sums. Of those fifty-four notes, only one was with someone definitely known to be neither a merchant nor an artisan. Clearly their contracts with businessmen assumed one nature while those with officers, civil servants and court officials assumed another. When the protested sum with the latter group *was* a rough number, it likely represented items delivered but not yet paid for, an "I.O.U." until the next pay day.

In almost half the contracts in which St. Petersburg merchants were holders, the contested sum ended in a zero. As noted above, contracts in denominations of tens or even hundreds could simply represent a rounding off of figures; but if St. Petersburg merchants were lending money, logic dictates that it was those merchants most involved in the trade in promissory notes who were doing so. Only seven St. Petersburg merchants protested more than fifteen notes during 1773. Of the one hundred forty-six notes held by these men, seventy-three had figures ending in "0," the average for all St. Petersburg merchants. The pattern of note-holding varied. Only two merchants held most of their notes against other merchants. Aleksei Khlebnikov, who protested the largest number (twenty-seven), had only three with merchants. His notes were made with army officers (eight), members of the guard units (seven), civil servants (six), non-commissioned officers (two), and princes (two). More than half the notes he protested were written in even numbers, and their average value was around 375 rubles. The St. Petersburg merchant holding notes second most frequently, Petr Dudin (twenty-three cases), had no contracts at all with merchants. He may have been delivering wares for payment later, because a third of his contracts were for amounts ending in odd kopeck values. Like Khlebnikov, he held notes against army officers (six), guards (nine, two against the young

Gavril Derzhavin), civil servants (three), and princes (two), besides foreigners (two) and a student (whose note was for a whopping 325 rubles!). The mean owed Dudin was 609 rubles, much higher than the average owed Khlebnikov. The highest average, 894 rubles, was owed Vasilii Ol'khin, who protested twenty-two notes against seventeen different people, only six of them merchants. The lowest was due to Timofei Kozlov, who protested twenty notes against nineteen different people, three of them merchants, at an average value of seventy-five rubles. All his notes not with merchants were with civil servants at the lower end of the service scale: *kantseliaristy*, *podkantseliaristy*, *kopeisty*, *sekretarei*, *pisarei*, and the like. Some, however, were in the fourteen ranks, among them *nadvornye* and *tituliarnye sovetniki*.[14] The one person in this group whose activity remained most tied to the original purpose of the note was Filip Kostsov. Of his nineteen protested notes, sixteen were with other merchants, all from other Russian towns, including Novgorod, Staraia Russa, and Pskov to the south, Kashin, Uglich, Kineshma, and Shuia in the area of the upper Volga and its tributaries, and Olonets on the far side of Lake Ladoga. This multi-directional involvement means that he engaged in trade not just with merchants from a former hometown, nor did he limit himself to traffic in goods along only one trading route from the capital. Whether Kostsov was exclusively a provider of short-term capital, or whether he dealt in a variety of wares or specialized in one type of product, we simply do not know from the evidence. It does seem clear, however, that the greater the involvement of a St. Petersburg merchant in note-holding, the greater the likelihood that he was taking cash value out of strictly commercial use. Other ways of putting their wealth to work proved more attractive. Or, to state the same thing another way, non-mercantile demands for short-term, small capital took precedence over mercantile.

---

[14]The "table of ranks" was created in 1722 by Emperor Peter I to establish equivalencies for officials at the higher rungs in the four main branches of governmental service: the military, guards, civil service, and courtiers. The table also eased transfer from one branch of service to another. With modifications, it lasted until the revolutions of 1917. The lowest rank, number fourteen, was the level of the lowest commissioned-officer rank. Rank number one was the field marshal in the military and the chancellor in the civil service. The positions held by the majority of governmental servitors, including chancellery clerks, junior chancellery clerks, copyists, secretaries, and scribes, did not entitle them to inclusion in the ranks. Court councillors and titulary councillors held ranks eight and nine, respectively.

Demand from merchants may have been insufficient to keep even this amount in circulation.

The pattern of involvement is wholly different when we examine the St. Petersburg merchants cited most frequently as payers. Here we find a much higher incidence of sums ending in kopecks (41.4% as opposed to 15.1%), a significantly lower percentage of contracts ending in "0" (30.3% vs. fifty percent), and a much higher frequency of notes in which the other party was a merchant (84.9% vs. 34.2%). This last comparison is the most dramatic. Not only did these men owe notes overwhelmingly to other merchants, but the vast majority were debtors to foreigners (98 of 129 notes). Among Russians, they were slightly less prone to indebtedness to those from the capital than from other towns.

Conclusion

Promissory notes were used for three purposes: to transfer cash; to postpone payment for goods until a later date; and as a monetary loan. The first and third functions are represented by rounded sums, especially in large denominations. The evidence of the second is found particularly in those awkward figures ending in kopecks. Foreign merchants appear to have been significantly more involved in trading in goods than in providing loans or cash transfers to Russians.

This brief discussion has omitted many other points about the eighteenth-century Russian economy on which the commerce in bills of exchange in St. Petersburg might shed light. Among them are the incidence and nature of joint economic ventures, the degree to which women were involved in business ventures, the apparent patterns of family ties in commercial and productive enterprises, and the representation of merchants among lower-level governmental functionaries. What *has* been shown is that the study of protested promissory notes can illuminate aspects of economic life which might otherwise be obscured. Our understanding of the eighteenth-century Russian business economy remains inadequate, but this new avenue of study is a means of adding a few more pieces to a most intriguing and captivating puzzle.

Shipowners and Iron Sailing Ships: The First Twenty Years, 1838-1857

David M. Williams and Jonathan M. Hutchings

The nineteenth-century maritime world was swept by a technological revolution as iron and steam replaced wood and wind. Although the transformation was sufficiently swift to be called "revolutionary," it nevertheless took more than a century. Moreover, there was no clear-cut shift from wooden sailing vessels to iron steamships. With hindsight, the secular trend is intelligible: steam and iron made steady inroads, ultimately gaining total ascendancy. In the short-run, however, the metamorphosis was more complex, mixing sail and steam and wood and iron. These took various forms: amalgams of power--steam vessels with sails and sailing vessels with auxiliary engines--and combinations of materials--"composite vessels" utilising wood and iron. In addition, there were mergers of old and new forms of power and materials. Until the 1860s wooden steamers were significant, and from the late 1830s iron sailing ships were built. Until almost the end of the nineteenth century, the new was neither technically perfected nor wholly proven, and the old was not entirely inferior. In addition, the characteristics of various trades ensured that the introduction of new technologies was gradual.[1]

This paper is concerned with one facet of mixed technologies--iron sailing vessels during the first twenty years or so of their existence--and the response of shipowners to this advance. Arguably, iron sailing vessels represented the outstanding form of mixed technology. While wooden steamships were significant until mid-century, they declined rapidly in importance thereafter. Composite vessels were never of any

[1]Little work has been done on the mixture of technologies in the early phase of the transition from wood and sail to iron and steam. A valuable short study is Sarah Palmer, "Experience, Experiment and Economics: Factors in the Construction of Early Merchant Steamships," in K. Matthews and G. Panting (eds.), *Ships and Shipbuilding in the North Atlantic Region* (St. John's, 1978), 233-247.

Research in Maritime History, No. 3 (December 1992), 115-133.

great account in terms of tonnage built and first registered in the United Kingdom and became irrelevant after 1870. Although doomed to eventual disappearance, the iron sailing vessel proved highly viable. Indeed, it was preferred to its wooden counterpart by many operators during what G.S. Graham termed the "ascendancy of the sailing ship."[2] In terms of tonnage of sailing ships built and first registered in the U.K. each year, iron first exceeded wooden sail in 1868 and continuously dominated from 1873 to 1890. In 1875, when total sail tonnage built and first registered totalled 241,600 tons--a figure only marginally surpassed in three years between 1787 and 1914--iron vessels comprised 198,800 tons, almost five times the tonnage of wood.[3] As long as sail remained competitive, the iron sailing vessel was of considerable significance.

Nonetheless, iron sail has never commanded the attention it merits. Contemporaries understandably were obsessed with the steamer, the most spectacular technological feature of the day. In writing about the mid-century, maritime historians have likewise regarded the steamship as the dynamic element of change or, if they focused on sail, have seen trans-Atlantic packets or "clippers" as the epitome of technological advance. Iron sail, for all its ultimate commercial significance, had neither the glamour of a new mode of power nor the romance of the final refinement of the wooden sailing vessel. Such subjectivity apart, early iron sail has perhaps failed to gain attention because of a lack of readily accessible statistical data. From the very outset of steam, governments assiduously assembled detailed figures; together with its dramatic attraction, this helps to explain the body of literature associated with early steam and the saga of the "first 1,945 steamships."[4] Iron sail did not enjoy this sort of generous statistical attention. An exhaustive search of British *Parliamentary Papers* unearthed no returns distinguishing iron from wooden sail before 1850. Thereafter, in material on shipbuilding and new registrations, a distinction was made between iron and wooden

---

[2]G. S. Graham, "The Ascendancy of the Sailing Ship 1850-85," *Economic History Review*, 2nd Series, IX (1956), 74-88.

[3]B.R. Mitchell and Phyllis Deane (comps.), *Abstract of British Historical Statistics* (Cambridge, 1962), 220-224.

[4]J.R.T. Hughes and S. Reiter, "The First 1,945 British Steamships," *Journal of the American Statistical Association* (1958), cited in Mitchell and Deane (comps.), *Abstract*, 232.

sail, but annual figures of total registered shipping, while separating sail from steam, failed to differentiate between wood and iron.[5]

As a consequence, although there have been studies of the technological aspects of iron shipbuilding, the early commercial use of iron sail has never been effectively examined. This paper seeks to redress this by posing a series of basic questions for Britain. When and at what pace were iron sailing vessels introduced? What were their characteristics, at what ports were they registered, and into what trades did shipowners put them? In endeavouring to provide some preliminary answers, the paper raises some significant issues concerning the wider aspects of defining sail and steam vessels in an age of transition.

At the outset, the researcher studying iron sailing vessels is confronted with the twin issues of definition and sources. The latter problem is hardly new; John Grantham, the Liverpool naval architect and shipbuilder and a leading advocate of iron, observed in 1858 that "to attempt to list the aggregate number [of iron vessels] built up to this time in the United Kingdom would be a work of no mean difficulty."[6] In the absence of adequate parliamentary returns, the obvious source would be the registers of the Registrar-General of Shipping. While a search of these records would yield complete details of every iron sailing vessel, it would also require a full survey of every port over a lengthy period. The enormity of this task helps to explain the lack of previous study and emphasises the virtual impossibility of such an exercise. Fortunately, the task is simplified by using *Lloyd's Register of Shipping* (popularly known as *Lloyd's Register*, though properly, *Lloyd's Book*). From 1843 to 1854, the *Registers* included special listings of iron vessels, with separate sections for steam and sail. Though separate enumeration ceased after 1854, the *Registers* in their main alphabetic sequence clearly differentiated iron vessels, thereby permitting analysis. Yet they only list vessels classed at Lloyd's. The obvious question concerns the comprehensiveness of the source. Fortunately, a check of its entries against available official statistics is reassuring and suggests that in this instance Lloyd's data are

---

[5]The first annual return of "vessels built and registered" to distinguish between wood and iron appeared in 1850. See United Kingdom, Parliament, House of Commons, *Parliamentary Papers* (hereafter *BPP*), 1851, LII, 567.

[6]John Grantham, *On Iron Ship-Building with Practical Illustrations* (London, 1858), 145.

reasonably complete.[7] A full justification for relying on the *Registers* as the prime source is contained in the Appendix.

The definitional problem lies in the development around mid-century of the auxiliary sailing vessel, with a steam engine to provide power when necessary. This immediately raises the question of what is a "sailing ship" or a "steam ship?"[8] Mixed technologies were common, since steam conferred great advantages but was not fully perfected. Hence, many steamers carried sails while many sailing vessels could resort to steam. Classifying such vessels is problematic, but most were committed to one principal source of power; contemporaries viewed them as one or the other rather than hermaphrodites. Lloyd's certainly followed this practice and its definition will be utilized. In all tables, columns headed "sail auxiliary" (abbreviated SL-AX) refer to iron vessels listed as sail, with steam engines to provide auxiliary power only. Lloyd's definition was unequivocal: for steamers, engine power was listed as HP; for sail with auxiliary engines, it was listed as AP.

While the history of iron shipbuilding began with canal barges in the late eighteenth century, it was not until after the Napoleonic wars that real development occurred. In 1818 an iron boat, the *Vulcan*, was built for work on the Clyde; three years later, the famous *Aaron Manby*, arguably the first iron steamer, was launched for use on the Seine, gaining much attention by sailing direct from London to Paris. Further iron steamers were constructed for use on the Shannon and the Mersey. In 1832, the *Elburkah* was produced by Laird and Sons for the Niger expedition, its passage to West Africa representing the first ocean voyage by an iron vessel. A handful of other iron steamers were constructed

---

[7]A point that must be emphasised when searching for vessels in *Lloyd's Registers* is the necessity of consulting a series of these documents. Irrespective of the fact that the annual *Register* ran from 1 July to 30 June and hence does not coincide with the calendar year, a search for references to vessels, built in, say, 1850, would require a scrutiny of the *Registers* not merely for 1850 and 1851 but also for a number of subsequent years. Of course a vessel might never appear in the *Registers*. However, in the case of iron sailing vessels in the period under review it would seem that most ultimately were listed at some time or other. For this survey of iron sail, 1838-1857, the *Registers* for the period 1838-1862 were surveyed--hence the source reference for each table.

[8]Basil Greenhill briefly raises this issue in his "An Introduction: The Development of Screw Propulsion for Steam Vessels," in Stephen Fisher (ed.), *Innovation in Shipping and Trade* (Exeter, 1989), 39.

later in the decade for coastal and channel work.[9] The first iron sailing vessel did not appear until 1838 when the 264-ton *Ironside* was launched in Liverpool. It attracted considerable contemporary publicity because of its novelty,[10] its successful maiden voyage to Rio de Janeiro and its status as the first iron sailing ship guaranteed by Lloyd's as "fit for the safe conveyance of dry and perishable cargoes."[11] Its appearance can be viewed as the birth of the iron sailing ship, which thereafter made slow but steady progress before enjoying a phenomenal expansion after 1853.

Table 1 depicts the progress of the iron sailing vessel during the first twenty years of its existence. Three major questions might be asked of the material. First, what were the significance of these craft in the context of total British shipping? This can be measured not only by its share of all vessels built and registered but also its proportion of all iron vessels. Until about 1852 iron sail was of little significance, representing only one or two percent of all vessels built and registered. But in 1853 it rose to five percent and from 1854 represented around ten percent. In tonnage terms the proportions were somewhat higher. Small though these percentages may have been, they were still significant. This is especially true in the context of all iron vessels. While up to mid-century sail annually represented about one-tenth of iron vessels built, from 1854 to 1857 it accounted for around half.[12] Thus, within the innovative sector of iron ships, sail was of considerable importance in the mid-1850s.

The second issue presented by Table 1 concerns the growth pattern of iron sail. Effectively there was a pioneering era followed by a dramatic take-off. Although some iron vessels had been launched in the 1830s, the 1840s represented the beginnings of commercial iron shipbuilding. Its novelty is apparent from the names of many early sailing vessels--*Ironside, Iron Duke, Iron Queen, Iron Prince, Iron Gem* and a number of *Vulcans*. The technology of iron ship construction was only

---

[9] On early iron shipbuilding see Richard Barker, "John Wilkinson and the Early Iron Barges," *Journal of the John Wilkinson Society*, No. 15 (1987), 1-34; Ewan Corlett, *The Iron Ship* (Bradford-on-Avon, 1974), 21-44.

[10] See the contemporary reports in *The Times* (London), 23 October 1838; 1 June 1839.

[11] Corlett, *The Iron Ship*, 27.

[12] Calculated from Mitchell and Deane (comps.), *Abstract*, 220-224.

then being perfected and although the rate of advance was swift--witness the enormous technological breakthrough of the *Great Britain*--there were still major problems of fouling and compass deviation. Yet if iron vessels were in a developmental phase, it must be admitted that in the 1840s sail made much slower progress than steam. One possible explanation is that despite the apparent success of *Ironside*, some other early iron sailing vessels fared less well. The *Iron Duke*, built in Glasgow in 1840, encountered steering and compass problems on her maiden voyage to Calcutta and was subsequently lost with a timber cargo from the Baltic. The *John Garrow*, launched in 1840 from an Aberdeen yard, took an inordinate time on a return voyage from Bombay and experienced major fouling.[13] Such widely-reported difficulties contributed to the crisis of "attitude" which was perhaps the chief reason for the relatively slow progress of iron sail. Both iron and steam, as complete breaks not only with the recent past but also with centuries-old traditions, required a mental re-adjustment which took decades. But in the 1840s, when they were still novelties and no real challenge to the traditional order, the *total* uniqueness of the iron steamer was easier to accommodate than was the iron sailing vessel, which to many flew in the face of nature. In other words, it is sometimes easier to accept total than partial innovation. John Grantham, looking back in 1858 over the first twenty years of iron sail, observed a greater opposition to iron sail than to iron steam, noting that

> they [underwriters] appeared to lend a willing ear to the unfounded objections which were raised, and when under the force of conviction, iron *steam* vessels were insured at lower rates than wooden vessels, iron sailing vessels found no favour with them and even where owners were willing to pay a higher rate for their *vessels*, shippers of goods were deterred from supplying them with cargo. This course was for a long time fatal to their progress, and it was not until lately that the inconsistency of it was fully apparent.[14]

---

[13]John Grantham, *Iron as a Material for Ship-Building being a Communication to the Polytechnic Society of Liverpool* (London, 1842), 29-44.

[14]Grantham, *On Iron Ship-Building*, 145.

While modest, progress was made: the table shows that the number of vessels built and first registered rose from nineteen in the first quinquennium (1838-1842), to thirty-two between 1843 and 1847 and to forty-seven in the period 1848-1852. Some perspective can be gained from the fact that in 1852 only 242 iron steamers were on the British register.[15] The growth of iron sail in its first decade and a half was moderate compared to the years 1853-1857, during which there was an almost ten-fold increase in output.

Table 1
Iron Sailing Vessels Constructed, 1838-1857

Year	Sail	SL/AX	Total	Year	Sail	SL/AX	Total
1838	1		1	1848	14		14
1839	2		2	1849	7	2	9
1840	3		3	1850	6		6
1841	6		6	1851	5	1	6
1842	7		7	1852	7	5	12
1838-42	19		19	1848-52	39	8	47
1843	2		2	1853	11	24	35
1844	8	1	9	1854	41	60	101
1845	5	3	8	1855	43	75	118
1846	7	1	8	1856	29	71	100
1847	5		5	1857	26	68	94
1843-47	27	5	32	1853-57	150	298	448
1838-57	235	311	546				

Source: Compiled from *Lloyd's Registers*, 1838-1862.

This remarkable advance resulted from a combination of factors. In part it reflected technological progress and attitudinal change, while at the same time it was due to a general upsurge in shipping. By the 1850s many early construction problems had been overcome, engineering techniques and materials had been developed, and significant centres of iron ship construction were established, notably on the Clyde, Mersey and Tyne. There was now a greater acceptance in commercial circles of the iron ship and a recognition of its many advantages, such as strength, stowage capacity, speed, durability and cost. Concerns over compass deviation had largely been resolved due to the work of Flinders, Barlow,

---

[15]Palmer, "Experience, Experiment and Economics," 233.

Johnson and, in particular, Airey. Above all, iron vessels had demonstrated their commercial utility. Perhaps in recognition of these developments, in the early 1850s Lloyd's regularised its rules for iron shipping. From 1838 the syndicate assigned characters to iron vessels; from 1844 it undertook more thorough surveys, though the "Iron Rules" remained vague and indeterminate. In 1854, following surveyors' reports and advice from the leading iron shipbuilders, formal "Rules for Iron Ships" were adopted. Even then, however, they were prefaced by the caveat "that iron shipbuilding is yet in its infancy."[16] No doubt all these factors would have led eventually to an expansion of iron shipbuilding, but in the 1850s the shipping market underwent dramatic change. In terms of the tonnage of new vessels, the 1840s had been stagnant. But from 1850 the market improved and between 1853 and 1857 boomed. Whereas in the 1840s ships built and first registered in Britain averaged around 125,000 tons per annum, between 1850 and 1852 this reached 150,000 tons, before doubling again between 1853 and 1857. The initial stimuli lay in gold discoveries in California and Australia and increased emigrant traffic, but the real impetus came from the Crimean War and the associated government demand for transports.[17] Moreover, Royal Navy orders for sizeable numbers of iron vessels (though not yet for battleships) enhanced confidence. As the need for shipping space and freight rates both grew in this age of optimism and activity, iron shipbuilding received a disproportionate incentive.[18]

The third issue to emerge from Table 1 concerns the huge growth of auxiliary vessels. Sailing auxiliaries appeared in 1844; the first such vessel listed in Lloyd's was the *Senator* of Hull, a schooner-rigged vessel of 160 tons fitted with a twenty-eight horsepower auxiliary engine. The

---

[16] *Annals of Lloyds Register being a Sketch of the Origin, Constitution and Progress of Lloyd's Register of British and Foreign Shipping* (London, 1884), 75-82; G. Blake, *Lloyd's Register of Shipping 1760-1960* (London, 1960), 42. A near-contemporary view is supplied by J. Grantham, "The Classification of Iron Ships," *Transactions of the Institute of Naval Architects*, II (1861), 128-140.

[17] As Table 8 reveals, a considerable number of iron sailing vessels found employment as transports.

[18] On the shipping boom of the mid-1850s, see J.R.T. Hughes, *Fluctuations in Trade, Industry, and Finance. A Study of British Economic Development 1850-1860* (Oxford, 1960), 207-219.

iron auxiliary made little progress before 1853, but thereafter became the predominant form of iron sailing vessel. Several explanations can be suggested. The development of the screw propeller, which could be accommodated within conventional vessels much more easily than paddle wheels, was clearly crucial, but perhaps more significant was that the auxiliary appeared to provide the best of both worlds. The engine conferred the advantage of steam yet limited the costs of additional crew and fuel, highly significant factors in owners' decision-making. The auxiliary proved particularly attractive on routes involving multiple ports of call, such as the coastal, Mediterranean and European trades. In the transition, when owners were faced with new choices, the auxiliary was the easiest and most logical compromise. Whatever the relative importance of different influences, by the mid-1850s sail had gained considerable acceptance and become the growth sector of iron shipping.

Table 2
Tonnage Distribution of Iron Sailing Vessels, 1838-1857

Tons	1838-42	1843-47	1848-52	1853-57	Total
0-100	4	8	17	5	34
100-199	6	6	7	14	33
200-299	5	7	2	23	37
300-399	2	3	4	21	30
400-499	1	1	1	25	28
500-749	1	2	5	11	19
750-999	-	-	3	25	28
1000-1499	-	-	-	25	25
1500+	-	-	-	1	1
Total	19	27	39	150	235

Source: See Table 1.

Having established the increasing numbers of iron sailing vessels, it is also possible to examine such basic features as tonnage and rig to ascertain if iron sail had any special characteristics. Tables 2 and 3 describe the tonnage distribution of iron sail and auxiliary vessels. The patterns varied over time and between sail and auxiliaries. While three of the earliest iron sailing vessels were over 500 tons, more than half of those built before 1852 were under 200 tons. Although a few small craft continued to appear, the trend was towards larger vessels. Almost half of the launches between 1853 and 1857 exceeded 500 tons and the

Indian, built in 1855, measured 1765 tons. Auxiliary iron sailing vessels were generally bigger: far fewer were below 200 tons, and in the great boom of 1853-1857 almost sixty percent exceeded 500 tons and over a tenth surpassed 1000 tons. In the main this reflected general trends in iron shipbuilding, and the later development of auxiliaries explains their higher tonnages.

Table 3
Tonnage Distribution of Iron Sail Auxiliary Vessels, 1838-57

Tons	1838-42	1843-47	1848-52	1853-57	Total
0-99	-	-	-	3	3
100-199	-	2	-	8	10
200-299	-	2	2	22	26
300-399	-	-	-	38	38
400-499	-	-	2	53	55
500-749	-	-	1	117	118
750-999	-	1	2	23	26
1000-1499	-	-	-	25	25
1500+	-	-	1	9	10
Total	-	5	8	298	311

Source: See Table 1.

Of far more interest than tonnage distribution is rig. Table 4 relates rig to tonnage, contrasting sail and auxiliary. The profile for sailing vessels was fairly predictable. Among those under 200 tons the schooner rig predominated; in the 200-500 ton class the barque was favoured; and above 400 tons the ship dominated. Indeed the pattern was as might have been expected except for the use of the schooner rig on some larger vessels. The profile for auxiliaries was somewhat different. While analysis is hampered because for about one-quarter of vessels rig details were not listed in Lloyd's, the picture is clear enough. Over half (two-thirds of those for which information is available) were schooner-rigged; the vast majority of the remainder, and especially those over 500 tons, were barque-rigged. The latter mirrored the contemporary trend towards rigging larger vessels as barques, but the wide use of the schooner rig raises interesting issues.

Table 4
Rig/Tonnage Distribution of Iron Sailing and Sail Auxiliary Vessels, 1838-1857

Tons	0-99	100-199	200-299	300-399	400-499	500-749	750-999	1000-1499	1500-2000	2000+	Total
Sail											
Brigantine	-	3	1	1							5
Brig	1	6	10	1							18
Barque	-	1	12	23	10	4	1	-	1		52
Ship	-	-	1	3	14	13	25	21			77
Smack	2										2
Sloop	2	1	1								4
Schooner	29	22	10	2	4	2	2	4			75
Snow	-	-	1								1
Not listed			1								1
Total	34	33	37	30	28	19	28	25	1		235
Auxiliary											
Brig	-	-	-	1	-	6					7
Barque			1		3	11	16	13	4	2	50
Ship					2	3	3	6		3	17
Smack	1										1
Schooner	1	8	20	27	28	67	4	2			157
Not Listed	1	2	5	10	22	31	3	4	-	1	79
Total	3	10	26	38	55	118	26	25	4	6	311

Source: See Table 1.

On pure sailing vessels the schooner rig was typically employed up to about 200 tons. Yet on iron auxiliaries this rig prevailed for craft between 200 and 750 tons. A logical explanation is that the schooner rig offered little wind resistance when engines were used. This is significant because if steam were used only occasionally it might be expected that a more appropriate rig relative to vessel size would have been utilised. The employment of the schooner rig suggests a regular use of engines to assist the vessel's passage. But if this were the case, can such craft be described as sail? Ultimately, the verdict must rest on the choice definition; in this instance, they have been included in the sail category, albeit always separately from pure sail. The justification is two-fold: first, because contemporaries described them as sail (witness Lloyd's' inclusion of them in lists of "iron sailing vessels"); and second, because of their tonnage/horsepower ratios. An examination of the 157 vessels categorised by Lloyd's as iron sailing vessels with auxiliary power and schooner rig reveals that tonnage to horsepower ratios averaged around 7:1, compared with a mean of about 3.5:1 for steamers.[19] Although auxiliaries may have made more regular use of steam than previously thought, they were neither fully-committed to it nor regarded as steamers by contemporaries. Nonetheless, this discussion is yet another reminder of the difficulty of defining vessels in a transitional era.

Thus far the analysis has been almost entirely impersonal and unrelated directly to ports or trades. One of the virtues of *Lloyd's Registers* is that they not only provide information on ports of registration but also on trades in which vessels were employed. Analyses of these variables reveal some interesting patterns, albeit not always easy to interpret. Tables 5 and 6 show the ports of registry of iron sail and auxiliaries, respectively. Both suggest the wide geographical distribution, especially when account is taken of the "others" category, which comprises ports in which only one or two vessels were registered. Yet although the first impression is of wide dispersion, closer scrutiny reveals significant concentration. Among sailing vessels, one-third were registered at Liverpool; Glasgow and the Clyde ports of Dumbarton and Greenock added an additional quarter; the northeast (Newcastle, Sunderland and Shields) contributed nine percent; and London registered

---

[19]Based on a random sample of 150 steamships listed in *Lloyd's Register* for 1854. Tugs, which had very low tonnage/horsepower ratios--sometimes as low as 1:1--were excluded from the sample.

8.5%. That these ports were centres for iron ships is understandable: they were major ports. Furthermore, as Table 7 shows, Glasgow, Liverpool and the Newcastle region were the major centres for iron construction, Clydeside in particular.[20] In such locales shipowners were likely to have close links with known builders and to possess far greater confidence in iron than owners more distant. Yet even taking these facts into account, two features stand out: the prominence of Liverpool and the relatively limited participation of London. While the former was significant for the building of sail, its registrations were almost twice the number of vessels built locally. London was both a minor builder and a relatively minor port of registry. These observations become more intriguing when the ports of registration of auxiliaries are considered.

Table 5
Ports of Registration of Iron Sailing Vessels, 1838-1857

Port/Period	1	2	3	4	Total
Aberdeen	2	-	2	1	5
Dundee	1	1	1	-	3
Dumbarton	-	1	1	1	3
Glasgow	4	-	13	31	48
Greenock	-	-	1	5	6
Hull	2	1	3	3	9
Kirkaldy	1	1	-	1	3
Liverpool	3	5	2	66	76
London	1	3	4	12	20
Newcastle	1	5	1	7	14
Shields	-	-	1	2	3
Sunderland	-	1	3	-	4
Others	4	9	7	21	41
Total	19	27	39	150	235

Note: Periods: 1=1838-1842; 2=1843-1847; 3=1848-1852; 4=1853-1857. Only ports with three or more vessels listed are included.

Source: See Table 1.

[20]On the principal centres of iron shipbuilding, see Fred M. Walker, *Song of the Clyde, A History of Clyde Shipbuilding* (Cambridge, 1984); D. Dougan, *A History of North-East Shipbuilding* (London, 1968); R. W. Sturgess (ed.), *The Great Age of Industry in the North-East* (Durham, 1981). Details on the builders of iron sailing ships may be found in a number of works by D.R. MacGregor: *Merchant Sailing Ships, 1815-1850: Supremacy of Sail* (London, 1984); *Merchant Sailing Ships, 1850-1875: Heyday of Sail* (London, 1984); *Fast Sailing Ships, 1775-1875* (London, 1973).

Table 6 shows even wider dispersal. Moreover, some ten percent of British-built vessels were exported and registered abroad. But closer examination reveals the significance of areas prominent in iron sail--Glasgow and the Clyde, the northeast, London, Liverpool and the Humber ports of Hull and Grimsby. The major port explanation above is valid here, as to a certain extent is the argument relating to place of build (although the principal areas for the construction of iron sail auxiliaries, Clydeside and Newcastle, built far more vessels than were locally-registered). Again, Humberside and London were significant; Liverpool, by contrast, built virtually no auxiliaries. Yet what emerges above all is the remarkable participation of London, which provided 26.4% of registrations, and the limited involvement of Liverpool with but 8.9%. This represents an almost complete reversal of their roles in iron sail. Why this was so is not wholly clear, although two factors may have some bearing. First, in adopting steam London was very much to the fore while Liverpool was somewhat laggard.[21] With some qualification, it is broadly true that the pace at which shipowners or ports responded to steam or any other innovation depended on the trades in which they engaged. The patterns of trade in Liverpool and London were very different and may well help to explain the contrasts observed. Table 8 shows the trades in which iron sail was placed, based on the entry in a vessel's first appearance in Lloyd's. While ensuring consistency, this approach also imposes a few limitations, since in some instances no destination was stated, while in others the voyage listed was coastal and could well have been a passage from its place of build to its port of registration. Although such vessels may have been engaged in the coastal trade, they have been designated as coastal delivery to distinguish them from vessels known to be genuine coasters.

The pattern of employment revealed by Table 8 shows a sharp contrast between sail and auxiliary vessels. Auxiliaries were chiefly employed in European trades, notably the "home trade" from Brest to the mouth of the Elbe, where cargo was relatively valuable and speed and regularity of some importance, and in the Mediterranean, where light and variable winds made auxiliary power especially attractive. The steamer had had already penetrated these trades significantly, and the same was

---

[21]P.L. Cottrell, "The Steamship on the Mersey, 1815-80, Investment and Ownership," in P.L. Cottrell and D.H. Aldcroft (eds.), *Shipping, Trade and Commerce* (Leicester, 1981), 137-164.

true for the coastal and northeast coal trades, which also attracted auxiliaries.[22] Yet these vessels had little impact on long-distance routes. They seem to have been effectively absent from all Atlantic routes and only the Australian trade was a significant source of employment. This Australian presence is somewhat surprising, as will be seen shortly.

Table 6
Ports of Registration of Sail Auxiliary Vessels, 1843-1858

Port/Period	1	2	3	Total
Belfast	-	-	4	4
Dublin	3	-	-	3
Glasgow	-	2	20	22
Grimsby	-	-	13	13
Greenock	-	-	5	5
Hartlepool	-	-	10	10
Hull	1	-	13	14
Leith	-	-	-	4
Liverpool	-	-	27	27
London	-	3	79	82
Newcastle	-	1	13	14
Shields	-	-	3	3
Sunderland	-	-	15	15
Stockton	-	-	4	4
Southampton	-	-	4	4
Wisbech		1	4	5
Others	-	1	47	48
Foreign				
Amsterdam	-	-	3	3
Bremen	-	-	5	5
Copenhagen	-	-	3	3
Marseilles	-	-	5	5
Rotterdam	-	-	5	5
Stettin	-	-	3	3
Others	1	-	9	10
Total	5	8	294	311

Note: Periods: 1=1843-1847; 2=1848-1852; 3=1853-1857. Only ports with three or more vessels listed are included.

Source: See Table 1.

---

[22] C.K Harley, "The Shift from Sailing Ships to Steamships, 1850-1890: A Study in Technological Change and Its Diffusion," in D.N. McCloskey (ed.), *Essays on a Mature Economy: Britain after 1840* (London, 1971), 215-237.

Table 7
Principal Locations for the Building of Iron Sail and Sail Auxiliary Vessels, 1838-1857

Location	Sail	Auxiliary
Clydeside	89	110
Eastern Scotland	21	-
Hull	4	25
London	10	32
Merseyside	39	9
Newcastle	25	68
Other North East	15	37
Others	32	30
Total	235	311

Source: Compiled from *Lloyd's Registers* 1838-62.

In contrast to the European and coastal emphases of auxiliaries, iron sail, although found in these trades, was favoured on long-distance routes. Remarkably, the Indian trade, which accounted for one-fifth of vessels, was of prime importance, as were the West Indian and South American trades (around a sixth each), and Australia (about one-tenth). What is surprising is that iron, as opposed to wooden, sailing vessels were put into these trades. As Graham remarked in his seminal paper,

> Although it could stand unlimited driving in high seas, had more room for cargo than the wooden ship of the same size, and was safer from fire, the iron ship could rarely equal the speed of the wooden on distant voyages, owing principally to fouling of the bottom.[23]

It was because of fouling that composite vessels--iron frames with wooden planking that could be coppered--were developed in the 1860s. While iron vessels had a reputation for slow passages, the extra duration of voyages and the costs in time and money of cleaning had to be balanced against the savings gained. In evidence before the Select Committee on Merchant Shipping of 1860 Charles Wigram, of the famous London

---

[23]Graham, "The Ascendancy," 76. For a near contemporary view of the fouling problem, see C.F.T. Young, *The Fouling and Corrosion of Iron Ships* (London, 1867).

shipowning firm of Money, Wigram and Sons, claimed that iron ships were "not particularly adapted for ocean voyages;" Richard Green, another leading London owner, was equally strong in his antipathy to iron vessels.[24] Yet, despite the opinions of London owners and the acknowledged problem of fouling, shipowners in Liverpool, and to a lesser extent Glasgow, placed iron sailing vessels into the Indian, Australian and South American trades. Possibly iron vessels were regarded as particularly suitable for the new bulk trades of rice and jute from India and wool from Australia, but the prominence of India and Australia in the employment pattern of iron sail (and to a degree of auxiliaries) deserves further investigation.

In the overall context of British shipping in the period and in light of the importance it attained after 1870, the iron sailing vessel was of little quantitative significance between 1838 and 1857. The first decade and a half were very much pioneering years and real growth only began from about 1852. Nevertheless, the first generation illustrated the pace of the response to innovation and its uneven nature in terms of shipowners in different ports and patterns of employment in different trades. It also raises a number of issues with significant implications for our understanding of the adoption of new materials and power sources.

Above all, this paper suggests the need to look more fully at iron and steam around mid-century. While the technology of iron construction has received much attention--albeit directed at steam rather than sail, and individual vessels rather than the entire fleet--far more investigation is required into the employment of iron vessels. On steam, fresh thought is needed about the definitions of steamships and auxiliary vessels. Engine size and more particularly tonnage/horsepower ratios deserve much closer attention, and it would be particularly valuable to know how and in what circumstances auxiliary power was used on voyages and how this varied between trades. Only when we have clearer definitions and a fuller appreciation of the way iron ships and steam power were utilised will we be able to understand the nature of the mid-century transition.[25]

---

[24] *BPP*, "Select Committee on Merchant Shipping 1860" (c.530), XIII, qs. 335, 950.

[25] We are indebted to our colleague Professor P.L. Cottrell for many discussions on this theme and his scrutiny of an earlier draft of this paper.

Table 8
Iron Sailing and Sail Auxiliary Vessels, 1838-1857: Patterns of Employment

	Sail					Sail Auxiliary				
Periods	1	2	3	4	Total	1	2	3	4	Total
Trades										
Africa-west	-	1	-	3	4	-	-	-	4	4
Africa-south	1	1	1	2	5	-	-	-	3	3
Canada	-	-	2	13	15	-	-	-	2	2
USA	-	1	1	1	3	-	-	-	1	1
West Indies	1	-	1	8	10	-	1	1	2	4
S. America	3	3	-	22	28	-	-	-	3	3
S. America (Pacific)	1	1	1	-	3		-	-	-	-
India	2	1	4	39	46	-	-	-	8	8
China	1	-	1	1	3	-	-	-	-	-
Australia	-	-	5	17	22	-	-	1	16	17
Europe-west	2	1	3	4	10	-	-	-	52	52
Scand./Baltic	3	2	2	3	10	-	-	-	25	25
Spain/Portugal	-	-	1	-	1	-	-	-	4	4
Mediterranean	2	2	-	13	17	-	1	-	44	45
Coastal trade	-	7	3	6	16	-	-	1	15	16
Colliers	-	-	-	-	-	-	-	1	11	12
Transports	-	-	-	2	2	-	-	1	20	21
Coastal delivery	2	7	11	5	25	-	3	1	47	51
No destination	1	-	3	11	15	-	-	2	41	43
Total	19	27	39	150	235	-	5	8	298	311

Note: Periods: 1=1838-1842; 2=1843-1847; 3=1848-1852; 4=1853-1857. India includes Aden; Mediterranean includes Egypt.

Source: See Table 1.

Appendix

Lloyd's Register Coverage of Iron Sailing Vessels

The limitations of *Lloyd's Register* are well-known. They are not complete registers of shipping but merely a compilation of vessels classified at Lloyd's. Shipowners were not obliged to have their vessels so classed and many did not, particularly with the growth of marine insurance outside London, notably the development of mutual insurance societies in the post-Napoleonic era. The extent of Lloyd's coverage has never been ascertained and it no doubt varied over time, and according to types of vessels and the practice of owners in particular localities. In consequence, any survey based on the *Registers* needs to address the question of how complete is the available data for the purpose being undertaken. Ideally, what is required is some official listing or statistics for the survey being made, against which entries can be checked.

In this instance, official material is not available prior to 1850. The development of the steamship seems to have been regarded as sufficiently spectacular to warrant a mass of regular listings from its earliest beginnings. Not so the iron sailing vessel, which gained scant separate coverage in official accounts and papers. The sheer wealth of material in the *Parliamentary Papers* and the limitations of all guides to it--whether contemporary catalogues or more modern compilations--makes it difficult to state categorically that no official data on iron ships exists. However, neither an extensive search of parliamentary papers in the 1830s and 1840s nor consultation with other scholars have unearthed any specific references. Only from 1850 does there appear to be any official data, and then not in the splendidly comprehensive form of full listings of all steamships, but simply a distinction between the materials of wood and iron in the annual returns of vessels built and first registered in the United Kingdom. Even so, this does mean from 1850 official statistics are available of iron sailing vessels built and first registered in each year. Such figures permit a check of the completeness of the information in *Lloyd's Registers*.

An examination of the official annual returns of vessels built and first registered in the United Kingdom provides a figure of 185 iron sailing vessels between 1850 and 1858. An investigation of these returns makes it apparent that they refer specifically to sailing vessels. An auxiliary, however limited the horsepower of its engine, was classified as a steamer, thus raising some queries about the composition of official statistics. But there is no ambiguity in the figures for iron sail. A survey of *Lloyd's Registers* for the years 1850 to 1862 produced a total of 168 iron sailing vessels built between 1850 and 1857, which represents ninety percent coverage. On this basis it would seem that Lloyd's coverage of iron sail for the period under review is largely complete.

The Growth of Norwegian Shipbroking: The Practices of Fearnley and Eger as a Case Study, 1869-1914[1]

Lewis R. Fischer and Helge W. Nordvik

In the past quarter-century our understanding of important aspects of nineteenth-century maritime history has improved dramatically. We know far more than before about topics such as the development of national fleets, the individuals who invested in them, the trades they plied, and the seamen who manned them. Scholars are even starting to examine the communities which spawned maritime actors and to situate their studies in the national societies and economies of which they were a part. Moreover, research is beginning to appear that analyses shipping comparatively within its international context. Yet there remain significant gaps in our knowledge. This generalisation is particularly apposite to those we might call "maritime middlemen," those intermediaries between buyers and sellers of shipping services. One of the occupations about which our comprehension is less than adequate is shipbroking. Virtually the entire literature on the historical development of this profession is in the form of either popular studies or commissioned histories on individual firms, most of which fail to meet the

[1]This paper is part of two larger projects. The first is a history of Astrup Fearnley, being written in collaboration with Gunnar Nerheim and Even Lange. The second is a larger international history of shipbroking being written by the senior author. We would like to thank our colleagues for assistance with some of the conceptual problems and Anders Martin Fon for helping with the research and much more. In addition, several past and present employees at Fearnley, especially Birger Nossum, former head of Fearnresearch, have rendered aid. We acknowledge support for the Fearnley project from both Astrup Fearnley and the Social Sciences and Humanities Research Council of Canada. The history of international shipbroking research is funded entirely by the latter agency.

Research in Maritime History, No. 3 (December 1992), 135-155.

standards of professional scholarship.[2] And even within this limited body of writing, almost nothing has been written about non-British brokers.[3] Indeed, even in Norway, a nation with a significant tradition of maritime scholarship, our ignorance is equally profound: the literature on this occupation is confined to only a few inadequate studies.[4]

Yet if there is a void in our comprehension of shipbroking firms, the literature is even more barren when it comes to examinations of the actual practice of broking. Indeed, the format most favoured by business historians--to describe and explain the success or failure of an individual

---

[2]The best scholarly study of a broker is Peter N. Davies, *Henry Tyrer: A Liverpool Shipping Agent and His Enterprises, 1879-1979* (London, 1979). For this period, in addition to the literature cited elsewhere in this essay, see Arthur Behrend, *Portrait of a Family Firm: Bahr, Behrend and Co. 1793-1945* (London, 1970); George Blake, *Gellatley's, 1862-1962: A Short History of the Firm* (London, 1962); W.M.L. Escombe, *Full and Down: The History of Escombe, McGrath and Company Limited* (London, 1953); Percy Harley, *My Life in Shipping 1881-1938. An Impression of Some of the Matters and Men I Have Met In It* (London, 1939); Hurford Janes, *Full Ahead. The Story of Brown, Jenkinson and Co. Limited 1860-1960* (London, 1960); Anne and Russell Long, *A Shipping Venture. Turnbull Scott and Company 1872-1972* (London, 1974); Augustus Muir, *Blyth, Jourdain and Company Limited, 1810-1960* (London, 1961); Philip Paul, *City Voyage: The Story of Erlebach and Company Limited, 1867-1967* (London, 1967); and Edward F. Stevens, *A Record of the History of Holder Brothers and Co. Ltd. from 1849-1950* (London, 1950). A marvellously useful handbook on late nineteenth and early twentieth century broking which includes much historical material is J.F. Myrhe, *About Chartering and Shipbroking Business* (Copenhagen, 1917).

[3]Perhaps the best of the studies of non-British firms is the anonymously-written *A Century of Ship Agency and Brokerage: Funch, Eyde and Co., Inc., 1847-1947* (New York, 1947).

[4]On recent Norwegian maritime writing, see Helge W. Nordvik, "Norwegian Maritime Historical Research during the Past Twenty Years: A Critical Survey," *Sjøfartshistorisk Årbok 1990* (Bergen, 1991), 241-278. The studies of brokerage houses in Norway have managed almost without exception to play down broking in favour of a concentration on shipowning. The worst may be Kr. Anker Olsen, *Mitt skip er lastet av: Winge og Co. gjennom 100 år* (Oslo, 1955), which devotes only a few sentences to the principal rationale behind the firm's establishment. See also Gunnar Christie Wasberg and Kaare Petersen, *Fearnley & Eger 1869-1969* (Oslo, 1971), and Lauritz Pettersen, Rolf Engelsen and Per Grieg, *The Sound of Grieg* (Bergen, 1984). Perhaps the best insights into a brokerage house are in Joachim Grieg, *Spredte erindringer om Bergens Skibsfart. Væsentlig om overgangen fra seil til damp* (Bergen, 1930). On a broking firm with twentieth-century roots, see T. Baalsrud and H.T. Gram, *R.S. Platou A.S 1936-1986. Fifty Years of Shipbroking* (Oslo, 1986).

enterprise--is part of the problem. From these studies a reader can learn a good deal about the experiences of a specific company but will find it next to impossible to gain an understanding of the development of the profession itself. While we make no pretext of breaking out of this paradigm completely--it is too early in our study for that and the secondary literature is too inadequate to support such aspirations--we do make a preliminary attempt to redress the problem. Although most of the evidence in this paper derives from an examination of a single firm, we try to shift the focus in two ways. First, our concern is to try to isolate factors which were likely crucial to Norwegian shipbrokers as a group rather than merely to the success or failure of an individual company. Second, using the records of Fearnley and Eger, an important house which by the First World War was the largest broker in Christiania and one of the most sizeable in Norway, we want to examine the practices and factors that enabled Norwegian shipbrokers to grow within the international arena. The word "grow" is crucial here, for Norwegian brokers did indeed expand. Yet it is important to recognize that prior to the war they did not really compete with foreign shipbrokers.

We pose two inter-related questions. First, we ask how to explain the timing of Norwegian entry into international shipbroking. In response, we posit an argument based primarily upon alterations in communications technology and the development of appropriate exogenous and endogenous structures to capitalise on these shifts. Second, we inquire about Norwegian broking practices--at least insofar as we can generalise about them from an examination of Fearnley and Eger--in an international perspective. We note the differences, such as a continuing dependence on local markets and a decided lag in adopting new broking strategies (including the adoption of time charters), and attempt to link them to a discussion of the pace of expansion in the prewar maritime world.

The profession that we discuss requires some delineation, since many maritime historians remain unclear about the functions performed by brokers. For the most part, shipbrokers historically have engaged in an identifiable range of activities. The most obvious was vessel chartering, bringing together the sellers of space (shipowners) with those requiring tonnage (consignors or consignees of cargo). The second was sale and purchase. Most commonly this involved either arranging the construction of a vessel or the sale of an asset for a shipowner; in the latter case, the vessel could be new or second-hand. Occasionally, brokers were asked by shipbuilders to find a buyer for tonnage constructed without a fixed contract, although as such speculative building declined in the second half of the century, so too did the demand for brokers to serve this function. A third activity in which brokers routinely engaged was to facilitate entrances and clearances in ports. By the nineteenth century, this most frequently meant acting as a customs' broker, easing the flow of goods across national frontiers. Shipbrokers were also often requested to arrange for ancillary services, such as the provision of insurance cover. In an especially sophisticated market, they might also be called upon to assist in arranging financing, although outside major shipping centres this type of activity was uncommon until after World War I. Finally, shipbrokers also frequently engaged in vessel management. Sometimes they did this as shipowners; at others, this was simply a service performed for a fee. But in the strictest sense, management and broking were distinct: while some brokers were also managers, most managers were not brokers.[5]

Individuals performing these tasks have existed in maritime nations, including Norway, literally as far back as we can chronicle. Indeed, prior to 1000 AD the Vikings had a position they called *brokunar-madr*, literally a "go-between" who facilitated contact between shipowners and merchants. In the modern era, the first Norwegian shipbrokers were formally licensed in Bergen in 1641, Trondheim (1660), and Christiania (1700). But because until about the mid-nineteenth century the majority of shipowners were themselves merchants, and the typical cargo consisted of goods carried for the owner's own account, the need for brokers remained relatively constrained. It was only in the bulk-carrying trades, such as the carriage of timber from Norway and the Baltic, that vessels frequently carried freights which were not the property of the owner. On such trade routes, there often was a market for broking services.[6]

---

[5]Perhaps the best nineteenth-century guide to broking practices is Thomas Edward Scrutton, *The Contract of Affreightment as Expressed in Charterparties and Bills of Lading* (First ed., London, 1886). For overviews of the functions of brokers see J. Bes, *Chartering Practice* (Amsterdam, 1960); Bes, *Chartering and Shipping Terms* (London, 1951); and Lars Gorton, Rolf Ihre and Arne Sandevärn, *Shipbroking and Chartering Practice* (London, 1980).For a superb overview of modern shipping economics which clearly highlights the role of shipbrokers, see Martin Stopford, *Maritime Economics* (London, 1988), especially 21-36.

[6]Baalsrud and Gram, *R.S. Platou*, 8 ff.

The repeal of the British Navigation Acts in 1849 and the subsequent movement toward free trade throughout much of the western world dramatically altered this environment by opening commerce with Britain to vessels regardless of nationality. Where shipowners had previously been limited to participation in fairly well-defined trades, they now had greater freedom to expand their interests. As other nations followed the British lead and lowered or abolished restraints to trade over the next two decades, they served as midwives to the modern international economy. In maritime terms these events had profound effects. By changing the rules of the game, western nations provided opportunities for shipowners to enter the cross-trades in significant numbers. This altered the nature of investment by giving rise to professional shipowners, individuals interested in owning (and perhaps managing) vessels rather than merely using them as adjuncts to their mercantile concerns. And as shipowners moved away from traditional trade routes and practices, this heightened the demand for shipbrokers.[7] It should be no surprise that many of the most established British brokers date from this period. Perhaps the best example is the London firm of H. Clarkson and Company, which was founded in 1852 and today is probably the largest shipbroking firm in the world.[8]

While the movement to freer trade had a noticeable and dramatic impact on Norwegian shipping, it did not immediately have the same effect upon broking as in Britain. There were two reasons for this, one having to do with domestic conditions and the other reflecting external realities. Internally, the growth of broking was constrained by the Brokerage Act of 1818, which severely limited the entrance of new people into the profession. Indeed, one curious provision of the

---

[7]The best study of the repeal of the British Navigation Acts is Sarah Palmer, *Politics, Shipping and the Repeal of the Navigation Laws* (Manchester, 1990).

[8]On the founding of Clarkson, see *The Clarkson Chronicles 1852-1952* (London, 1852). The anonymous author credits the California gold rush and the Crimean War for the timing of the establishment of the firm. While the former had some impact, it is dwarfed by the repeal of the Navigation Acts in its impetus to shipping. The latter, which did not begin until 1854, could hardly have been a factor in the decision of Henry Clarkson to enter broking. On the relative impacts of the various causes of the shipping boom of the early 1850s, see Lewis R. Fischer and Helge W. Nordvik, "Maritime Transport and the Integration of the North Atlantic Economy, 1850-1914," in Wolfram Fischer, R. Marvin McInnis and Jürgen Schneider (eds.), *The Emergence of a World Economy, 1500-1914* (Wiesbaden, 1986), 519-544.

legislation seemed to suggest that broking was not a valuable occupation by describing those who ought to be admitted as "such subjects as by mischance, through no fault of their own, have lost their capital in trade."[9] While the act was widely ignored, its mere retention on the statue books served to deter some capable individuals from choosing broking as a career.

The external deterrent, however, was more serious. The problem was that in shipping terms Norway was rather isolated on Europe's northern periphery. Since Britain was the centre of the nineteenth-century shipping world, brokers in the United Kingdom had an obvious advantage over competitors elsewhere. Part of this derived from the fact that British brokers were close to the largest pool of clients, but an even more important benefit accrued from being at the nexus of important information flows. Brokers in London or Liverpool generally had the best and most recent information and thus could serve the interests of shipowners with ambitions beyond domestically-oriented commerce better than potential competitors in towns like Christiania or Bergen.

Both these disincentives were removed about the same time. The laws limiting entrance into broking were repealed between 1871 and 1885.[10] The problem of isolation was eased by the completion in 1869 of the North Sea cable, which allowed Norwegian brokers virtually instantaneous access to the same information available to their colleagues in Britain. That the external disadvantage was the more serious barrier to the expansion of Norwegian shipbroking can be seen by the timing of the founding of Fearnley and Eger.[11] Thomas Fearnley established himself as a broker in 1869, the same year that the cable came into operation, but two years prior to the formal repeal of the restrictions upon brokerage activities in Christiania. Fearnley had spent four and one-half years in London working for the brokerage house of Rücker Offor and Co. The timing of his return to Christiania can only be

---

[9]Norway, Storting (Parliament), Meglerloven, 8 September 1818.

[10]The Norwegian parliament in 1870 repealed the national law, while allowing individual municipalities to retain restrictions. In Christiania the local provisions were ended in 1871, while they remained on the books in Bergen until 1885.

[11]At first, the firm merely existed in the name of Thomas Fearnley, becoming Fearnley and Eger in 1874 when Fearnley invited his cousin, Johan Engelhardt Eger, to become a partner.

explained by reference to the completion of the cable. Indeed, for all Norwegian brokers it is the consummation of the cable project, followed shortly thereafter by the repeal of the Brokerage Act of 1818, which enabled them to become potential competitors to the British.

Yet the completion of the cable, important though it was, did not by itself automatically confer upon Norwegian brokers the advantages necessary to become competitive. Instead, its principal impact was to heighten the importance of several other traits which determined success or failure. The first was access to information. The facts that a broker outside the United Kingdom needed were now available, but only if he knew how to gain access to them. The obvious solution was a good relationship with a well-connected firm in Britain, where most news arrived first. The second characteristic was analysis. Facts, in shipping or any other industry, do not speak for themselves; they need to be interpreted and put into some kind of coherent framework before they acquire significance. If shipbrokers could now obtain much more current information than previously, they still had to interpret it. This put a new premium on developing the skills necessary to translate raw data into coherent strategies and recommendations. Third, even if a broker could obtain and analyse information, he still had to have clients willing to pay for his advice. To gain this clientele required both access to shipowners and the ability to convince them that the broker's data and evaluation would generate profits. While "salesmanship" was always essential to a shipbroker's success, the communication revolution epitomised by the cable lowered the barriers to entry into the profession. By the turn of the century, there were more than one hundred shipbrokers in Christiania. If an individual broking firm could not satisfy its clients, it was no longer very difficult for a shipowner to find a replacement. And the tonnage glut which appeared by the mid-1870s and the resulting pressure on revenues provided shipowners every inducement to do this quickly if a broker failed to perform to their satisfaction.[12]

These three criteria, if fulfilled, would have allowed Norwegian brokers to grow within the domestic market. As we will see, Fearnley and Eger certainly exhibited all these traits prior to 1914. But there is a

---

[12]Lewis R. Fischer and Anders M. Fon, "The Making of a Maritime Firm: The Rise of Fearnley and Eger, 1869-1917," in Lewis R. Fischer (ed.), *From Wheelhouse to Counting House: Essays in Maritime Business History* (St. John's, 1992), 303-322. For information on the brokers, see Oslo City Archives, Christiania Address Books, various years; Oslo City Archives, Tax Lists, various years.

fourth characteristic which was essential to being truly competitive internationally and which to our knowledge no Norwegian broker developed in this era: independent access to international contacts other than through the intermediation of British brokers. On the eve of the war, Fearnley and Eger (and perhaps Grieg in Bergen) were on the verge of developing it, but it took the dislocations brought about by wartime conditions to enable the breakthrough to occur.

Nonetheless, the experience of Fearnley and Eger demonstrates how crucial each of the first three factors was to the early development of broking in Norway. Access to overseas sources of information was especially vital. Thomas Fearnley's most important contacts were with the London brokerage firm of H. Clarkson and Company. He first established these while he was employed at the rival London house, Rücker Offor and Co., between 1864 and 1869. The choice was fortuitous. By the 1860s Clarkson was increasingly becoming a specialist in Scandinavian shipping. Achieving prominence in the chartering of Norwegian shipping at the time was no easy task. In 1860 this market was dominated by two other large British concerns, Charles Northcote and Co. and W.S. Lindsay and Co. Neither firm, however, apparently was as assiduous in courting Norwegian interests as Clarkson. Indeed, Clarkson's offices became a favourite meeting place for Norwegian captains waiting for their vessels to be readied for sea. It is likely that Thomas Fearnley made a number of the contacts upon which he later built in Clarkson's "Captains' Corner."[13]

Central to the development of Clarkson's Scandinavian business were Carl August Granlund, a Swede from Hernösand, and Henry Benham, both of whom later became partners. Fearnley befriended them both. While Granlund appeared to take the young man under his wing, the contact with Benham may have been even more important, since he was on exceedingly good terms with Wilhelm Wilhelmsen, the Tønsberg shipowner who was then beginning his phenomenal rise in Norwegian shipping circles. It is likely that Benham either introduced the two or provided Fearnley with a letter of introduction. Regardless, Wilhelmsen would become one of Fearnley's most loyal customers and for a while

[13]Wasberg and Petersen, "Fearnley & Egers historie," 28; *The Clarkson Chronicle*, 14-24.

a partner in a shipowning venture, Fearnley and Wilhelmsen, founded in 1916.[14]

We do not know precisely when Fearnley began working with Clarkson on broking, but it must have been shortly after his return to Christiania.[15] For reasons that are not altogether clear, Fearnley apparently was dissatisfied with his existing relationship with Rücker Offor. At the same time, Clarkson appears to have perceived some advantage in working with Fearnley. In the early 1870s, the principal Clarkson connection in Norway was Ferdinand Breda. The fact that Breda was the largest broker in Christiania at the time underscores the importance of access to information as a primary determinant of competitiveness. Yet by 1872 Fearnley had apparently reached some sort of agreement to receive a share of Clarkson's broking business. As he wrote to Gunder Aas at Clarkson in April of that year,

> I can of course not for one moment doubt that you are in earnest regarding the principle of dividing commission as proposed...[yet] you can not class me with your sole and exclusive agents who have a share of everything you do with their respective towns whether they do it direct or indirect even if the business is done through other agents. I believe I have here to compete with Breda, who is placed on perfectly equal terms with me...[16]

Sometime in 1873 Clarkson appears to have agreed that at the beginning of 1874 Fearnley would become its exclusive agent in Christiania.[17] This was confirmed in a revealing letter that Fearnley

---

[14]On Wilhelmsen, see Leif B. Lillegaard, *Over alle hav. Wilh. Wilhelmsens rederi* (Oslo, 1986); Kr. Anker Olsen, *Wilh. Wilhelmsen i hundre år* (Oslo, 1962); Jan Petter Syse, *Wilh. Wilhelmsen 1861-1977: A Brief History* (London, 1978).

[15]Fearnley to Clarkson, 21 May 1869, Thomas Fearnley Copybooks, Fearnley and Eger Collection (hereafter F&E), Norwegian National Archives (Riksarkiviet). In this letter, Fearnley indicated that he had succeeded in fixing a Clarkson vessel and noted that the British firm had "booked 1.1/4% to me."

[16]Fearnley to Aas, 17 April 1872, Thomas Fearnley Copybooks, F&E.

[17]Fearnley to Clarkson, 18 September 1873, Thomas Fearnley Copybooks, F&E.

penned to Gunder Aas early in 1874: "Well, henceforth then we begin working exclusively with each other. On condition that you break off with Breda, we agree not to fix direct with any merchants in England."[18] From this point on, Fearnley and Clarkson attempted to dominate the freight market throughout eastern Norway. From Fearnley's perspective, this meant that he would share in any commissions involving Clarkson-chartered vessels trading to or from Norway, whether he actually performed any brokerage services or not.

Along with the broking relationship, of course, came a sharing of information. Fearnley routinely reported to Clarkson on the state of the Christiania market and at the same time regularly received up-to-date information from his British partner. Some came by letter, especially when it was not vital to help procure business. But much of it also used the new undersea cable. Just how vital this link was can be seen in a letter he wrote to the state telegraph company in March 1872 complaining about delays in delivering messages from the central telegraph bureau to his office. To prove that the delays were unconscionable, he enclosed a list of all telegrams received during the first two weeks of the month. The average delivery time--forty-seven minutes--he judged "excessive."[19]

Having gained access to the required information, Thomas Fearnley and his Norwegian colleagues next had to perfect techniques to interpret it. In a modern economy, the quickest method of securing this expertise would have been to purchase it from outside the firm. But in the early 1870s such proficiency was rare in Norway. This meant that in the first instance broking companies would have been forced to develop these skills internally. Since all the firms were small, a premium was placed upon the skills of the principals. Here Thomas Fearnley had an advantage in that he had spent a decade in learning his trade, first working on shipping-related matters for his uncle, N.A. Andresen, and then spending time with Rücker Offor in London.[20] Most of his competitors, on the other hand, had practical experience at sea but no

---

[18]Fearnley to Aas, 10 January 1874, Thomas Fearnley Copybooks, F&E.

[19]Fearnley to Den Norske Telegraph-Direction, 14 March 1872, Thomas Fearnley Copybooks, F&E.

[20]Wasberg and Petersen, *Fearnley & Eger*, 27; Thomas Fearnley, "Recollections," F&E.

real training in broking. In Christiania, both Rudolph and Axel Winge, who founded Winge and Company in 1855, had spent time at sea. When Axel withdrew in 1867, he was replaced by Plade Stranger, an ex-captain. Joachim Grieg, the founder of what was to become Bergen's largest broking house, also was a former master.[21]

Had Fearnley been able to concentrate solely upon broking, it is possible that he might have been able to utilise his expertise effectively to provide the needed analysis; it is certain at the very least that he would have enjoyed a substantial competitive edge over his rivals. But again the nature of the country in which he was based made it impossible for him to survive simply as a broker. Norway was in many respects just embarking upon the process of modernisation.[22] One of the economic characteristics of this type of society is a relative lack of specialisation. Among Norwegian brokerage firms, this was reflected in the fact that none in this period concentrated solely upon broking. While all were to a certain extent also interested in shipowning--a logical outgrowth which was characteristic of most brokerage firms outside Norway as well--the unspecialised nature of the commercial economy led most to dabble in other businesses. Fearnley provides a useful example. From the outset, much of his energy was devoted to attracting foreign companies for whom he could act as agent. Some of the agencies he established fit well with broking. Representing the British firms Vivian and Sons and D. Andersen of Company, both of which sold shipbuilding materials, copper and anti-fouling devices, made sense. So too did serving as a purchasing agent for a number of foreign timber merchants, including Tondeur, Lempriere and Co. of Paris and its Australian arm, O. Tondeur and Co. of Melbourne (1869); Wright, Dahl and Co. of London (1872); and With. Webster and Co. and London (1873). He also was heavily involved in insurance, representing a variety of life and marine insurance companies before founding its own insurance firm, Fearnley and Egers Assuranceforretning, in 1916. In 1869 he became the agent for the Eagle Insurance Company of London, which specialised in life insurance. By 1874 the firm had become the Norwegian agent for one of the leading

[21]Olsen, *Mitt skip er lastet av*, 131; Pettersen, Engelsen and Grieg, *The Sound of Grieg*, 8.

[22]The best study of the nineteenth-century Norwegian economy is Fritz Hodne, *Norges Økonomisk historie, 1815-1970* (Oslo, 1981).

Swedish insurance companies, Sveriges Allmänna Sjöforsäkrings-Aktiebolag; two years later, the firm became the agent for both Norway and Sweden for the Scottish Imperial Insurance Companies. The company also came to represent two Norwegian marine insurance companies, Den Gjensidige Dampskibsassuranceforening of Grimstad (1879-1900) and Den Vestfoldske Skibsassuranceforening of Tønsberg (1876-1883).[23] Others agencies, however, were far removed from his main maritime interests. Wine importing and distribution for firms such as Wisdom and Warter of London, A. Jordan of Koblenz, W. and J. Graham of Oporto, Eschemauer, Bennecke and Co. of Bordeaux, and Perrier, Jovet and Co. of Espernay became a speciality. He also sold raisins, nutmeg and figs for William Huelen and Co. of Malaga, candles for De Nederlandsche Palmitinefabriek of Amsterdam, and coffee for M. Mathiesen and Co. of Altona.[24]

This type of frenetic search for outside business obviously limited the time he could devote to data analysis. In this context the relationship with Clarkson takes on a slightly different nuance. The agreement to share commissions jointly provided Fearnley with valuable income with which to expand his staff and to train others to undertake the necessary analysis. In this respect, the hiring in 1878 of Carl O. Lie was likely the most important decision Thomas Fearnley ever made. When Lie joined the firm, he was only fifteen. Yet while he may have been young, he was sufficiently precocious that two years later when the firm decided to establish a separate chartering department he was selected as its first head. For the next forty-one years Lie more than anyone was responsible for the success that Fearnley and Eger enjoyed in shipbroking. Indeed, when the Fearnley and Eger Chartering Company was separated from the shipping firm in 1917, Lie was named the first managing director, a post he held until his retirement in 1921. When he died in 1924, Olaf Dahl in his eulogy called him a "born shipbroker" who was both "competent and respected." Perhaps Carl Lie was born for his profession, but the evidence suggests that he was trained by Thomas Fearnley. Equally

---

[23]These investments are summarized in Wasberg and Petersen, *Fearnley & Eger*, 37-38. For further examples of his interest in agency work, see Thomas Fearnley to Duncan and Shaw, 12 February 1869, Fearnley Copybooks, F&E; Fearnley to H. Clarkson and Company, 21 May 1869, Thomas Fearnley Copybooks, F&E.

[24]Background material to Arne Kildahl, "Fearnley & Egers historie, 1869-1944" (Unpublished mss., F&E).

important, he instructed others: by the early 1890s the firm employed nine full-time brokers and by 1905, eleven, all of whom had been trained in analysis by Lie.[25] It was by this process that Fearnley and Eger developed the ability to provide its customers with the necessary analysis.

The final part of the equation was an ability to market the product. The most important factor was to recruit and retain clients. In this regard, Fearnley began with a decided advantage over the domestic competition. He began recruiting clients by building upon contacts already developed. He commenced with his mother's family, the Andresens, an important Christiania banking and business family, who responded by immediately naming him the exclusive broker for all vessels in which they had shares. He also brought back with him the agency for Rücker Offor, which provided prestige albeit disappointingly little business. His contacts with Norwegian captains and owners were apparently more lucrative and hence better cultivated: during his first year in Christiania he visited Drammen three times, Fredrikstad once, and Tønsberg, the home of Wilhelm Wilhelmsen, on two occasions. From the beginning, Wilhelmsen was his most prestigious client: in 1869 Fearnley arranged charters for at least four Wilhelmsen vessels, the *Hakon Adelsteen*, *London Packet* (chartered from Fredrikstad to London with 550 tons of ice), *Axel*, and *Skjold*, which was chartered for Australia with timber for O. Tondeur and Co., while the next year he orchestrated about a dozen more.[26] And hovering in the background, never far from the surface, was the relationship with Clarkson. Indeed, even in his first year of operations, when the two firms had no formal arrangement, letters to Clarkson dominated his copy book. As far as we know, Fearnley's only formal dealings with Clarkson in 1869 were in the chartering of the *Nymphen* and a commission earned for helping Henry Benham buy a one-tenth share in the 536-ton newbuild *Vasa*, but the potential was too important for him to ignore.[27]

In 1870 Fearnley began a strategy that ensured growing revenue for his broking business: he started to invest in vessels. For a shipbroker to turn to investments in vessels was hardly unique, either in Norway or

---

[25] Box 39, F&E.

[26] Background material for Kildahl, "Fearnley & Egers historie," F&E.

[27] Fearnley to Gunder Anton Aas, 17 April 1872, Thomas Fearnley Copybooks, F&E; Balance Sheets, 1869 and 1870; F&E; Kildahl, "Fearnley & Egers historie," I, 20.

abroad. Indeed, some of Norway's more important shipowners, including Wilhelmsen, began this way. And internationally, the mixing of broking and owning was always typical. Such a strategy was eminently rational, since the barriers to entry in broking--in particular, the capital requirements--were obviously much lower. But the lure of shipowning--and likely the potentially high profits that could be earned--soon convinced most would-be brokers to concentrate upon ownership. Nonetheless, it is important not to lose sight of the fact that Thomas Fearnley, and later Fearnley and Eger, continued to depend upon broking as the backbone of the firm.[28] These earliest investments in vessels demonstrate an important feature of the strategy that would be followed throughout the years. Fearnley's pattern of investment was exceedingly conservative. In none of these vessels did he invest by himself; in each case, he was a minority shareholder. Indeed, we do not know of a single instance prior to World War I in which the company acquired an entire vessel on its own account. This behaviour, of course, had the advantage of spreading risks in an industry in which the peril of watching helplessly as a valuable asset was lost was always very real. If it placed obvious limits on capital accumulation, it also helped to ensure that the firm would not be imperilled by a single unforeseen occurrence. Moreover, this strategy made sense for a company that was especially interested in shipbroking. By owning a share in a vessel, Fearnley practically guaranteed himself the chartering business. While a vessel in which he had a share *might* generate profits, it would *certainly* yield commissions from chartering.

For most of the prewar period, Fearnley and Eger's clients were either domestic shipowners or individuals engaged in trade to or from Norway. In choosing to specialise in this way the firm was adopting a strategy that was at once both safe and dangerous. It was circumspect in that it avoided the possibility of ruffling the feathers of the larger brokers outside the country. It also enabled Fearnley--and other Norwegian brokers, all of whom appear to have adopted similar strategies--to develop strong relationships with their clients. But it was hazardous in that it made Fearnley and Eger a captive of the investing and deployment practices of Norwegian shipowners. Indeed, in order to comprehend why the pattern of Norwegian broking developed in the way it did requires an examination of the predilections of domestic owners.

---

[28]The shipowning side of Fearnley and Eger's activities is discussed in great detail in Wasberg and Petersen, *Fearnley & Eger*.

One of the characteristics of Norwegian shipping in the last third of the century was a continuing reliance on sailing vessels. Shipowners in various countries responded to the prospects and challenges of steam in very different ways. Some nations, such as Britain, Germany, France and Belgium, were relatively quick to adapt steam technology; the merchant marines of all these nations were more than sixty percent steam by 1890. Others, like Canada, the United States, and Finland, were slower to make the transition. Norway was in this second group. By 1869, its shipowners had responded almost imperceptibly to the technological challenge; only 1.5% of its vessels and 1.2% of tonnage lay in the holds of steamers. Not until 1890 would Norwegians begin to invest in steamers to any great degree, and even in 1900 steam vessels accounted for only about a third of the fleet's carrying capacity.[29] Instead, Norwegian shipowners clung to an older technology--the wooden sailing vessel. They had a good deal of success with this strategy, wresting often impressive profits.[30]

From this investment pattern also followed particular characteristics of deployment. The first was a continuing dependence upon the home market. As a small country with limited absorptive capacity and few bulk exports, Norway provided a freight market which was relatively protected from more technologically-advanced competitors and hence a secure employment base for domestic shipowners. Second, Norwegians were able to dominate the carriage of the lowest grade of bulk cargoes. Timber, in particular, was a commodity for which older Norwegian sailing vessels were well-suited. Commanding low freight rates and flexible delivery horizons, wood products provided virtually a guaranteed cargo. Third, with a fleet by and large non-competitive on many of the world's trade routes, Norwegian shipowners as a group were forced to act entrepreneurially in seeking out specialty trades. For sailing vessels,

---

[29]Helge W. Nordvik, "The Shipping Industries of the Scandinavian Countries, 1850-1914," in Lewis R. Fischer and Gerald E. Panting (eds.), *Change and Adaptation in Maritime History: The North Atlantic Fleets in the Nineteenth Century* (St. John's, 1985), 117-148; Lewis R. Fischer and Helge W. Nordvik, "Floating Capital: Investment in the Canadian and Norwegian Merchant Marines in Comparative Perspective, 1850-1914," *Scandinavian-Canadian Studies*, III (1988), 17-42..

[30]Lewis R. Fischer and Helge W. Nordvik, "From Broager to Bergen: The Risks and Rewards of Peter Jebsen, Shipowner, 1864-1892," *Sjøfartshistorisk Årbok 1985* (Bergen, 1986), 37-68.

this to a great extent meant long-distance trades, especially those which also utilised primitive loading facilities; sail continuing to dominate such commerce until the First World War. And when Norwegians began investing in steam, they frequently sought out other niches, such as the Central American fruit trade, the carriage of pilgrims to Mecca, and Chinese coasting.[31]

These investment and deployment traits had several consequences for shipbroking. The first was that Norwegian brokers likely derived a greater share of total income from the sale and purchase of second-hand vessels than did their typical British counterpart. And given the predilection of Norwegian owners to operate their wooden sailing vessels until they were no longer seaworthy, it is probable that it was in the purchase rather than the sale of assets that the most money was to be made. We do not possess sufficiently good accounting data to test these conclusions empirically for the entire period, but scattered evidence seems to support it. The year 1873 may have been more or less typical. In that year we know that Fearnley was involved in the sale of the schooner *Sakuntala*, which fetched 3600 speciedaler in May. In July, the barque *Nelly* was sold for 8600 speciedaler. Also handled were contracts for the 171-ton brigantine *Lucinda* and the 389-ton schooner *Louise*. The 163-ton schooner *Marie*, which was sold in November 1873 but not formally transferred until January 1874 for 5650 speciedaler, earned Fearnley and Eger a one percent commission. While it is unclear whether this represents all the sales and purchase activity for the year, we can nonetheless make some calculations. If we assume that all the transactions earned a one percent commission, and if we assume that the *Lucinda* and *Louise*, for which we do not know the sale prices, fetched the same price per ton as the *Sakuntala* (both of which were also schooners), Fearnley would have earned about four hundred kroner in commissions. This would have represented about 1.5% of the value of

[31]For a complete discussion of the patterns of Norwegian vessel deployment in this period, see Lewis R. Fischer and Helge W. Nordvik, "New York, Rio or Batavia? The Deployment Patterns of the Canadian and Norwegian Merchant Marines, 1860-1900," in Lewis R. Fischer and Helge W. Nordvik (eds.), *Across the Broad Atlantic: Essays in Comparative Canadian-Norwegian Maritime History, 1850-1914* (St. John's, 1992), forthcoming.

the company, including all his stakes in vessels, a goodly sum for a developing company.[32]

A second consequence was that chartering reflected national deployment patterns. We have been able to quantify the surviving charter parties only for the years 1871-1875 and 1891, but the results are instructive. In the first period, an analysis of the 412 surviving agreements shows some definite patterns. First of all, during the entire five-year period there was not a single time charter; all were for specific voyages and cargoes. It was not unusual in this period for shipowners to reject the security of a time charter for the potential windfall profits of voyage charters. With freight rates high and rising, such behaviour is understandable. Yet the complete absence of time charters among Fearnley and Eger's agreements is also a reflection of the dependent position of Norwegian brokers. To arrange lucrative employment required far better contacts than Norwegian brokers had. Instead, it was the British brokers who led in this type of business. By 1880, for example, one estimate is that fully half of all charter parties arranged by London brokers were time charters; Fearnley and Eger would not reach this threshold until after World War I.[33]

Moreover, every surviving agreement was for a sailing vessel. As Fearnley admitted in 1876, "we ourselves [are]...mostly engaged in the managing of sailing vessels." Not surprisingly, wood was by far the dominant cargo, accounting for eighty-eight percent of all the charter parties. Eighty-five percent of the wood charters were from three locales: Norway (41%), the Baltic (36%) and Canada (15%). In 1871, almost sixty percent were from Norway, but in the years 1872-75 the majority of charters were from the Baltic. Throughout, the preponderance of these charters (44%) went to Britain, which is hardly surprising given both the demand in the British market and Fearnley's particular connections. Another twelve percent went to France, where Fearnley had developed especially strong connections with firms such as Orlog and Berner in Paris. The French market had always been potentially important to Fearnley. In fact, in early 1870 he commented that he intended to visit France to ensure that a greater share of chartering for vessels in the

---

[32]Box 39, F&E.

[33]See the discussions in Blake, *Gellatley's*, chapter 2; and Long, *A Shipping Venture*, 32-41.

timber trade to France was moved to Christiania, "where it belongs." A final ten percent of wood cargoes went to the Netherlands. No other cargo came close to rivalling wood in Fearnley's business dealings.[34]

In 1891, wood remained the dominant cargo, accounting for thirty-six percent of the extant charter parties. Wood pulp, a new cargo, contributed an additional twelve percent. But even their combined contribution was considerably less than the share accounted for by wood and wood products in the 1870s. The reliance upon Norway remained, however: three-quarters of all timber charters originated in Norwegian ports and all the wood pulp agreements were for cargoes originating domestically. About forty-six percent of the wood charters were destined for the United Kingdom and twenty-eight for France, suggesting that the firm's connections in those areas remained strong. Among the wood pulp charters, fifty percent were for England and thirty-four percent for France.

If wood were less dominant than it had been in the firm's dealings in the 1870s, coal had clearly assumed a greater importance. Almost twenty-seven percent of all charter parties were for coal. All originated in England; seventy-seven percent of the voyages were destined for Norway and another ten percent to either Sweden or Denmark. Most of the Norwegian agreements were with H.A. Paulsen and P.O. Holter in Christiania.[35]

While no other cargo contributed significantly to Fearnley and Eger's chartering business, what is striking is the increased breadth of cargoes in which the firm now chartered. While most still involved trade to or from Norway or the immediate region, there was some evidence of spatial dispersion to more distant parts of Europe and overseas. Moreover, about two percent of all charter parties were now for time charters, another obvious difference compared to the 1870s. The reliance upon Norwegian cargoes and owners remained strong, but it was less pronounced than it had been a decade and a half earlier.

By the early 1890s Fearnley and Eger had exploited their comparative advantages to become an important presence on the Christiania broking scene. As Norwegians began to invest in steam over the next two decades, the focus of shipowning began to shift away from

---

[34] *Ibid.*

[35] *Ibid.*

ports like Bergen toward the capital. The firm was thus ideally situated in the last years before the war to begin to break out of purely domestically-oriented broking and into the international arena. Along with Grieg in Bergen, it did just that over the next few years.

An understanding of this process requires a brief flashback. Thus far we have discussed only contacts with Britain. Important as these were for initial growth, it appears clear that British brokers were more interested in gaining access to the opportunities presented by the large Norwegian fleet than they were in fostering competitive brokers in Norway. To admit this, of course, is only to suggest that British brokers had a keen grasp of their own self-interest. To see how this dependency was maintained, we can examine Fearnley and Eger's first attempts to establish a relationship with a non-British broker. This was with the firm of Benham and Boyeson in New York. The Norwegians introduction to the firm came through Clarkson. Henry Benham, one of Thomas Fearnley's patrons, had a brother named Isaac, who had operated as a grain shipper in the Danubian port of Ibrail. In the early 1870s he apparently gave up this business and went to London to consult with his brother about future options. While there was no room for Isaac Benham at Clarkson, Henry conceived the idea of sending him to New York as a shipbroker. But since Isaac's experience as a broker was negligible, the two recruited Boye C. Boyeson, the London representative of Norske Veritas, as a partner. Henry Benham went to New York with his brother and Boyeson to establish the firm; after some initial difficulties it flourished.[36]

Given Thomas Fearnley's close relationship with Henry Benham, he might have expected that the relationship with Benham and Boyeson would flourish. Yet while Fearnley and Eger had a number of dealings with the New York brokers over the years, most of it was in sale and purchase rather than chartering. As long as Norwegians remained interested in buying second-hand sailing vessels, Thomas Fearnley was an important man to know. But given the world-wide glut of tonnage in this period, it was not in the self-interest of either his London or New York friends to allow him to have an independent position in chartering. While Fearnley and Eger was able to arrange some employment for Norwegian vessels through Benham and Boyeson, the relationship did not fundamentally alter the nature of the firm's broking, as the 1891 charter

[36] *The Clarkson Chronicle*, 28.

party analysis above showed. As with so much else, World War I would change the nature of this relationship.

But even before the war, the firm began to make some progress in breaking out of the dependent relationship with Clarkson. Some of this was a result of the continuing enlargement of the staff in Christiania, which freed brokers to travel more and hence to make new contacts. About the turn of the century, for example, Carl Lie developed a remunerative business in chartering vessels in the timber trade to Egypt. More significantly, as early as 1910, the firm developed an interest in the groundnut trade from West Africa. This developed into a major broking activity from 1912 when Sverre Lie, Carl's son, made a trip to Bordeaux to put the chartering of vessels on a firm footing. Indeed, this West African commerce developed into a Norwegian specialty, with Fearnley and Eger occupying a central place. Shortly before the war the firm also entered the Asian market for the first time by negotiating several charter parties with the Shanghai broker, Wallem and Co.[37]

The first real success in denting the American market also occurred shortly before the war. After 1904 Fearnley and Eger developed a working relationship with the New York brokers, Winchester and Co. in New York. We do not know precisely how this developed, but it is clear that it was not through the intercession of Clarkson. A reasonable hypothesis would go something like this. Winchester had been successful at gaining lucrative contracts for the carriage of coal to Colon during the construction of the Panama Canal. This was a trade in which sailing vessels were still dominant, which made Norwegians logical sources of tonnage. Since Fearnley was the most visible broker in Norway with access to large amounts of sailing tonnage, an agreement was reached. Regardless, the relationship with Winchester not only strengthened the firm's connections with the growing port of New York but also enabled Fearnley and Eger for the first time to break the dependence on Clarkson. An added bonus was that Winchester had no stake in keeping a Norwegian firm out of time chartering. For the first time, Fearnley and Eger began to write a significant amount of this kind of business.[38]

---

[37]Interview with Ole Boe, 19 January 1944, F&E.

[38]*Ibid.*

When the First World War broke out, Norway was of course the leading owner of neutral tonnage.[39] As German U-boats took their toll on allied--and particularly, British--shipping, firms like Clarkson were no longer able to shut out competitors. Wartime exigencies enabled Norwegian brokers, including Fearnley and Eger, to become truly competitive in the international arena for the first time. With the return of peace, it proved impossible for British brokers to reconstruct their antebellum dominance.

This paper has tried to isolate the factors that enabled Norwegian brokerage firms to grow in the half-century prior to 1914. There were two preconditions which enabled domestic brokers to engross a larger share of their own market: the completion of the North Sea cable and the abolition of the Brokerage Act of 1818. Firms which became successful, like Fearnley and Eger, were able to exploit the new opportunities by creating important comparative advantages. The first was gaining access to the market information made available by the new technology. In the case of Fearnley and Eger, this came through an alliance with an important--and rapidly growing--British brokerage house. After gaining the information, successful firms devised strategies for analysing it. For Fearnley and Eger, this meant expanding the broking staff and developing sufficient expertise in competent people. Finally, by making alliances with important domestic shipowners, the firms that prospered were able to engross sufficient business to grow impressively. Yet as we have seen, prior to World War I there were very real constraints on this growth. Most broking was done either in partnership with larger British brokers or in relatively narrow trades for domestic owners. As Norwegian shipowners altered their investment and deployment habits--and as the international milieu changed--Norwegian brokers were finally able to enter the international arena as full-fledged competitors rather than dependent handmaidens of larger British houses.

---

[39]While the total carrying capacity of the U.S. fleet was larger than the Norwegian, American ocean-going tonnage was considerably smaller. Indeed, the American deep-sea fleet had stagnated after the Civil War; the growth that occurred was almost entirely in the coastal and Great Lakes' fleets. See Jeffrey J. Safford, "The Decline of the American Merchant Marine, 1850-1914: An Historiographical Appraisal," in Fischer and Panting (eds.), *Change and Adaptation*, 51-85.

Captain John Deane: Mercenary, Diplomat and Spy

Richard H. Warner[1]

In 1892 Count Evgenii Putiatin purchased a curious manuscript from a London bookseller entitled *A History of the Russian Fleet during the Reign of Peter the Great by a Contemporary Englishman, 1724*. Three years later he published a Russian translation of the document, which aroused interest in England when the Naval Records Society brought it out in its original form in 1899. Neither Putiatin nor the Naval Records Society editor were able to identify the author, the mysterious "Contemporary Englishman."[2] In 1934 a second account came into the possession of another maritime book collector, Captain Bruce Ingram. It was dedicated to King George I by a Captain John Deane and included an extra chapter entitled "The History Continued to the Commencement of 1725." Fortunately, *Mariner's Mirror* ran a notice of the authorship and printed the additional chapter, for when Ingram died in 1966 his manuscript was sold at auction and vanished once again.[3] This setback to scholarship has been compounded recently by the disappearance of the Putiatin version from the collection of the London School of Slavonic Studies. While Deane's *History* has endured as the finest account in any language of the emergence of the Russian Baltic fleet, little is known about the Captain's unique career as a mercenary, diplomat, and spy.

---

[1]The research in St. Petersburg for this paper was funded by a grant from the International Research and Exchange Board.

[2]E. Putiatin (trans.), *Istoriia Russiisskago flota v tsarstovannie Petra Velikago* (St. Petersburg, 1897). E.A. Cazalet, review of Count Poutiatine [sic], *The History of the Russian Fleet during the Reign of Peter the Great* in *Proceedings of the Anglo-Russian Society*, XV (1899), 27-31. Sir Cyprian A.G. Bridge (ed.), *History of the Russian Fleet during the Reign of Peter the Great (1724)* (London, 1899), XV.

[3]"The Authorship of the History of the Russian Fleet under Peter the Great," *Mariner's Mirror*, XX (July 1934), 373-376.

Research in Maritime History, No. 3 (December 1992), 157-173.

Most British naval officers who entered Russian service in this era were Jacobite refugees or persons whose careers had stalled in the demobilisation at the close of the War of Spanish Succession. The timing was perfect for the Tsar, for he was able to tap a talented pool of foreign combat officers when his need was greatest in the war against Sweden.[4] But Deane entered in 1711 as a lieutenant, before the demobilisation and at a lower rank than most, for he had no record of service as an officer in the British navy. Not a Jacobite, he was a refugee of quite a different sort. He fled to Russia to escape his reputation, which had been destroyed in one of the most infamous sea disasters of the era, the wreck of the *Nottingham Galley* on Boon Island off the New England coast in the winter of 1710. As master, Deane was responsible for the decision to cannibalize a dead crew member, an event which created a sensation when various accounts of the voyage were published in 1711.[5] Consequently, he welcomed the opportunity to enter Russian service and to disappear for eleven years. In a new career and a new country, he established himself as a daring and effective frigate commander, one of the leading commerce raiders of the Great Northern War.

The year 1712 was a watershed in the history of Russian naval development--the year after the Turkish victory on the Pruth forced Peter to abandon his plans for naval expansion in the south. As a result, the Tsar turned from the Black Sea toward the Baltic in order to consolidate his conquests in Livonia and to carry the war to the Swedes in Finland. Recognising that both objectives required the development of a deep-water fleet in the eastern Baltic, he began furious efforts to build ships at St. Petersburg, to purchase others abroad, and to man both with qualified officers. Deane was one of many officers promoted after the

---

[4]For an explanation, see Richard H. Warner, "Peter the Great's Combat Admiral, George Paddon, Captain R.N.," *Mariner's Mirror*, LXXV (February 1989), 7-18.

[5]The three versions of the wreck are Deane's first-person narrative published by his brother Jasper, *A Narrative of the Sufferings, Preservation, and Deliverance of Capt. John Deane and Company in the Nottingham Galley of London Cast Away on Boon Island near New England, December 11, 1710* (London, 1710); Christopher Langman [the mate], *A True Account of the Voyage of the Nottingham Galley of London, John Deane Commander, from the River Thames to New England, near which Place She was Cast Away on Boon Island, December 11, 1710* (London, 1711); and Deane's third person, "revised" edition, *A Narrative of the Shipwreck of the Nottingham Galley, Captain John Deane, Commander* (London, 1726).

great galley fleet victory at Hango Head in 1714.[6] Several months later he received command of the *Iaqudil*, a new fifty-two gun man-of-war, and was instructed to sail it from Archangel for service in the Baltic.[7] After a harrowing voyage, Deane was reassigned to the *Samson*, a thirty-two gun frigate on which he earned a reputation as one of the most successful combat commanders in the fleet.

During 1717 the diplomatic situation changed rapidly. As plans for an allied invasion of Sweden were abandoned, the Tsar visited Paris and Amsterdam in an effort to undermine Sweden diplomatically and to speed the development of his navy. He also began to explore the possibility of a negotiated settlement to the war; by winter he sent emissaries to the Åland Islands.[8] To strengthen his position, Peter inaugurated a campaign in the eastern Baltic to put the enemy on notice that the Russian navy had developed an offensive capability. In advance of the fleet the *Samson* reconnoitred the harbour and fortifications at Ostergarn on Gotland Island before rejoining the main armada later in the season. Deane won the admiration of Admiral Apraskin and in the winter was assigned to the squadron of Captain-Commodore van Hooft at Reval. The assignment was fortuitous for the Åland negotiations broke down and the Tsar decided to initiate a vigorous campaign against

---

[6] Deane's service record is in F. Veselago (ed.), *Obshchii morskoi spisok* (13 vols., St. Petersburg, 1885), I, 131-132.

[7] Tsentralnyi gosudarstvennyi arkhiv voenno-morskogo flota (Central State Historical Archive of the Navy) St. Petersburg (hereafter TGAVMF), 233/1/131/111, *Ukaz* of Count Apraskin to Captain Ivan Siniavin, 6 March 1715. This *ukaz* was published in F.M. Elagin (ed.), *Materialy dlia istoriia Russkago flota* (4 vols., St. Petersburg, 1887), I, 598-599.

[8] J.F. Chance, *George I and the Northern War* (London, 1909); L.A. Nikiforov, *Russko-angliiskie otnosheniia pri Petra I* (Moscow, 1950); Nikiforov, *Vneshniaia politika Rossii v poslednie gody severnoi voiny: Nishtadskii mir* (Moscow, 1959); J.J. Murray, "Scania and the End of the Northern Alliance (1716)," *Journal of Modern History*, XVI (1944), 81-92; R.E. Lindgren, "A Projected Invasion of Sweden, 1716," *Huntington Library Quarterly*, VII (1943-1945), 223-246; S.A. Feigina, *Alandskii Kongress: Veshnniaia politika Rossii v kontsu Severnoi voiny* (Moscow, 1959).

Swedish commerce from his base at Reval in 1718.[9] That spring, *Samson* put to sea with sealed orders to sail in the company of van Hooft on the *Pearl* "to cruise at large on the enemy coast, to hinder all trade with Sweden, and to take prizes of ships of all nations, French and Hollanders excepted."[10] Deane had extraordinary success, capturing eight vessels in three raids. Two were taken near Burgs Vik on Gotland Island, where he entered the harbour posing as a Swedish man-of-war, by his own account "amusing the people on the Swedish batteries with Swedish colours and friendly discourse."[11] On another occasion, after the *Samson* had forced a Swedish privateer to run aground, Deane dispatched a boarding party which stripped it of its ammunition and cannon.[12] At the close of the season, the *Samson* took several prizes near Pillau in the Gulf of Danzig, leading to complaints from Prussia and a confrontation with British and Dutch naval vessels.[13]

Commerce-raiding was complicated by enemy merchantmen, which frequently flew neutral flags and secured foreign passes, as well as by neutrals transporting goods to and from Sweden. Indeed, England and Holland added to the difficulties by using their navies to protect their mercantile interests from both Swedish privateers and Russian men-of-

---

[9]Apraksin to Prince Menshikov, 6 March 1717, in Elagin (ed.), *Materialy dlia istoriia*, I, 208; Apraksin to Peter I, 5 and 17 April 1717, *ibid.*, II, 196, 200; Capt. Sievers to Apraksin, 22 June 1717, *ibid.*, II, 228; van Hooft to Apraksin, 21 October and 4 November 1717, *ibid.*, II, 252, 254. See also Bridge (ed.), *History of the Russian Fleet*, 53-54.

[10]Bridge (ed.), *History of the Russian Fleet*, 58.

[11]TGAVMF 233/1/163/211, Deane to Apraksin, 21 May 1718.

[12]Bridge (ed.), *History of the Russian Fleet*, 57-58; TGAVMF 233/1/163/239-241, van Hooft and Deane to Apraksin, 3 August 1718.

[13]Bridge (ed.), *History of the Russian Fleet*, 60-61; Deane to Peter I, 20 August 1718, in Elagin (ed.), *Materialy dlia istoriia*, II, 306-307; Apraksin to Count Golovin, 20 February 1719, *ibid.*, II, 330-333. TGAVMF 233/1/255/286, Apraksin to Mardefeld, 2 November 1718, is a response to the Prussian minister's complaint about the ships seized at Pillau, reminding him of the state of war between Sweden and Russia.

war.[14] The incident in the Gulf of Danzig reflected all these factors. In late summer Deane had been ordered to enter Pillau to search for Captain Samuel Armitage of the *Prince Aleksander*, who had been arrested and had his vessel interned by the commandant of the port for taking a prize within sight of the harbour. This was frustrating for the Russians because Prussia was engaged in a lively commerce with their enemy. Unable to find the ship, Deane took two prizes, although his lieutenant was arrested on the same charges as Armitage. Leaving Pillau, Deane turned the prizes over to another ship. Then on 5 September, ten miles off Bruster Ort lighthouse, the *Samson* took two more prizes, which were identified by their papers as Swedish even though their masters produced passes claiming they were Dutch and English traders. While Deane was dividing his crew between the ships, an English frigate and a Dutch man-of-war appeared and demanded their release. The *Samson* was at a considerable disadvantage: with sails down, its crew separated and no junior officers, it faced two ships under full sail, with full complements of officers and men and twice as many guns. Deane was eventually forced to agree to a conference aboard the man-of-war at which he was compelled to forfeit his prizes.[15]

Though the incident did not provoke an immediate inquiry, it later led to Deane's court-martial, reduction in rank, and eventual dismissal. But in 1719 he was promoted to Captain and entrusted with a much bolder enterprise and greater responsibility. With the *Pearl* under van Hooft, he was employed once again for reconnaissance, this time off the great Swedish naval base at Carlskrona. There he took three prizes before being detached with the frigate *Landsdown* to intercept packet boats between Visby and Stockholm. The two cruised the entrance of the Stockholm inlet for seven days, taking fourteen prizes, including several

---

[14] David Aldridge, "The Navy as Handmaid for Commerce and High Policy, 1680-1720," in Jeremy Black and Philip Woodfine (eds.), *The British Navy and the Use of Naval Power in the Eighteenth Century* (Leicester, 1988), 64.

[15] A large amount of material relating to this incident appeared in testimony at Deane's trial and will be discussed below. One of the most interesting documents is Deane's log entry from 5 September 1718 in TGAVMF 1720/60/II/702.

packets.[16] Returning to Reval, Deane was reassigned temporarily to deliver the *Devonshire* to Kronstadt. On the journey two other vessels ran aground and were lost in foul weather. Though Deane conducted himself properly, his association with the incident was unfortunate, for he was called to account for the affair of the prizes in the Gulf of Danzig the year before and was charged with accepting a huge bribe for their release.[17]

On 30 October 1719, Rear-Admiral Sievers wrote to the Admiralty that "while he was taking prizes at Danzig, Captain Deane, formerly of the frigate *Samson*, freed them for a payment of 500 chervonets."[18] In the new year Sievers was directed to conduct an investigation, including an examination of the officers of the *Samson*; in May he was ordered "to convene a court martial without delay."[19] Deane argued that the incident had occurred "almost two years since," that he "had no reason to believe that it would be called a second time," and that his "actions were later approved by other officers."[20] He was no doubt aware that conditions had changed considerably in the interim and that he was caught in the larger web of political rivalry triggered by the recent death of Rear-Admiral Paddon which cost the English officers in Russian service their patron while the older Dutch and Dano-Norwegians saw theirs, Captain-Commodore Sievers, advance to command of

---

[16]Apraksin to van Hooft, 7 April 1719, in Elagin (ed.), *Materialy dlia istoriia*, 345; Veselago (ed.), *Obshchii morskoi spisok*, I, 131-132; Bridge (ed.), *History of the Russian Fleet*, 64-75. A convenient summary of the 1719 activity is TGAVMF 233/1/177/237-238, Deane and Alexander Apraksin to Admiral Apraksin, 18 May 1719. Alexander Apraksin, the Admiral's nephew, was in command of his first ship and Deane's support won the Admiral's gratitude. See also Great Britain, Public Record Office (PRO), State Papers (Foreign), Russia (Misc.), SP 91/107, Captain John Deane's Account of Affairs in Russia, June and July 1725.

[17]Veselago (ed.), *Obshchii morskoi spisok*, I, 131-132; Bridge (ed.), *History of the Russian Fleet*, 58.

[18]TGAVMF 233/1/177/56, Sievers to Apraksin, October 30, 1719, excerpted in Elagin (ed.), *Materialy dlia istoriia*, 441.

[19]*Ibid.*

[20]TGAVMF 212/1720/60/II/750-752, Final Statement of Captain John Deane for his Court Martial, 9 July 1720.

the fleet. Sievers catered to his own constituency and to the junior Russian officers, who were offended by the recently arrived British and who themselves coveted promotion and command.[21]

In the investigation, eleven officers from the *Samson* provided similar written testimony describing the difficulty of the *Samson's* position. Though none faulted Deane, all seemed encouraged to comment that he had not attempted to resist. Most telling, however, no one accused him of accepting money for the release of the prizes.[22] Admiral Sievers cross-examined Deane in December and allowed him to write a separate explanation for boarding the Dutch warship. Deane added a final statement, arguing that "because of the presence of the English fleet at Bornholm and that our fleet was at sea, I felt it would not be wise to create an incident which might cause conflict."[23] When asked if he "had served his own interests," Deane responded unequivocally that "I swear that I have never taken money or gifts for release of the prizes."[24]

In his closing statement, Deane made an eloquent appeal for consideration of his record as commander. He wanted to leave Russian service with his reputation intact and attempted to lay the foundation for this. A year earlier he had discussed the possibility with Ambassador Jeffereyes, and in the course of the investigation he hoped that Admiral Apraksin might intervene on his behalf. The admiral thought well of Deane both for his performance and most particularly for the kindness he had shown his nephew.[25] On 8 December, before he had even given testimony, the admiral granted Deane a pass "releasing him from service

---

[21]Warner, "Peter the Great's Combat Admiral," 15-17.

[22]TGAVMF 212/1720/60/II/711-727, Testimony of the Over and Under Officers of the *Samson*, 8 January 1720.

[23]TGAVMF 212/1720/60/II/703-704, "Reasons Why I Went Aboard the Dutch Man-of-War on September 5, 1718."

[24]TGAVMF 212/1720/60/II/739, Admiral Sievers' Cross-examination of Captain John Deane. See also TGAVMF 212/1720/60/II/750-752, Closing Statement of Captain John Deane at his Court Martial at St. Petersburg, 7 July 1720, in which he wrote that "I never decidedly acted anything to the prejudice of His Majesty's interests."

[25]See note 16.

at his own request to return to his homeland."[26] But he never got a chance to use it.

Deane was found guilty "of ignorance of the calling of an officer, for abandoning his ship and command,...for failure to hold prizes taken and for being himself taken prisoner." The court recommended dismissal from service and a year in prison, which the Tsar reduced to demotion to the rank of lieutenant and service in Kazan.[27] After the peace of Nystadt, Deane was released but not rehabilitated. In November, he was formally dismissed from service and expelled from the country with the ominous warning from the tsar's own manifesto that "...he never be permitted to return to Russia."[28] Curiously, the following February Apraksin interceded and wrote a letter providing him with another passport on which he was again described as *Captain Deane*, "...who has served for the past several years in his Tsarist Majesty's fleet as a captain, is by his own request separated from service, to return to his homeland or wherever he desires without restriction."[29] Deane thus left Russia as a Captain, a title he used for the rest of his life, with no mention of any malfeasance, judicial action, or exile on his record. For the last time Apraksin had shown him a sign of favour and patronage, permitting him an honourable departure from Russian service.

Captain Deane returned to England in 1722 and disappeared from public view until the spring of 1725, when he was employed by the British Foreign Office to act as commercial consul in Saint Petersburg. In 1722, Deane republished *The Shipwreck of the Nottingham Galley* and wrote his *History of the Russian Fleet under Peter the Great*, using the books to promote himself in government circles.[30] He came to the

---

[26]TGAVMF 212/1720/60/II/737, Passport given to Captain Deane, 8 December 1719.

[27]TGAVMF 212/1720/60/II/728, *Ukaz* of 11 May 1720; TGAVMF 212/1720/60/II/920, *Ukaz* of 9 August 1720.

[28]TGAVMF 212/1721/4/346, *Ukaz* of 15 November 1721.

[29]TGAVMF 233/1/259/24, Passport given to Captain Deane, 5 February 1722.

[30]This account of the wreck was identical to the 1711 edition except that it omits Jasper Deane's introduction. It seems that the wreck that destroyed his reputation in 1711 had become an asset by 1722. See Captain John Deane, *A Narrative of the Sufferings...as it was printed in 1711 and now reprinted in 1722* (London, 1722). This version of the

attention of persons at the pinnacle of government, including Robert Walpole and Lord Townshend, head of the Northern Department.[31] Haunted by the spectre of a Jacobite plot, these men felt deficient in Russian intelligence after the recall of their ambassador in 1722.[32] The timing could not have been more perfect. George Tilson, Under Secretary of the Northern Department, noted that he "undertook to be useful to us and showed a letter from Admiral Apraxin [sic], who seemed to be of power in that country, which persuaded us he might render service."[33] Although he was appointed commercial consul at Saint Petersburg, Townshend defined another more special duty, indicating that "he has a commission of consul from His Majesty to serve as a colour, but his true business is to transmit hither what intelligence he may be able to get for His Majesty's service."[34] Two months later Deane left for St. Petersburg.

From Elsinor on 26 May he sent a dispatch about the passage of three Russian ships through the Sound that further persuaded his superiors that the Russians were preparing to assist the cause of the Pretender.[35] While Deane may have dramatized his first dispatch, when the three mysterious ships later made port in Scotland before sailing on to Spain apprehension over Russian Jacobitism turned to alarm in the British Foreign Office.[36]

When Deane landed at Kronstadt on 2 June, he was immediately detained and interrogated by several officers, including his old patron,

---

History was the Putiatin manuscript (see note 2). The Ingram version was written and dedicated to George I in 1725.

[31]Cambridge University, Cholmondeley (Houghton) Mss. 1250, Townshend to Newcastle, 2 October 1725.

[32]Paul S. Fritz, *The English Ministers and Jacobitism between the Rebellions of 1715 and 1745* (Toronto, 1975), 130-131.

[33]PRO SP 43/9/239-240, Tilson to Townshend, 17 July 1725.

[34]PRO SP 95/37/211-212, Townshend to Points, 7 July 1725.

[35]PRO SP 91/9/387-388, Deane to Townshend, 26 May 1725.

[36]J.F. Chance, *The Alliance of Hanover* (London, 1923), 139; Fritz, *The English Ministers and Jacobitism*, 130.

Admiral Apraksin. The scene was confrontational. Deane first tried to conceal his commission, arguing that he "had come into Russia on [his] own private affairs." But the Admiral warned that if he "did not produce some commission, he should be obliged to use [him] ill." The following day on board Apraksin's flagship Deane was required to reveal his mission and to write what he claimed were his verbal instructions from Lord Townshend.[37] The Admiral turned less threatening, but despite several private expressions of friendship, did nothing more than facilitate the Captain's transportation to Saint Petersburg. In the capital Deane was interviewed by Chancellor Golovin and Count Tolstoy, denied accreditation, and quickly deported.

On the day of Deane's arrival, Apraksin notified the Empress, sending copies of his note to Golovin and Tolstoy.[38] On 8 June, Golovin replied that

> ...Deane served in the fleet and committed many crimes for which he was removed from service and sent to Kazan. He was released by the kindness of His Imperial Majesty, sent out of the country, and warned never to return. Why then should Her Imperial Majesty set aside what the Emperor ordered before?[39]

Golovin notified Apraksin that Deane would be given his passport.[40]

Deane later recalled that "after it was determined that I should be sent away, my chief study was how to gain future intelligence, besides what might be expected from Dr. [Thomas] Consett."[41] Engaging a man

---

[37]PRO SP 91/9/390-391, Deane to Townshend, 8 June 1725. This is a brief dispatch about his arrival and does not contain the richness of his reflective report in PRO SP 91/107, "Captain John Deane's Account of Affairs in Russia, June and July 1725." The "verbal instructions" from Lord Townshend that he was forced to produce were translated into Russian and sent to St. Petersburg; see TGAVMF 233/1/239/11, 4 June 1725.

[38]TGAVMF 233/1/239/6, Apraksin to Golovin, 2 June 1725; TGAVMF 233/1/239/6-7, Apraksin to Tolstoy, 4 June 1725.

[39]TGAVMF 233/1/289/20-21, Golovin to Apraksin, 8 June 1725.

[40]PRO SP 91/9/392-393, Deane to Tilson, 16 June 1725.

[41]PRO SP 91/107, "Captain Deane's Account of Affairs in Russia."

named Trescoud, formerly a seaman and a man of some education who kept a tavern in Saint Petersburg, he offered his services to attend to the schooling of the man's son in England. In return Trescoud assisted in getting him "privately in the company of an Irishman, a relative of General Lacy...named O'Connor [sic]" who had been "very active...for that party in different parts of the world for some years."[42] Through O'Conner the Captain was later able to claim a huge success for his mission, which appeared to have been such a disaster on the surface.

Convinced of his failure, Deane frantically warned Townshend and Tilson that "endeavours will be made use of to asperse and blacken me in order to justify these as well as former proceedings," and that "my adversaries have found means...of representing me a monster."[43] He portrayed himself as the victim of a sinister Jacobite conspiracy to undermine and destroy his mission for its own dark purposes. Knowing that his superiors shared this obsession and that such an explanation would be credible and convincing, he wrote that the Jacobites were "too powerful for a person so much suspected as I was."[44] Although Deane's Jacobite enemies were real, there was opposition from another quarter, which he mentioned just as prominently. The Russia Company merchants did not want a consul at all, and certainly not one that they had not chosen. The governor of the company, Benjamin Aylosse, challenged the right of the Foreign Office to make such an appointment, while another spokesman, Nathanial Gould, warned Lord Townshend "that Deane is very obnoxious to the Russian government and for which reason...his coming may prove very prejudicial to our mercantile affairs."[45] The English envoy in Sweden, Stephen Points, and Reverend Thomas Consett, the minister for the British factory in St. Petersburg, both wrote

---

[42]*Ibid.*

[43]PRO SP 91/9/398, Deane to Tilson, 5 July 1725.

[44]PRO SP 84/579, Deane to Tilson, 24 August 1725.

[45]PRO SP 91/107, Aylosse to Townshend, 2 July 1725; PRO SP 91/107, Gould to Townshend, 2 July 1725.

that the merchants were intertwined with the opposition and had allied themselves with the Jacobites.[46]

Deane wrote two reports in 1725. The first was his detailed "Account of Affairs in Russia, June-July 1725," a reflective political narrative compiled when he reached Hanover. It is a formal record of his mission and was directed to Lord Townshend.[47] The second was an intelligence report, replete with maps, entitled "The Present State of the Maritime Power of Russia," designed for use by the Admiralty.[48] Through these writings he was able to promote his interests, to justify all his actions and to prove his loyalty to "King and Country." Indeed, he pointed to a new direction where he could perform service. Despite the opposition, Deane's twenty-day sojourn in Russia proved more successful than he realized, for Lord Townshend offered the Captain his protection and patronage, even shielding him from the barbs of his own diplomats.[49] This led immediately to a new assignment in Amsterdam, then a second mission to the Baltic with Admiral Wager in 1726, and finally to a permanent post as commercial consul in Ostend for the ports of Flanders. Far from destroying his career, the mission to Russia in 1725 assured him one.

The "Account of Affairs in Russia" is a chronological description of Deane's mission, but it is most interesting for its perspective on politics and allegiances in the volatile period immediately after the death of Peter the Great. Deane noted that "upon my arrival in the country His Majesty's friends rejoiced believing that it might facilitate the reconciliation and be a check on the insolence of the Jacobites." But he warned that "the disaffected both in Russian service as well as in the Factory had on the news of my arrival spoke very positively that I should

---

[46]PRO SP 95/38/31-32, Points to Townshend, 7 July 1725; PRO SP 95/38/41-42, Points to Townshend, 14 July 1725; PRO SP 95/38/101-102, Points to Townshend, 4 August 1725; PRO SP 91/9/396-397, Consett to Townshend, 30 June 1725.

[47]PRO SP 91/107, "Captain John Deane's Account of Affairs in Russia."

[48]British Library (BL), Map Collection, K. Mar. II.51.5, "The Present State of the Maritime Power of Russia," accompanying maps, K. Mar. 51.1, Ladoga Sea; K. Mar. 51.3, Retusari (Kronstadt); K. Mar. 51.4, St. Petersburg.

[49]Townshend wrote to Points that "You know Capt. Deane as well as I do. I take him to be an honest man;" PRO SP 95/37/211-215, 7 July 1725.

not be admitted" and "that set of men...[endeavoured] to prevent a reconciliation betwixt the two crowns." They were not only treasonous to the government of their origin but also affiliated with the worst elements in Russian politics. According to Deane, he encountered a "united front of Holsteiners and the Jacobites, which were caballing and studying ways to frustrate my design."[50]

His report on maritime affairs was written for intelligence purposes and was quite capably done, providing detailed sailing instructions to Kronstadt, a complete description of its fortifications and armaments and an account of the manning of the fleet at all ranks. It featured the construction of vessels and a current standing of the fleet accompanied by a list of ships; though lost, the latter was probably identical to the revised list found in the second version of the *History*, written a few months later. He revealed that though many ships were unfit for sea, they were kept at Kronstadt because "the Czar takes infinite delight to view his ships in harbour, and [to] have the lists, when exaggerated, appear aboard." This did not present a problem, Deane reported, because "he has twice as many as he can man" and because "he will never cease to increase their number."[51]

What Lord Townshend valued most about Deane's service in 1725 was not what was conveyed in his reports or dispatches but what was conveyed in person once he reached Hanover. While in St. Petersburg, Deane had convinced a Jacobite courier, Edmund O'Conner, to betray the cause for the promise of "a good economic reward in proportion to his services and a pardon for what is past."[52] Since the whole affair played directly into the government's obsession with the Jacobite menace, Deane was immediately commissioned to meet O'Conner in Amsterdam to take delivery of correspondence from Russia.[53] So began an extraordinary winter of espionage involving Deane, O'Conner, and the notorious Jacobite agent, John Archdeacon.

A cousin of the mercenary General Lacy, Edmund O'Conner had gone to St. Petersburg to use his relatives' connections to obtain a

---

[50]PRO SP 91/107, "Captain John Deane's Account of Affairs in Russia."

[51]BL, K.Mar. II.51.5, "The Present State of the Maritime Power of Russia."

[52]PRO SP 84/579/139-140, Townshend to Deane, 2 October 1725.

[53]*Ibid.*

commission in the Russian army. Finding the rank offered unacceptable, he decided to seek better fortunes in Spain. Through Lacy, he was introduced to the Jacobite community in St. Petersburg and agreed to deliver correspondence in Amsterdam, Bordeaux and Madrid. Deane made contact with O'Conner in St. Petersburg through the tavern keeper Tresoud and arranged a rendezvous in Amsterdam.[54] After both had left the Russian capital, Reverend Consett, now Townshend's only remaining agent, warned that O'Conner had visited a prostitute prior to departing and may have jeopardised the entire affair. "He being very drunk and partly asleep, let some words drop, which she caught hold of," Consett reported, adding that she "did go to his cousin, General Lacy, and told him that O'Conner designed to betray their cause, and to make his own peace. But she is a woman of so bad reputation and he supposed to be so firmly attached to that party that it was not credited."[55] When Townshend received another report that the Jacobites had sent someone overland to intercept O'Conner, he immediately dispatched Deane to Holland to collect the correspondence.[56]

Deane made haste, writing that his objective was "to be here before my friend from Russia, which I thought might enable me to prevent...him making ill use of anything should he be inclined to act a double part." Deane later recalled that he "laid wait" for O'Conner "to be with him from the first minute in order to prevent his disposing of any letters without his letting me have sight of them." O'Conner made his delivery, assisted the Captain in copying them for Townshend, and then resealed them for delivery to Archdeacon in Rotterdam.[57]

---

[54]PRO SP 84/579/134-137, Deane to Townshend, 2 October 1725.

[55]*Ibid.*

[56]PRO SP 84/579/141-142, Townshend to Deane, 4 October 1725; PRO SP 91/9/396-397, Consett to Townshend, 30 June 1725; PRO SP 91/9/407-410, Consett to Townshend, 17 July 1725; PRO SP 91/9/411-412, Consett to Townshend, 9 August 1725.

[57]PRO SP 84/579/131, Deane to Townshend, 18 September 1725.

The correspondence confirmed the worst suspicions of those at the top of the British government.[58] Townshend immediately asked Deane to send O'Conner to Hanover for a personal interview and afterwards wrote Newcastle that the letters were genuine. He also noted that when coupled with other intelligence they constituted conclusive proof of a plan for a Jacobite attack in the spring, which might have been "fatal if it had not been discovered in time." There was a flurry of correspondence, as Walpole and his secretaries watched another Russian ship suspiciously pass the Sound.[59]

At the centre of the imbroglio, Deane wrote Townshend with a bold plan to penetrate the Jacobite conspiracy even further. He proposed to send O'Conner to Archdeacon in Rotterdam as originally agreed in St. Petersburg. This would preserve O'Conner's cover. Since he was well known to Archdeacon, he could reseal the letters in one of his own and mask the interception. Deane hoped that O'Conner might "get something from Archdeacon" and then if possible proceed to Gordon in Bordeaux before setting out for Spain or perhaps even Ireland, where he was well known.[60] Townshend decided not to risk discovery, but instead recommended that O'Conner be kept in hiding in Holland. He was well pleased and provided O'Conner with a pardon and one hundred pounds for his services, writing Deane that "you have upon this occasion done great service and may depend upon being well rewarded."[61]

In the spring of 1726 Deane was given a new assignment--to join Admiral Sir Charles Wager's fleet in the Baltic. The British government was panicked by reports that the Russians were preparing their fleet and a large expeditionary force for some unknown purpose. Wager was instructed to check any Russian attempt to assist the Duke of Holstein's

---

[58]PRO SP 46/6/145-150, Townshend to Newcastle, 2 October 1725; PRO SP 46/6/211-214, Townshend to Newcastle, 4 October 1725. The intercepted letters are in PRO SP 91/107, Thomas Gordon to Robert Gordon (Bordeaux merchant), 26 July 1725; William Hease to Messrs. Hease and William Waters (Paris bankers), 25 July 1725; and Sir Henry Stirling to Messrs. Butler and Kelly (Madrid merchants), 25 July 1725.

[59]PRO SP 84/579/171-172, Townshend to Deane, 19 October 1725; PRO SP 43/7/211-215, Townshend to Newcastle, 4 October 1725.

[60]PRO SP 84/579/134-137, Deane to Townshend, 2 October 1725.

[61]PRO SP 84/579/141-142, Townshend to Deane, 4 October 1725.

cause against Denmark or the Pretender's designs on England. Deane spent a peaceful summer aboard the flagship, *Torbay*, mostly anchored near Nargen Island off the port of Reval, where he consulted with the Admiral on Russian and Baltic affairs and established a close personal friendship with Wager that served him well in the future.[62]

At Reval, he again came into conflict with Thomas Saunders, the port admiral who had caused him such problems in 1725 and who now barred him from going ashore. Deane humorously reported that Saunders expressed

> much satisfaction at seeing me in Russia, which I (with equal truth) told him was occasioned by the great desire I had to see him and the rest of my good friends in this country. He compared me to Mercury by my quick removal from England to Petersburg, Stockholm, Hanover, the Hague, England, and now again to Reval.[63]

Deane's duties as before were to provide what his superiors wanted most in Russia, a network of agents able to keep a close watch on the Jacobite community. For that purpose he travelled to Helsinki aboard the frigate *Port Mahon* to gather intelligence and to recruit local officials as informers. He encountered little success.[64]

The most interesting result of the mission with Admiral Wager was a brief report entitled "The Present State of the Danes, Swedes, and Russians in Respect to One Another and to the English Fleet in the Baltic in the Year 1726."[65] Though signed with the initials "C.W.," J.F.

---

[62]Deane wrote seven dispatches while on the cruise from 26 April to 11 October 1726. They are filed with those of Sir Charles Wager in PRO SP 42/77. When the voyage was finished Wager wrote Tilson from Spithead on 30 December 1726 that "I fear [Deane's] money is all out. I wish my Lord would remedy this. I think him a very honest man."

[63]PRO SP 42/77, Deane to Tilson, 20 July 1726.

[64]PRO SP 25/77, Deane to Townshend, 14 June 1726.

[65]PRO SP 43/77.

Chance is probably correct in suggesting that Deane was the author.[66] Despite its title, the report was not a comparison of the fleets in the Baltic but an analysis of the political events of that summer. It describes the "apprehensions" of the Danes over the Holstein parties in Sweden and Russia and the political rivalries and instability in both countries in the wake of the deaths of Charles XII and Peter the Great. When the mission was over the report reassuringly concluded that "it is wonderful to see the Swedes...tremble at the name of the Russians" and that "it does not seem at all to be the interest of the Russian nation to begin a new war, which might probably end to their disadvantage." The report testified to the great economic and political problems caused by over two decades of conflict, so that even the victorious Russians "have already more conquered country than they know what to do with." The report indicated that the mission of threatening the Russians in their own territory in the summer of 1726 had worked splendidly.[67]

Even if some of the enterprise was fanciful, Deane had proved his worth to his superiors and was rewarded with the post of commercial consul for the ports of Flanders. For a decade he was first Townshend's and then Harrington's "watchful eye" and played a major part in the suppression of the Ostend East India Company.[68] He later retired in Nottingham, living to the age of eighty-three and dying in 1762.

While in Russia, Amsterdam and the Baltic, Captain Deane established himself as a resourceful and effective spy and won praise from his superiors, who were grateful for his ability to track the shadowy Jacobite movement abroad. He also established himself as a knowledgeable expert on Russian naval affairs and was recognized as such by being employed in the fleet in 1726 as an advisor to the commanding admiral. Deane's *History of the Russian Fleet under Peter the Great* and his other reports testify to his competence and justify his designation as the first expert on Russian naval affairs.

---

[66] J.F. Chance, *The Treaty of Hanover: A Study of British Foreign Policy in the Last Years of George I* (London, 1923), 348.

[67] *Ibid.*

[68] PRO SP 77/75-86 contains an enormous body of material on Deane's service in Flanders.

Her Majesty's Coastguard

Walter Minchinton

One organisation which occupies the interface between land and sea--comprised of those who normally live on shore but whose work regime is determined by the deep--is the coastguard. Known in the past by various names, the term "coastguard" has won acceptance in most nations to describe organisations with a range of responsibilities, the precise composition of which depends upon needs and available facilities. Although they also have other functions, most are now principally concerned with lifesaving and search and rescue.

Although in Britain the Board of Customs long had responsibility for collecting duties and preventing the evasion of payment by smugglers, the Coastguard was established in 1822 as the result of a report[1] which recommended that since the existence of separate agencies led to a duplication of effort, a new service comprising the Preventive Water Guard,[2] the Revenue Cruisers,[3] and the Riding Officers[4] should be

[1]See Great Britain, Parliament, House of Commons, *Parliamentary Papers* (hereafter *BPP*), "Twelfth Report of the Commissioners...for Securing and Improving the Revenue" (1822), XI, 82-98. The full story of HM Coastguard has yet to be told, but see William Webb, *Coastguard! An Official History of HM Coastguard* (London, 1976). For a list of Parliamentary papers regarding the Coastguard, see *Subject Catalogue of the House of Commons Parliamentary Papers, 1801-1900* (Cambridge, 1988), V, 522-524.

[2]This service was established in 1809 to apprehend vessels which evaded the revenue cruisers to operate in coastal waters. The coasts of England and Wales were divided into three districts: from London to Land's End; from Land's End to Carlisle (including the Scilly Isles); and from London to Berwick. There were twenty-three cruisers and forty-two boats on the southern coast; ten cruisers and thirteen boats in the west; and nine cruisers and thirteen boats on the east coast (*BPP*, [1822], XI, 90). They were placed under the control of the Treasury in 1816.

[3]These were operated at sea under the control of the Admiralty.

Research in Maritime History, No. 3 (December 1992), 175-189.

combined as the Coast Guard (initially spelled as two words).[5] This amalgamation was designed to provide a triple cordon around Britain to prevent smuggling and to monitor the wartime movement of passengers, intelligence and correspondence. The report also recommended that the new force should operate under the Board of Customs, although the Admiralty was to appoint its officers. Since 1822 the Coastguard has been the subject of numerous reviews designed principally to make it more efficient while reducing costs. These changes have regrettably resulted in the dispersal and loss of records, which render it difficult to write a proper history of the service. Nonetheless, we at least are able to determine that its functions have altered over time. Its operation is best described in three phases, which to some extent overlap. In the first phase its main role was to protect the revenue; from the mid-nineteenth century until the 1920s it served as a Naval reserve; and finally, since 1925 its main function has been search and rescue.

The Protection of the Revenue

With income from import duties providing the main source of government revenue and a complicated (and often high) tariff schedule, smuggling became a major industry. While for centuries officials had tried to check this activity, their efforts met with little success. At the end of the Napoleonic wars there was a great revival in smuggling; to deal with this a Coastal Blockade, consisting initially of ninety-two officers and men, was established in 1817 to provide special protection to the most vulnerable portions of the Kent and Sussex coasts between the Isle of Sheppey and Beachy Head.[6] In addition, the Navy provided ships and men for revenue duties to supplement the work of the three branches of the Preventive Service.

---

[4]These were founded in 1699 after lengthy discussions between the Board of Customs and the Treasury to prevent goods being smuggled inland. Originally under Treasury control, the 299 officers were stationed along the coasts of Kent, Sussex and Hampshire. They remained in operation under the Board of Customs until 1865.

[5]The term "coastguard" does not seem officially to have been employed as a single word until the Coastguard Act of 1925.

[6]*BPP* (1822), XI, 87-88.

The earliest and most complete survey of the original Coastguard was provided in the 1822 report, which itemized the size and cost of each of the services to be amalgamated (see Table 1). In addition, 2375 naval personnel aboard ships at Plymouth, Portsmouth, Sheerness and Leith were to be employed at a cost of £154,399. Possibly because the numbers were calculated differently, the total strength of the Coastguard after amalgamation amounted to 3000 men, to which in 1824 were added the 200 members of the Preventive Guard, then under the direction of the Comptroller-General (England).

Table 1
Size and Costs of the Maritime Revenue Services, 1822

Service	No. Persons	Salaries £	s	d
Riding Officers (Land Guard)	157	19507	17	1½
Preventive Water Guard	1250	92003	9	2
Revenue Cruisers (Admiralty)	1553	158089	8	1
Cruisers under Revenue Board	97	7373	3	3
Coastal Blockade	1276	89152	8	4½
Total	4333	366126	6	0

Source: Great Britain, Parliament, House of Commons, *Parliamentary Papers* (1822), XI, 84.

In the early 1820s fierce skirmishes occurred between smugglers and government forces; every smuggler carried firearms which he was prepared to use. In February 1821 the two sides battled at Brookland, between Romney and Rye, with at least 240 smugglers involved, and other brutal conflicts the same year took place at Shorecliffe, Dymchurch, Lydd and Margate.[7] To deal with this lawlessness, the Coastguard was formed. Although the frays continued, the Coastguard's activities had some deterrent effect, especially in Kent. To fulfil its mandate, the men were provided with muskets and cutlasses and advised to wear tin hats and camouflage clothing while on patrol. To consolidate further the government forces, the Coastal Blockade was absorbed into

[7] "An Account of the Number of Lives Lost in Conflicts and Affrays between, Revenue, Coast Guard, Coast Blockade and Smugglers on Coasts of Kent and Sussex, 1821-1824," *BPP* (1825), XVIII, 385.

the Coastguard in 1831, but even this failed to stop the chaos. The smugglers were active in Hastings, St. Leonards, Eastbourne, Bexhill and Worthing in 1832 and 1833. In November 1833 two smugglers were killed and five captured (and subsequently sentenced to transportation to Tasmania) at the Battle of Pevensey Sluice. This stern action finally ended the disorders. Thereafter the smugglers changed their tactics, and goods were brought in through ports using concealment and bribery rather than being landed on the beaches.

Table 2
Strength of the Coastguard and Mounted Guard, 1839

Position	England	Scotland	Ireland
Chief Officers	275	33	153
Chief Boatmen	307	35	180
Commissioned Boatmen	795	42	349
Boatmen	1322	106	798
Mounted Guard	158		
Total	2857	216	1480

Source: William Webb, *Coastguard! An Official History of HM Coastguard* (London, 1976), 33.

By the end of the 1830s, the size of the force was virtually stagnant, reflecting the government's assessment that the problem was well in hand. In the next decade, this appeared to be the case: smuggling declined for a number of reasons, including a reduction in duties. Moreover, the Coastguard proved less susceptible to smuggling tactics while the frequent outrages of the outlaws cost them public sympathy. At the same time, the growth of nonconformist sentiment, particularly Methodism, changed public attitudes toward smuggling: for the first time in British history the smuggler became discredited. Since the Coastguard had enjoyed considerable success in the battle to safeguard the revenue, the sixty years prior to World War I were its most peaceful.[8]

What types of men comprised the Coastguard? Although *Punch* described Coastguard stations as "castles of idleness, where able-bodied men spend their time looking through long glasses for imaginary

---

[8]See Neville Williams, *Contraband Cargoes: Seven Centuries of Smuggling* (London, 1959), 187, 204-221.

smugglers," this was a travesty of the truth. Both on shore and afloat the men spent long hours in onerous conditions under strict discipline and often at considerable risk. Old coastguardsmen, Henry Shore recorded, remembered that

> The work was terrible...in the winter months we had to be on our guards by dusk, which meant leaving home at four or half-past, and we never got back again till nearly eight next morning. The only "nights in" we got was when our turn came round to be day watchmen at the station--once in ten days or so; and perhaps two nights before the full moon and two nights afterwards; though, even then, we seldom got more than half nights off, and if smuggling boats were expected off the coast, of course all the crew had to be out. I've often been that done up that I could scarcely walk home, and many is the time I've gone down to the water and washed my face to keep my eyes open. Oh, it was enough to kill a horse, I can tell you; only a strong man could stand the work![9]

To make conditions more bearable, stations were provided with books--a total of 52,000 were distributed among them.[10]

Although it had been intended that Coastguard personnel be experienced seamen, others were admitted, probably through influence and attracted by the prospects of prize money. At one point it was discovered that the service included shoemakers, tailors, coopers and gentlemen's valets. Volunteers for the Mounted Guard (to replace the Riding Officers) were recruited from cavalry regiments.

Regulations issued in 1831 ordered that "the vacant situations of Boatmen [in the Coastguard] will be filled up, from time to time by Seamen, as Ships of War are paid off." Applicants were to be not more than thirty years of age and at least five feet five inches tall. It was also mandated that seamen belonging to the Revenue Cruisers could occa-

---

[9]Henry N. Shore, *Smuggling Days and Smuggling Ways* (London, 1892), 141.

[10]It would be interesting to know what books were provided.

sionally be received.[11] As a result of dissatisfaction with recruitment standards, the Lords of the Admiralty in 1839 issued a notice which stipulated "that no more landsmen, either for general service or for particular ships, may be entered by the Officers of the Coastguard."

Because the Coastguard was required to operate in isolated places at unsocial hours and were often unpopular with the local population, accommodation was provided for the men.[12] Some coastguards were housed in the Martello towers built along the south and east coasts during the Napoleonic wars or in old hulks which had been hauled up on the beach. But stations were also rented. The boathouse and watchhouse at Hope Cove in Devon were rented from the Earl of Devon for £2 per year. Later in the nineteenth century it was decided to purchase the stations rather than rent them.

A Reserve for the Navy

With good progress being made against smuggling, the Admiralty decided that the Coastguard should become a reserve for the Navy, although without proper consideration of the consequences.[13] In 1845 recruits were required to sign an agreement to serve aboard Royal Navy ships if required and in 1853 all were made liable by statute for naval service in emergency. Such a crisis occurred the following year with the outbreak of the Crimean War, when about 3000 coastguardsmen were drafted into the Navy to form the backbone of the crews in the Baltic.[14] Although it was reported that they proved of great use in forming the untrained crew of many ships, Admiral Sir Charles Napier was less impressed when he sailed on the *Nile* in 1854. He reported that when the

---

[11]Webb, *Coastguard!*, 31-32.

[12]The station at Rickham (Prawle Point) in Devon was one of those built with windowless walls as a defence against smugglers. It is now part of the Gara Hotel.

[13]For the pamphlet debate about the Coastguard, see John S. Bromley (ed.), *The Manning of the Royal Navy: Selected Public Pamphlets 1693-1873* (London, 1974), especially the pamphlets by Captain Matthew Connolly, Admiral William Bowles, Vice-Admiral W.F. Martin, and Admiral the Hon. Sir F.W. Grey.

[14]George Butler Earp, *The History of the Baltic Campaign of 1854* (London, 1857), 19.

chaplain held services and the crew took off their caps, nearly every one was bald; most also needed spectacles and were unfit to go aloft.[15] The recruitment of coastguardsmen for naval service of course also removed them from their coast-watching duties.

Such problems led to a review of the role of the Coastguard in 1856. As a result, control by the Admiralty was reaffirmed and the permitted maximum complement was raised to 10,000. The coast was divided into eleven districts, with a guardship in each to serve as headquarters; on the books of these ships were placed all the young and active ex-naval men. Entry was henceforth restricted to naval men of the highest character under thirty-seven years of age with at least seven years' service. Because of these barriers, recruitment was slow; by 1859 only about 5600 men had enroled.[16] Of these, more than 2000 were ex-naval men, another 1900 had experience at sea, and 2756 (of whom 1491 were from the Navy) had received gunnery training. But only 2000 were under thirty-five; the rest were probably too old for active service at sea and many would have lost their sea legs.

The 1856 act stipulated that the Coastguard was to have three duties: coastal defence; a source of seamen for the Navy in the event of emergency; and protection of government revenue.[17] In practice, only the second role was truly implemented. Coastal defence fell to the Navy, while the transfer of the Coastguard to the Admiralty virtually severed the traditional association with revenue protection, which henceforth became a minor responsibility.

The change in the Coastguard's role brought with it the creation of its own squadron, and a number of vessels were stationed along the coast for this purpose. There was also a greater emphasis upon seamanship and training at sea. The first test for the organisation came in 1878 when there was a threat of war with Russia. The Coastguard was embarked upon seventeen ships and was afloat for ninety-eight days. From 1885 the Coastguard squadron was mobilised annually.

---

[15]Webb, *Coastguard!*, 36; Great Britain, Parliament, House of Commons, *Parliamentary Debates* (hereafter *Hansard*), Third Series, CXL, 863.

[16]R. Taylor, "Manning the Royal Navy: The Reform of the Recruiting System, 1852-1862," *Mariner's Mirror*, XLV (1959), 46.

[17]19 and 20 Victoria, cap. 83.

In the first years of the twentieth century there was further discussion about the way in which the Coastguard should be organised. Again there was concern about cost. To reduce expenditure the number of coastguardsmen was reduced. In the late nineteenth century there had been 533 stations which were estimated to cost over £200,000. Between 1904 and 1905 thirty-five were shut down, and in the latter year the Coastguard comprised 4135 officers and men. By 1911 the number had fallen to 3085, with savings of £124,000.[18] Taking note of public concern about this decline, the Board of Trade unsuccessfully protested about the policy.[19]

With Admiralty control came administrative changes. Coastguard officers were assigned naval ranks and a review of the system for promotion and pensions was undertaken. When Admiral Sir John Fisher became First Sea Lord a scheme to give coastguardsmen better sea training was introduced. With the outbreak of war in 1914 the defect of treating the Coastguard as a naval reserve was immediately revealed. Many men were dispatched to serve on old reserve vessels which were no match for the German High Seas Fleet or the U-boats, and the vast majority lost their lives. As a result, a gap was created in the services for which no provision had been made. Since there were insufficient men to man the lookout and watch system, civilians (including Boy Scouts) had to be recruited. The experience made it clear that the Coastguard was needed on shore, among other things, to deal with the greatly increased telephone traffic and to dispose of mines washed up on shore. Experience proved that the use of the service as a naval reserve was unworkable.

In addition, in the late nineteenth century the Coastguard had acquired a variety of further responsibilities, including assisting vessels in distress, taking charge of wrecks, operating lifesaving apparatus, participating in the lifeboat service, searching for mines and torpedoes, and performing sundry duties in connection with signals, telegraphs, buoys, lighthouses, wild birds and rare fish washed ashore.[20]

---

[18]Webb, *Coastguard!*, 54.

[19]Winston Churchill, then First Lord of the Admiralty, took a different view. He suggested that stations not required for wireless purposes should be used by the newly-formed Royal Naval Air Service; *ibid.*, 55.

[20]Public Record Office, *Record of HM Coastguard* (1988), 1.

Lifesaving

Even before the Coastguard was officially founded, lifesaving was a responsibility of the Water Guard. In 1821 the Water Guard was instructed that "when a wreck takes place...every officer and man on the spot...is to afford every assistance for the purpose of saving the lives of the persons aboard."[21] In 1841 it was further mandated that

> it is the duty of the cruizers [sic] and coastguard stations to render all possible assistance to vessels in distress, and in case of shipwrecks to use their utmost endeavours to save the lives of the persons on board, and to save and protect from plunder and embezzlement the rigging, sails, stores and cargo.

Under the Merchant Shipping Act of 1854 the Board of Trade became responsible for issuing lifesaving apparatus to the Coastguard. A number of attempts were made to produce satisfactory equipment, the most widely-adopted being the Boxer Rocket, produced in 1865.[22] But since the number of coastguards was limited, a problem arose as to whom should operate the equipment. The solution was found in the formation of volunteer companies, which were first organised in the northeast in the 1860s. The idea spread rapidly; at its peak in 1913, there were 404 brigades or companies manned by over 5000 volunteers throughout the country.[23]

When the First World War ended in 1918 many of the additional duties performed by the Coastguard during hostilities were no longer

---

[21]Webb, *Coastguard!*, 56.

[22]*Ibid.*, 56-65. After experiments in the 1790s by John Bell, the first successful breeches buoy was developed by George William Manby in 1810. Improvements followed, leading to the production of the Boxer Rocket, which remained in use from 1865 until 1950. The modern rescue rocket for use with the breeches buoy was introduced in 1948.

[23]By 1923 there were only 261 and today only three remain--at South Shields, Sunderland and Tynemouth.

required and the number of men was greatly reduced.[24] Because of the wartime difficulties a committee was appointed "to enquire into what establishment is necessary for carrying out the civil duties of revenue protection, life-saving, coast-watching, etc., now discharged by the Coastguard."[25] The panel concluded that it was no longer appropriate for the Coastguard to act as a naval reserve, since its men were no longer qualified to man modern warships. As far as the protection of revenue was concerned, a continuous watch over stretches of the coast was no longer necessary, since the Customs service was more appropriate for the task. On the other hand, the coast-watching and lifesaving services of the Board of Trade had increased in importance. To perform these functions, the Coastguard was instructed to maintain a complete chain of posts, with 935 men manning 322 stations in Great Britain and Northern Ireland. It was estimated that these and related services would cost £183,214 per year, with the Coastguard housed at the expense of the state.[26]

Accordingly the Coastguard was transferred to the Mercantile Marine Department of the Board of Trade on 1 April 1923. The Coastguard Act of 1925[27] gave legislative sanction to this change. As a result, for the first time in history Britain possessed a specialised force primarily devoted to coast-watching, lifesaving, wreck salvage and the administration of the foreshore. To maintain surveillance, the coast was divided into twelve divisions, each with an Inspector, and these were further split into fifty-one districts, each under a District Officer.

Recruitment, it was decided, should be from past and present members of the old Coastguard, plus retired officers and pensioners. As the supply of such men was soon exhausted, the service then began to recruit directly from the seaman class of the Royal Navy. The Board of Trade commented that:

---

[24]A series of registers of discharges in 1919 is to be found in Public Record Office, Admiralty 175/91-96.

[25]Webb, *Coastguard!*, 92.

[26]*Ibid.*, 93-94.

[27]10 George V, cap. 88.

> A large proportion of the Admiralty Coastguard force was recruited from the Royal Marines and stoker ratings but these men are not now regarded as suitable for service in His Majesty's Coastguard because they have not the seamanship which the Board of Trade regard as essential. It is considered very important that men employed to watch the coast should have a training in seamanship and its requirements as good as possible. Stokers, Royal Marines, etc. have not the opportunity of acquiring the knowledge that Seamen and Signalmen naturally secure and the Board think that the policy they have adopted in connection with recruitment will raise the general level of the qualifications of the Coastguard personnel above previous standards.[28]

The Board also agreed to recruit officers and men from the mercantile marine provided they had served in command or as chief officers of large merchant vessels. Between 1923 and 1936 great improvement was made in housing, which was regarded as important to maintain good morale within the service.

On the nature of the Coastguard's work, the Chief Inspector commented in 1931 that

> The enemy of the Coastguard is monotony, particularly on the quieter portions of the coast. It must frankly be recognised that, human nature being what it is, a very high degree of conscientiousness is necessary on the part of men who, night after night, are required to maintain watch by themselves, in a darkened hut, often in a very isolated position, if they are, throughout the length of their watch, to maintain unceasing vigilance. It is necessary to guard against the attention wandering, even momentarily, as it is conceivable that at that juncture mariners in peril may burn an inefficient signal of distress--it may be their last one. Next morning bodies and wreckage may be washed up on the beach. A single watchman, owing to a momentary aberration, may, even

[28]Webb, *Coastguard!*, 98.

> if life is not lost in consequence, very seriously prejudice the Service in the eyes of the public--and the Coastguard are the servants of the public--who are prone, in such cases, to ignore the innumerable instances of good work.[29]

A report in 1931 recommended that the number of stations be reduced from 252 to 217, while auxiliary stations be increased from ninety-eight to 142. Regular Coastguard personnel would be decreased from 820 to 772. As well as providing a service for fishing and small trading vessels, the Coastguard in the 1930s increasingly dealt with accidents on small yachts and motor cruisers. For rescues, the Coastguard was supported by the motor lifeboats of the Royal National Lifeboat Institution (RNLI), with which a good working relationship was established.

When war threatened in the late 1930s it was decided that the Coastguard should remain with the Board of Trade and not come under Admiralty jurisdiction. Nonetheless, it was to add the duties of a War Watching Organisation (WWO) to its lifesaving role and to act on instructions agreed by both ministries. The number of staff was increased to put all stations on constant watch. At the end of 1939, the Coastguard became the responsibility of the Ministry of Shipping; in May 1940, while its successor, the Ministry of War Transport, retained administrative control, the Admiralty became responsible for the WWO as well as the distribution and allocation of stations and lookouts, the mounting of patrols, and the dissemination of intelligence. The coastguardsmen were armed, given khaki uniforms and their numbers strengthened. By the end of 1940 the Coastguard was manning 371 stations, 355 coast-watching posts and 199 coast-searching posts, assisted by nearly 5000 auxiliary coastguardsmen.[30] The important role for the Coastguard had thus reverted to the first duty laid down in the 1856 act--coastal defence. In addition, it continued to perform its lifesaving role, made more difficult by the mining of the beaches and the ban on the firing of maroons.

---

[29] *Ibid.*, 107. The Chief Inspector was Captain V.S. Rashleigh, who served from 1926 to 1945.

[30] *Ibid.*, 118-119.

When the threat of invasion ended in 1944, the future of the Coastguard was again discussed. The Director of Local Defence at the Admiralty urged that it should remain under Admiralty control. He contended that the 1925 act was flawed because

> so far as can be ascertained it had and has no advantage or avowed object except to satisfy disarmament cranks by transferring the financial cost of the Coastguard from the Naval Estimates to the less contentious Shipping Estimates.

"The security of the coast," he claimed, "was much impaired for many months."[31]

The Chief Inspector of the Coastguard refuted these allegations and the Ministry of War Transport supported his views. As the Ministry put it, "In the years following 1923 there was a vast improvement made in the life-saving organisation...we must be sure that the Coastguard returns to us."[32] Thus on 1 October 1945 the Coastguard became the responsibility of the Ministry of (War) Transport. The next June it was given back its traditional blue uniform and in 1948 it was decided that coastguardsmen should become "established civil servants," thus guaranteeing enhanced status and a pension at the end of their service.

In 1949 the Ministry of Transport established a working party to see whether any changes were needed in the operation of the Coastguard. The report, published in 1952, agreed that its role was civilian and that the coast-watching service should continue to be organised as at present. But it recommended a reduction in the number of regular stations from 183 to 161 and of auxiliaries from 366 to 312. The number of regular staff was to be reduced from 667 to 485. The report also urged that a new rescue rocket system be installed.[33] A recommendation that the Coastguard should take over the lifeboat service was rejected on the grounds that the RNLI "does an excellent job at no cost to the Exchequer." A proposal that the Coastguard be concentrated in large

---

[31] *Ibid.*, 122.

[32] *Ibid.*, 123.

[33] As a result, a new Schermuly type of rocket was introduced into service in 1974.

stations of eighteen to twenty men was dismissed as impractical. But the disposal of houses not required by the reduced staff was an economy measure later regretted when additional accommodation was needed.

Administrative changes continue. In October 1964 the Coastguard was transferred to the Department of Trade, the eighth ministry to be responsible for the service in the 140 years since its creation. Subsequent administrative alterations have mainly reflected changes in Whitehall. The Coastguard was under the Department of Trade and Industry between 1970 and 1974; the Department of Trade from 1974 to 1983; the Department of Trade and Industry briefly again in 1983; and the Department of Transport since 1984. Meanwhile there were further studies, most notably by the Laver Review in 1974, which was concerned with whether the 1925 act provided an adequate legal basis for the Department of Trade (and hence the Coastguard) and the Rayner Review of 1982.[34] In March 1992 a further coastal review stated that

> Her Majesty's Coastguard is responsible for the initiation and co-ordination of civil maritime search and rescue within the United Kingdom search and rescue region. This includes the mobilisation, organisation and tasking of adequate resources to respond to persons either in distress at sea, or to persons at risk of injury or death on the cliffs or shoreline of the United Kingdom.[35]

Because of technological developments and shifting needs, the Coastguard has been reorganised since the 1970s. It now consists of 485 regular coastguardsmen operating from twenty-one rescue centres and some 3500 auxiliary coastguards--since 1970 including women as well as men--who form over 300 rescue teams around the coast. The coastline of the United Kingdom is now divided into six search and rescue regions with headquarters at Aberdeen, Yarmouth, Dover, Falmouth, Swansea

---

[34]The position of the Coastguard also found a place in the Sea Fisheries Act of 1968, paragraph 7 (1) f. By the Convention of the High Seas (1958) and the International Convention for the Safety of Life at Sea (1974), the Coastguard became the appropriate United Kingdom maritime search and rescue agency.

[35]*Hansard*, Sixth Series, CCV, 410. It should be noted that the Coastguard is now concerned with persons in distress or at risk of injury or death.

and Clyde.[36] Each region is partitioned into districts, headed by a station manned by established personnel under the management of a full-time Coastguard officer. All calls go to district headquarters, which alerts the local search and rescue facilities. In the review currently under way, there are moves to reduce the equipment supplied to smaller auxiliary stations, using their personnel to check the situation before calling out the necessary rescue services.

Conclusion

When its role was the protection of the revenue, the Coastguard combatted smugglers in the waters and on the coasts of the United Kingdom. In the second phase it provided a coast-watching force and a reserve for the Navy, helping to man warships in emergencies while also performing a wide range of other duties. In the third phase the Coastguard has been concerned primarily with lifesaving, at first by visual sighting and breeches buoys and in the past decade with telecommunications, lifeboats and helicopters, being responsible for search and rescue over a wider area than hitherto. As people of the sea, Coastguard personnel have widened their horizons, monitoring events by satellite; overseeing traffic through the English Channel and the Straits of Dover; and operating all around the coasts of Great Britain and Northern Ireland. In addition, search and rescue has now become a combined national and international concern. The task of monitoring traffic through the English Channel and Straits of Dover is shared with France and the area of responsibility off the west coast extends for 1000 miles into the north Atlantic to adjoin the area covered by the US Coast Guard. In addition to formal areas of responsibility, the various coastguard organisations in the world cooperate on an *ad hoc* basis according to convenience and telecommunication and satellite reception facilities in particular incidents. These are changes which have affected the number of coastguards required, the array of skills appropriate, and their relationship with the sea.

---

[36]The Coastguard also maintains cliff rescue teams and a fleet of inflatables for inshore emergencies. At Sumburgh in the Shetlands, Stornoway in the Outer Hebrides and Lee-on-Solent, it has helicopters on contract for search and rescue.

Coastal Life, "Nordic Culture" and Nation State: Reflections on the Formation of the Nation State and Maritime History

Poul Holm

Maritime history fascinates large segments of the public; the success of maritime museums and nautical archaeology are but the most spectacular expressions of this phenomenon. Ironically, it is precisely this interest which often arouses the scorn of professional historians. To quote Frank Broeze,

> many people, and not only outside the field, believe that maritime history is all about ships and navigation, and about nothing else. All too often, this very narrow field was and still is tainted by the brushes of hero-worshipping (of ships as well as of individuals) and antiquarianism--the desire to know detailed facts for the sake of detail...[T]he considerable achievements of maritime archaeology and maritime museums...have not always had a beneficial effect, as artifacts more often than not are closely linked to ships and shipwrecks and well-nigh inevitably, rarely add up to a complete story, let alone a full addressing of historically important issues.[1]

Maritime history enjoys the anecdote and suffers the drawbacks. I am sure that many historians envy us for having beautiful objects like the *Wasa* to put on display. On the other hand, others will retort that there

[1]Frank Broeze, "From the Periphery to the Mainstream: The Challenge of Australia's Maritime History," *The Great Circle*, XI (1989).

Research in Maritime History, No. 3 (December 1992), 191-204.

are phenomena more central to the human experience than an error-filled naval reconstruction.

I believe that it is vital to conceive of maritime history as a truly international discipline that is sufficiently open to shed the shackles of national boundaries and confident enough to draw insights from a whole range of disciplines. In this essay I would like to make some observations based on recent developments in Nordic historiography to demonstrate not only some of the potential but also some of the pitfalls of adopting this type of broad approach.

The first question to be addressed is why maritime history is so crucial. Certainly it is not because those with maritime orientations were a majority. From a purely numeric perspective, maritime people have been almost everywhere a small minority. Even in a seagirt country like Denmark, the active maritime male population, including everyone from dockers to farmers who derived some income from fishing, numbered only about 35,000 at the turn of this century. Counting their families, they comprised perhaps 140,000 people in a population of three million, or less than five percent of the total. The ratio was less than in Norway, but higher than in Sweden. Peasants dominated Denmark, and Danish historians often write as if the country had a continental position like Switzerland, albeit with the mountains excluded.

The point of course is that it is dangerous to equate quantitative and qualitative importance. The intrinsically interesting thing about maritime people is that they cross borders, since coastal people live on the margins of the state. Usually (but not always) the state has accepted this transgression as desirable. As a result, the history of coastal populations has had a disproportionate impact and significance. Maritime people are simultaneously influenced by foreign impulses and conscious of their identity, which they shape by interacting with strangers. The meeting of cultures should therefore be a central concept to an understanding of maritime history.

Maritime people are also conduits between the agrarian population and aliens. Coastal life represents freedom and opportunity compared to agrarian conditions, which often restrict geographic (and social) mobility. A generation or two ago, cultural historians used the characteristic mobility in coastal regions to justify the exclusion of maritime people from their studies. Since many believed that "true culture" could be found only in stable communities, they discovered their "ideal types" in the remote farmsteads of Norwegian Setesdalen or on the good claylands in the middle of Zealand. By contrast, a new generation of historians is suggesting that an examination of coastal areas might be equally fruitful. It is with this acceptance that maritime history assumes a peculiar importance. And when scholars interested in coastal populations begin to generalize from their findings, this attracts the attention of quite a different historical sub-discipline, the history of nationality.

Examinations of the formation of nation states and the development of national identity have evoked intense interest in recent years, as many historians have come to realize that politics exert a decisive and at times disastrous influence on all facets of life. A decade ago the fashion was to write the "history of everyday life" with the politics omitted (except perhaps trade union politics); today a growing number of scholars recognize the intimate connection between the mundane components of economic and social life and "politics." No group has experienced the importance of politics more directly than coastal people.

Maritime history has played a significant role in the building of national identity in many countries. Despite the fact that it is almost by definition an international discipline, we should not forget that most often it has been used to construct nationalistic images. We may not like it, but we would betray our profession not to reflect on the way in which it has been utilized. For my part, I would distinguish between a search for historical roots, which I believe is perfectly legitimate, and a construction of nationalist history, which I find totally illegitimate.

For the post-World War II generation of Nordic historians questions of national identity (or prejudices) were taboo. The monstrosities of the 1930s and 1940s convinced them that some very real aspects of historical identity were best ignored. In the last decade, however, the strictures have been lifted. One of the first scholars to tackle the subject was the ethnologist Åke Daun, who for his troubles was sharply criticized at the Nordic Ethnological Conference in 1982 for speaking about Swedish identity as perceived by immigrants. Nonetheless, a number of studies soon followed by both ethnologists and historians. In Denmark analyses by the ethnographer Anne Knudsen on Corsica and the historian Uffe Østergaard on European nation states have reflected general trends in Western thought about the formation of nations and national identity. The latest and most comprehensive manifestation is the research project directed by Ole Feldbæk on "The History of Danish Identity."[2] I believe these studies are innovative and pathbreaking.

Perhaps because of its relative intellectual isolation, maritime history has not been directly linked to this general trend. Yet several books have been published in Scandinavian languages arguing that Nordic culture is best defined by the all-prevailing influence of the sea. That was indeed the point of the very first textbook in maritime ethnology, edited by Olof Hasslöf.[3] The focus of maritime ethnologists has been concentrated on small communities, which have been studied in significant works by people such as Orvar Löfgren and Bjarne Stoklund.[4] In recent years, however, this Scandinavian school of eco-history or community studies has turned towards regional and national studies, in the process abandoning maritime studies. Nonetheless, the work of Svein Molaug, the former director of the Norwegian Maritime Museum, on Norwegian coastal culture may be seen as an example of generalization from community studies to national maritime culture.[5] In the preface he argued that the coast was the formative zone of national culture because it was there that rural ideas confronted cultural impulses from abroad. By explicitly presenting his work as a tribute to Norwegian identity, I think he crossed the divide between a history of national formation and nationalist history.

While Molaug was content to present the fruits of a generation's work in museums, the ambitions of the most recent contribution to this genre are much higher. I refer here to Kirsten Hastrup (ed.), *Den nordiske verden* (*The Nordic World*), published in 1992. It is the result of a Nordic-wide research project begun in 1985 and supported by the

---

[2]Ole Feldbæk (ed.), *Dansk Identitetshistorie* (5 vols., Copenhagen, 1991-). See also Anne Knudsen, *En ø i historien. Korsika: historisk antropolgi, 1730-1914* (Copenhagen, 1989); Uffe Østergaard, "Hvad er en nationstat?" (Unpublished paper, Centre for Culture Studies, Aarhus University, 1988).

[3]O. Hasslöf, *et al.* (eds.), *Sømand, fisker, skib og værft* (Copenhagen, 1970).

[4]Orvar Löfgren, "Resource Management and Family Firms: Swedish West Coast Fishermen," in Raoul Andersen and Cato Wadel (eds.), *North Atlantic Fishermen* (Toronto, 1972); Bjarne Stoklund, "Economy, Work and Social Roles. Continuity and Change in the Danish Island Community of Læsø, c. 1200-1900," *Ethnologia Europaea*, XV (1965), 129-163.

[5]*Vår gamle kystkultur* (Østerås, 1985).

Nordic Research Councils. Its aim was to "clarify the concept of 'Nordicness.'" The authors come from various disciplines (although most are ethnologists) and were chosen to present "a broad cultural historical perspective on the Nordic world." In the preface, Hastrup stresses that it is possible to comprehend the "Nordic world" as a single entity, albeit with minor local differences. Maritime culture is discussed in contributions by Jóan Pauli Joensen and Brit Berggreen.[6]

Den nordiske verden is very different from most histories. For starters, the editor disavows any obligations regarding chronology.

> We have consciously wanted to break away from traditional chronological thinking that focuses the narrative on major events and historical disruptions. This choice is connected with our Nordic point of departure, in as much as the Nordic character may be identified everywhere in history and reveals its contours in the details of everyday life.

She adds that "chronological examples differ from one chapter to another. The Nordic character is not clearly to be seen at all times and in all areas of life." One conspicuous result of this selective view of history is that the authors manage to write more than 500 pages spanning ten centuries without referring once to the incessant warfare between the Nordic states--except for references to the Vikings, who conveniently play the role of barbaric ancestors to the more contemporary and peaceful Nordic folk.[7] Consequently, readers will not find any reference to navies in the seventy pages about the influence of the sea on Nordic mentality, except for a single reference to the fact that women are now allowed to enter naval service.

---

[6]Other sections of the book deal with time, landscape, agriculture, language, law, household, and people. I must point out that the following remarks only apply to the maritime sections; the book includes other scholarly contributions which do not conform to the basic perspective that I discuss in this essay.

[7]In propagating the myth of the peaceful sea-people of Scandinavia, *Den nordiske verden* continues the line of thought developed in the introduction to Arne Bang-Andersen, Egil H. Grude and Basil Greenhill (eds.), *The North Sea. A Highway* (Stavanger, 1985).

The reason for this striking omission is that the editor denies the importance of national allegiances compared to the deeper importance of the Nordic character.

> In a long historical perspective national allegiances are less constant and often irrelevant compared to being a Northerner and sharing so many experiences that political boundaries often seem accidental. Boundaries have changed up to this century; Norway opted out of the union with Sweden in 1906 [sic], and Iceland broke the ties to Denmark in two turns by 1918 and 1944.[8]

In this kind of analysis events lose weight and mental structures become all-important. The methodological result is that examples tend to be selected almost at random as they suit the author's whim. And this is exactly what it takes to construct the "Nordic world."

Curiously, the authors never define the concepts of "Nordicness" or "Nordic identity." Instead, they base their arguments on dualistic concepts well-known in social anthropology, such as culture/nature, inside/outside and homestead/wilderness. While these are without doubt relevant to understanding culture anywhere in the world, they maintain that there was a special Nordic mediation. As a result, their basic concept only becomes clear when the chapters are analyzed as a whole.

As I read Kirsten Hastrup, the Nordic economy was characterized by economic pluralism, allowing people to subsist on the various natural resources available. Still, the centre of Nordic life was the homestead, which was formed in the Iron Age when a basic household unit that was to exist until this century took shape. The Nordic mentality was contoured by the need to uphold the homestead. When economic pluralism forced most people to be mobile, ideology placed a premium on stability. Stable peasants came to dominate thinking about the "good society," as hunters, lumberers and fishermen were perceived to be on the margin, mediating culture and nature in the wilderness.

In a separate contribution to the volume Hastrup and Orvar Löfgren present what they believe to be the key to understanding the

---

[8]Kirsten Hastrup (ed.), *Den nordiske verden* (2 vols., Copenhagen, 1992), II, 205. The year of the dissolution of the Norwegian-Swedish union was 1905. This blunder is indicative of the editor's loose approach to the temporal dimension.

Nordic mentality: the notion of "limited luck." Luck should be understood as an explanatory metaphor for economic success; since peasants believed luck to be a limited good, the price of luck for one was another's mishap. You could have fish luck, butter luck, cattle luck or any other kind of luck. Hastrup and Löfgren describe this as a peculiarly Nordic phenomenon: "The interesting thing is that we are dealing with a special *Nordic* conceptual world that has a very long history." If the notion of "luck" as a limited good were unknown in other societies, this might make sense. But in fact there are a number of anthropological studies of "limited luck" in other societies.[9] Although they obviously know them, Hastrup and Löfgren fail to acknowledge their existence. The uninitiated reader, on the other hand, is only directed by their footnotes to Scandinavian sources. Unfortunately, this method is also used by several other contributors. By omitting references to non-Nordic occurrences of so-called "Nordic phenomena," Hastrup and Löfgren save themselves from having to falsify the record.

Although Hastrup maintains that the Nordic world was one, she divides it into two halves, "summer north" and "winter north." Through this dichotomy she differentiates the grain-growing south (present-day Denmark, southern Sweden, and sometimes southern Finland) from the pastoral north. The "summer north" was characterized by manors, aristocracy, and social hierarchy; by implication the "winter north" was more egalitarian. Hastrup also suggests that a distinct Nordic form of economic pluralism allowed for strong female participation in husbandry and for a generally robust female position in the family.

Brit Berggreen takes this conceptual model one step further. She maintains that "the history of the North cannot be understood without the sea. It is the sea and its maritime life that gives the North its most distinct character, and that defines it in the eyes of the surrounding world."[10] She also believes that "contacts between the Scandinavian countries and the Nordic insular settlements in the sea have been both dense and continuous; there has been a comprehensive Westbound traffic ever since the first colonization of the promising Atlantic isles in the

---

[9]George M. Foster, "Peasant Society and the Image of the Limited Good," *American Anthropologist*, LXVII (1966), 293-315; James R. Gregory, "Image of Limited Good or Expectation of Reciprocity?" *Current Anthropology*, XVI (1975), 73-92.

[10]Hastrup (ed.), *Den nordiske verden*, II, 15.

Viking age." Moreover, she hints that there probably was more contact with Greenland in the late middle ages than "official history" would allow. Her only reference, however, is to Didrik Pining's obscure journey in 1472 to Greenland and possibly Newfoundland, which is normally perceived as a rediscovery rather than evidence of continuing contact.[11]

Unfortunately, Berggreen's literary style is more suggestive than informative. For example, she writes that

> The sea defines the Northerners; the "others" have come to them across the sea, and the Northerners have found their way to the "others" across the sea. In that way the limitless ocean has characterized the relations of the North to the world. And internally it has left its mark on all circumstances of life; economically, socially, and culturally the sea bears the Nordic World.[12]

Although the passage is ambiguous, the drift of her argument seems to be that the sea has been the great Nordic unifier.

Jóan Pauli Joensen's contribution is clearer, relating for the most part to Faroese experiences on which he is an unrivalled expert. But on the general argument he seems to be in accord with Berggreen.

> Summer or winter, the sea has always united the North. In the Viking age the Northerners were masters of the sea. The Kattegat and the Skagerrak united the coastal peoples of a large area of Denmark, Norway and Sweden. Ethnologists and folklorists have also proven a cultural unity between Norse settlements in the Atlantic, not just regarding language, but also in house construction and popular ideas, which prove the existence of close economic and cultural contacts for a long time

---

[11]Cf. "Opdagelsesrejser," *Kulturhistorisk Leksikon for Nordisk Middelalder* (Copenhagen, 1956-1978).

[12]Hastrup (ed.), *Den nordiske verden*, II, 17-18.

> after colonization, contacts that were maintained by local people right up until the end of the sixteenth century.[13]

Joensen is too good an ethnologist to conjure up a Nordic boat-building tradition in his contribution on sailing. He explicitly draws attention to the fact no such thing ever existed, and that material culture was anything but unified. His contribution may be read as a simple statement that Nordic maritime society was both local and international. In this respect the term Nordic loses all but its geographic content.

In a further contribution on fishing, however, he accepts the Hastrup/Löfgren idea of a peculiarly Nordic type of luck, as he discusses fisherman's luck as a uniquely Nordic phenomenon. The crux of the matter, of course, is that there is no evidence adduced to sustain the argument. Indeed, there cannot be, since Reginald Byron has described the phenomenon in much the same way in a non-Nordic setting.[14]

In a final contribution on "The Woman's Sea," Brit Berggreen takes up another line of the general argument. Hastrup maintained that women were more visible in the Nordic pastoral economy than was usual in Europe; Berggreen suggests that women were also of economic and cultural importance in shipping and fishing. While no one would deny this assertion, the problem is the imprecision that occurs in trying to imagine the extent of women's participation in maritime affairs. Since she makes no attempt at quantification, Berggreen's suggestive prose paints a picture that I believe grossly exaggerates the actual presence of women aboard merchant and fishing vessels. A growing number of studies show that skippers' wives were often present on deep-sea trips, but the average mariner was never accompanied.[15] Berggreen believes that "if Nordic women today have more equal opportunities than other women, it is natural to see a continuity from a traditionally freer position, which was only interrupted by a period of restrictions on female

---

[13]*Ibid.*, 23-24.

[14]Reginald Byron, "Luck and Leadership. The Management of Decisions in Shetland Fishing Crews," *Maritime Anthropological Studies*, I (1988), 3-14; Orvar Löfgren, "The Reluctant Competitors. Fisherman's Luck in Two Swedish Maritime Settings," *ibid.*, II (1989), 34-58.

[15]Morten Hahn-Pedersen (ed.), *I storm og stille den sikre havn* (Esbjerg, 1992).

activities."[16] Perhaps, but Berggreen never shows that Nordic women were actually freer than other northern European females, and I doubt that it is possible to generalize about the status of Nordic women given the present state of knowledge. I would argue that it is more accurate to describe eighteenth and nineteenth-century women, at least in the Kattegat-Skagerrak area, as bound within a patriarchal gender system.[17]

Den nordiske verden is in important ways a culmination of certain trends in Nordic ethnography. Many historians--and I would hope also ethnographers--are likely to be put off by its chronological carelessness and unrigorous analysis. Regardless, there is a more important point here for maritime history: the kind of Nordic-centred analysis attempted. By simply asserting that general trends are peculiarly Nordic, Hastrup, Löfgren, Berggreen, and to some extent Joensen conjure up a world that never existed. That may be a kind of history which is popular with some politicians, but it lacks any kind of scholarly credibility.

One wonders why scholars of international reputation would produce a work that seems to revive old nationalistic ideas in a new Nordic form. I believe that there is a continuity in the theoretical models employed in Nordic ethnography that can explain this seeming anomaly. In *Kystfolk. Kontakter og sammenhænge over Kattegat og Skagerrak* (*Coastal People. Contacts across the Kattegat and Skagerrak*), I discussed the underlying ideas of Nordic maritime ethnology, which adheres to a school of thought that I labelled the "criticism of civilisation" approach. Common to the authors whom I have discussed is a basic abhorrence of capitalist forms of organisation, which are presumed to be destructive of local communities and to lead to serious moral decline. This basic attitude can be seen in a whole series of historical-cultural studies written in this century. While there is insufficient space here to explicate this theoretical model, it is important to note several of its assumptions. It links industrialisation with serious human and cultural loss and is basically pessimistic regarding the development of industrial society. In the same way, capitalism is linked with a distortion of the relations between men and women, destroying a society in which women in "democratic" fishing communities played central and

---

[16]Hastrup (ed.), *Den nordiske verden*, II, 65, 76.

[17]Poul Holm, *Kystfolk. Kontakter og sammenhænge over Kattegat og Skagerrak, 1550-1914* (Esbjerg, 1991).

respected roles as the pivots of family life and enjoyed a certain economic independence.

I believe that *Den nordiske verden* represents a continuum in this line of thought. There is very little discussion of modern Nordic societies in the book, but Hastrup does mention the existence of dangers to the Nordic model, concluding that the Nordic mentality will live as it encounters new cultural challenges. I suggest that the idea of a "Nordic world" has replaced the old notion of a popular democratic culture. The twist of the argument is that the "Nordic mentality" survives in industrial society. Thus the temporal dimension of history becomes meaningless to Hastrup. There is no longer a dreadful loss of culture as industrialization changes everyday life. Indeed, post-industrial times are alleged to revive the "Nordic mentality," as Berggreen triumphantly notes the reinstatement of the rights of Nordic women within the family.

The book alludes to a research project on the coastal peoples of the Kattegat and Skagerrak as an example of the unifying role of the sea in the Nordic experience. I perceive this to be a misunderstanding of the project that I summarized in *Kystfolk*. The questions my colleagues and I posed were reasonably simple: How important were contacts across the sea and inland for the coastal population? Were there special relationships between certain coasts? How did contacts develop over time? What were the consequences of warfare for the coastal population? Could contacts continue in spite of naval warfare or customs barriers? Did people marry across the sea?

The strength of the project was that we departed from traditional national perspectives that conceptualize the nation as a natural whole with the capital as the centre of all aspects of life. Instead we assumed the perspective of the actors and investigated the contact horizon of the coastal populations. The result was that we found a relatively homogeneous coastal culture until around 1840. Coastal communities were by no means totally similar, but they did share certain consensual assumptions about ecological adaptation, social stratification and mental horizon. Even when Sweden conquered the eastern coast of the Kattegat and Skagerrak in 1645 and 1658, coastal life retained old patterns. After 1700 national characteristics became more apparent as the realms were transformed into nation states. The shipping of Halland and Bohuslän was constrained to stay within Swedish territory and a conscious language policy was established through a Swedification of the countryside. From around 1750 national identities became more apparent in Denmark-Norway as well. Let me illustrate this point by one Norwegian example.

In 1795 Mary Wollstonecraft visited several Danish, Swedish and Norwegian cities around the Kattegat and Skagerrak. Among the things she noticed was that southern Norwegian cities were strikingly modern compared with their counterparts in Sweden and Denmark.[18] Danish historian Albert Olsen commented on this modernity in his study of Denmark-Norway in the eighteenth century:

> Already by the year 1750 literature mentions the growing knowledge of the Norwegian peasant...[who] would read earlier and with greater proficiency than the Dane. Furthermore, Norwegian peasants, many of whom would sail and fish besides tilling the soil, had a closer contact to foreign countries and foreign thinking. By 1795 an "enlightened peasant" proverbially was a peasant with coffee in his house wearing a wig, and in 1784 Hans Strøm commented on the English republican spirit that seems to have beset everyone trading with England...In parts of Norway a different kind of peasant was about than the one you met in Denmark. Here hardly any peasants were beset by the English or republican spirit or would wear a wig. Particularly in the second half of the century, the Norwegian peasant was probably closer to bourgeois culture than the Danish were.[19]

At the end of the eighteenth century the Danish-Norwegian realm was still controlled by a unifying state. But the maritime trades of Norway were beginning to foster a separate identity. Open trade was a channel through which a variety of impulses could enter Norwegian society, which accepted them faster than Denmark. While Denmark was dominated by German culture until the Schleswig War of 1848-1850, Norway was oriented towards British culture by shipping.

There is an interesting contrast in Ole Feldbæk's discussion of the formation of Danish national identity. Feldbæk has shown that national sentiments were stirred as ambitious Danes with good educations

---

[18]Mary Wollstonecraft, *Letters Written during a Short Residence in Sweden, Norway, and Denmark* (Lincoln, 1976).

[19]Albert Olsen, *Danmark-Norge i det 18. Aarhundrede* (Copenhagen, 1936).

found their path to the apex of the civil service blocked by Germans with a virtual monopoly on the posts.[20] National ideas were the product of so-called enlightened Danish writers of the second half of the eighteenth century. The parallel trend in Norway was to awaken national sentiments for the advancement of financial institutions and centres of learning that would enable the Norwegians to reap the profits of maritime trade with Britain.

The Norwegian peasant was considered to be the best subject under eighteenth-century Danish-Norwegian absolutism. Indeed, there is hardly a better expression of this idea than the decision of naval officers to sail on a ship called *The Norwegian Peasant*. I would venture a counterfactual claim: mutiny would have threatened had the King named one of his ships *The Danish Peasant*. The archetypal Danish peasant was known for his clumsiness and slow wit. The Norwegian peasant, on the other hand, embodied a grander stature. He was, as Albert Olsen remarked, "half-maritime." While maritime activities did not shape a distinctive Norwegian identity, shipping and trade were the conduits through which new impulses and ideas reshaped peasant culture.

Early Norwegian modernity was neo-puritan, as reflected in Haugian revivalism. The hallmark of early Haugians was their astonishing mobility; they bought and sold farmsteads and moved from village to village, thus spreading the good news from the coast into deep Setesdal. The background of this mission was an expanding coastal economy. The four decades after 1840 were characterized by a lengthy boom for deep-sea shipping in southern Norway, a time of plenty of work and broadening perspectives. People naturally associated economic growth with the prevalent ideology, which stemmed from English Victorianism. The strong Anglo-Saxon influence on southern Norway in this period was no coincidence. The open shipping communities were forerunners of missions to the heathens (which were themselves expressions of widening perspectives), missions to sailors and buildings of worship.

The breakthrough of religion on the Danish coast was quite different. Revivalism took an additional generation to manifest. One reason was that religious language was not acceptable to all members of society as an expression of existential problems. But another fact was perhaps as important: while the Norwegian mission originated on the

[20]Ole Feldbæk, *Clashes of Culture* (Copenhagen, 1991).

Printed and bound by CPI Group (UK) Ltd, Croydon, CR0 4YY
16/09/2026
14963469-0001

Introduction to Medical Virology